WITHDRAWN

More than Kings and Less than Men

More than Kings and Less than Men

Tocqueville on the Promise and Perils of Democratic Individualism

L. JOSEPH HEBERT, JR.

LEXINGTON BOOKS
A division of
ROWMAN & LITTLEFIELD PUBLISHERS, INC.
Lanham • Boulder • New York • Toronto • Plymouth, UK

Published by Lexington Books
A division of Rowman & Littlefield Publishers, Inc.
A wholly owned subsidiary of The Rowman & Littlefield Publishing Group, Inc.
4501 Forbes Boulevard, Suite 200, Lanham, Maryland 20706
http://www.lexingtonbooks.com

Estover Road, Plymouth PL6 7PY, United Kingdom

British Library Cataloguing in Publication Information Available

Library of Congress Cataloging-in-Publication Data

Hebert, L. Joseph, 1975–
  More than kings and less than men : Tocqueville on the promise and perils of
democratic individualism / L. Joseph Hebert.
      p. cm.
  Includes bibliographical references and index.
  ISBN 978-0-7391-3374-3 (cloth : alk. paper)
  ISBN 978-0-7391-3376-7 (electronic)
  1. Tocqueville, Alexis de, 1805–1859. De la démocratie en Amérique. 2. Tocqueville,
Alexis de, 1805–1859.—Political and social views. 3. Democracy. 4. United States—
Politics and government. 5. Individualism. I. Title.
  JK216.T7193H47 2009
  321.8—dc22   2009034694

♾™ The paper used in this publication meets the minimum requirements of American
National Standard for Information Sciences—Permanence of Paper for Printed Library
Materials, ANSI/NISO Z39.48-1992.

Printed in the United States of America

To my Mother and Father

Contents

Acknowledgments

This study is the fruit of many years of research, beginning with my dissertation at the University of Toronto, completed in 2003, and extended through projects conducted while a member of Brown University's Political Theory Project and St. Ambrose University's Department of Political Science and Leadership Studies. During that time, my understanding of Tocqueville has benefited from the advice, example, support, encouragement, and criticism of more individuals and institutions than I could possibly acknowledge here. I must therefore begin by begging pardon of those whose influence I have omitted or understated.

I became aware of the desire to grasp what Tocqueville calls the "admirable order of all things" through the influence of great teachers. I am especially grateful to Charles Reed, Gayle Curtis, Fred Jones, John Emerson, and James Nahra for their early encouragement. I am deeply indebted to Steven Cohn for his inspiring example, generous guidance, and unflagging friendship. I owe my love of political philosophy generally, and appreciation of Tocqueville in particular, to the teaching and example of Michael Palmer. Though I never had the opportunity to study Tocqueville with Michael, he bequeathed me nothing less than the intellectual milieu into which I have attempted to fit the thought of this great author. Without Michael's original direction and continued support, I would neither have dreamed of attempting this feat, nor would I have been capable of accomplishing it in any measure. I am also grateful to William Small, Michael Howard, and Jefferson White for their generosity.

I first picked up *Democracy in America* at the prompting of Khalil Habib, who eagerly unearthed for me some of the hidden treasures it has to offer. For this, and for his continued encouragement of and collaboration in my efforts to continue the hunt, I owe him more than I could ever express. The same goes for Carl Eaton, whose lifelong companionship and willingness to accompany me on my intellectual journeys has constantly sustained me. I am deeply indebted as well to Aaron King and James Sexton for their generosity over the years and to Willow Wetherall and Monique Bouchard for their inspiration and friendship.

My dissertation on Tocqueville was written under the wise and patient supervision of Clifford Orwin. His tireless review of proposals and drafts, combined with judicious praise and blame, rescued me from many follies and immeasurably honed not only my arguments, but my very ability to think with precision. Cliff's teaching, and that of Thomas Pangle, rigorously shaped my approach to political philosophy, and their combined influence pervades this study far beyond any specific advice they have given me. I am grateful to both as well for their continued support of my work. It was also my great fortune to have on my dissertation committee Ronald Beiner, Donald Forbes, and Sanford Kessler, each of whom provided a unique and valuable perspective on my research. Their constructive criticism, sound advice, and cheerful encouragement informed and strengthened my resolve to complete the project then and to build upon it since. I also thank Sandy for his continued efforts on my behalf.

Another happy circumstance of my graduate years was the company of friends whose conversation informed and advanced my search for truth. I am especially grateful to Bill Parsons, Gabriel Bartlett, Tom Powers, Chris McClure, Alexander Orwin, and Rory Schachter for their sustained interest in and assistance with my studies, to John Szczerkowski, William Melek, Alexei and Catalina Trochev, and David Nguyen for their friendship and support and to Frank Monozlai and Fr. Thomas Trottier for their profound guidance.

One of the most significant differences between this book and my dissertation is my present focus on individualism. This fruitful restructuring of my argument was inspired by my experiences in the Political Theory Project at Brown University under the direction of John Tomasi. John's kind interest in my work and future career, combined with his wise counsel, admirable example, and generous assistance, helped me to develop a mature and fruitful vision of the future course of my studies. I am deeply grateful to him and to the others in the Political Theory Project who generously shared with me their insights and enthusiasm, especially Keith Shaw, Carmen Pavel, Ross Corbett, Mariah Zeisberg, and Adam Tebble, as well as to the many students at Brown who shared their energy and intelligence with me, especially Stephen Beale and Sheila Dugan. My progress at that time was also due in no small part to my participation in Notre Dame University's 2004 Erasmus Institute Summer Seminar and in the 2005 Lehrman Summer Institute hosted by Robert George of the James Madison Program at Princeton University, as well as to the kindness of Fr. Kevin Fisette, Fr. Joseph Santos, David O'Connell, Allen Maynard, Ken Garrepy, and the late Daniel Storti.

Over the years, several scholars have taken an interest in my work or shared their research with me in inspiring ways. Thanks are due especially to Paul Carrese, Phillip Gray, Steven Michels, Jon Schaff, Scott Yenor, Peter Lawler, Will Jordan, and Jim Ceaser for their generosity in this regard.

Writing this book has been a joyful challenge thanks to the care and assistance of those around me. Its content and style have been greatly enriched by the influence of Devin Schadt, who generously lent his ear to and shared his thoughts on every page of its draft. His loyal friendship and love of truth have been an inspiration to me in my scholarship and beyond. I am also grateful to Dustin Schadt and Scott Rains for their feedback on previous projects. While writing this book I profited from the wise direction and friendship of Fr. Michael Driscoll and the kind counsel of Fr. J. M. Logan, Fr. Bruce DeRammelaere, and Fr.

Scott Lemaster. I also benefited greatly from the strong support of my colleagues and superiors at St. Ambrose University. Nathan Schlueter and Rand Wonio eased my transition with their experience and expertise, while Bill W. Parsons has been as kind a mentor as a junior professor could hope for, and has had more of an influence on my work than he may realize. I owe much as well to Andy Swift, Ron and Linda Wastyn, Regina Stephens, Bea and Paul Jacobson, Dean Marple, Randy Richards, Jim Van Speybroeck, Ryan Dye, Katy Strzepek, Daniel LaCorte, Sandy McKinley, David Diamond, Matt Halfhill, Brenda Peters, Lance Sadlek, Stella and Carl Herzig, Tadd Ruetenik, Mary Waterstreet, Tom Yang, John Madsen, and Nancy Hayes for their kindness, to Aron Aji and Lori Rodrigues-Fisher for their inspiration and support, and to my students for everything they have taught me. I am indebted to Mark Kremer for his probing questions on an earlier version of my fifth chapter, to Matthew Holbreich for his feedback on a related project, to Joseph Parry, Jana Wilson, Victoria Koulakjian, and Ashley Baird of Lexington Books for being so gracious during the many stages of preparing this manuscript, and to Brian Danoff, whose insightful suggestions have made this a significantly better book. I am also grateful to Ben Nonnenmann, Steve Johnson, David Rericha, Daniel Ade, Stephen Perenich, Greg Franich, and Bret Robinson for their interest and encouragement.

Most of all, I am grateful to my wife, Elena, whose unwavering love and understanding, coupled with timely counsel and assistance, have made me a far better scholar, and man, than I would otherwise be; to my brother Justin and sisters Jennie Martel and Jill Ellis, whose steadfast love has informed all of my endeavors; to my mother-in-law, Alexandra Riabinina, for her constant support; to my children, Sophia and Nicholas, who daily remind me what a precious gift life is; and to my parents, whose self-sacrificing love and example have shown me what it means to be grateful for that gift.

My graduate work on Tocqueville at the University of Toronto was facilitated by the generous support of the Bradley, Earhart, and John M. Olin Foundations; my postdoctoral fellowship at Brown University was funded by the William H. Donner Foundation; my teaching at St. Ambrose University has benefited from the kind assistance of the Lehrman Institute; two related conference presentations were supported by the St. Ambrose University Faculty Development Committee; and the Introduction, first chapter, and proposal for this book were made possible by a grant from the Frank and Jane Folwell Fund.

It goes without saying that none of those listed above are responsible for the faults I have not been able to expunge from this work.

Meliora sunt vulnera diligentis
quam fraudulenta oscula odientis.

Introduction
Why Tocqueville? Why Individualism?

Why Tocqueville?

For Alexis de Tocqueville (1805-1859), democracy was in question. After the French Revolution (1789), which had ushered in democracy (and then tyranny) by such bloody means; the reign of Napoleon (1799-1814), who manipulated the ideals of freedom and equality to found an empire; the brief restoration of the Bourbon dynasty (1814-1830); and Louis-Philippe's attempt to rule as "the Citizen King" and "King of the French [people]" (1830-1848); what Frenchman would not have had questions about democracy? In the European society of Tocqueville's day, one had to question (if one did not blindly assert) whether democracy was eternal or ephemeral, providential or diabolical. As a consummate rhetorician writing for a broad European audience, Tocqueville was prudent to adopt this quizzical stance in his great work, *Democracy in America* (1835-1840). In fact, Tocqueville attributed the celebrity he achieved through his first volume largely to the perception that he had probed the strengths and weaknesses of democracy without showing partiality to the "great parties" (royalist and republican) then dividing the political scene (400).[1]

Yet Tocqueville's impartiality was no mere pose designed to elicit easier acceptance among a divided readership. Nor was it the result of an ambivalence, real or feigned, to the phenomenon of democracy and the questions his contemporaries were asking about it. Tocqueville's balanced stance was rather the fruit of the passion, genius, and erudition he brought to these same questions. In tracing the path of democracy, examining its penchants, pointing out the achievements that it promotes or impedes, and judging "what we ought to hope or fear from" democracy, Tocqueville strove "to see, not differently, but further than the parties" (13, 15).[2] He declined to adopt a reflexive view, regarding democracy as all good or all bad, or to take for granted its ultimate effect on European society. Tocqueville thought there was more, not less, to say for both sides of the debate over democracy than was evident in the usual arguments. He was very much concerned with the question of how democracy could be made "prof-

1

itable to man," as its proponents promised it would be, and yet he felt a "religious terror" at the prospect that the forces unleashed by democracy might prove "fatal to humanity," as its opponents warned (6, 13). Tocqueville saw both a peculiar promise and definite dangers in democracy, and he considered the realization of both to be possible, while regarding neither as wholly inevitable. In his writing he sought to articulate a "new political science" capable of enhancing democracy's benefits and avoiding or mitigating its harms (7, 676).

At first glance it may seem that democracy is not in question for us. Contemporary parties in the United States and Europe do not question the merits of democracy or propose it as anything new. In those parts of the world where democracy is new or nonexistent, many—Americans, Europeans, and local citizens—assume that democratization is the only path compatible with the public welfare. Iraq presents a striking example: in the vociferous debate over the United States' decision to depose Saddam Hussein, few questioned that the transition from tyranny to legitimate government in Mesopotamia, if possible, meant the establishment of democracy rather than the restoration of a (once) legitimate monarchy.

At second glance the status of democracy today may not be so obvious. The troubles in Iraq have given prominence to the question, always relevant in modern international affairs, of democracy's exportability. Oddly enough, the nation that believed its manifest destiny was to bring democracy to its own continent and foster it abroad is now painfully unsure of the conditions for establishing democracy and how they might apply to its present foreign commitments. Domestically, democracy is also not as secure as it may seem. In America, the left and right are increasingly divided, not over whether we should have democracy, but over what it entails in such fundamental life spheres as religion, science, and family relations. In Europe, the traditional setting of democracy in the nation-state is giving way to the evolving institutions of the European Union, which has plausibly been accused of running a "democratic deficit." Countries that have recently transitioned from communism to democracy face the decision whether to cling to the authoritarian past, cede significant elements of self-government for the sake of EU membership, or attempt to chart some other route to freedom and prosperity. Everywhere, the competence of democratic states to handle global issues is being challenged by the influence of multinational corporations and international organizations.[3]

In light of these facts, it may be easier now than ever before to see the advantage in returning to an author like Tocqueville, for whom democracy was very consciously and profoundly in question. Still, one might doubt whether a book finished in 1840 can teach us much that is relevant to contemporary problems. To this reasonable doubt there are at least two decisive answers.

First, Tocqueville is far more than a nineteenth century writer. He is an author of immense intellectual stature who, in writing *Democracy*, applied his powers for almost ten years to the study of American democracy, the nature of modern democracy in general, and the future of democracy in the modern world. In his day Tocqueville was celebrated by both conservatives and progressives,[4] and is still admired by figures on the left and right in ours. His magnum opus, *Democracy in America*, is almost universally regarded as the greatest book on America ever written.[5] Readers have perennially been impressed not only by Tocqueville's impartiality, but also by his prescience.[6] Passages of *Democracy* that seemed fanciful when he wrote them came to sound like descriptions of contemporary events. Though many have quibbled with details of Tocqueville's account, his reputation for sagacity has largely increased with time.[7]

The best explanation for Tocqueville's far-sightedness is nothing but the depth of his vision. Pierre-Paul Royer-Collard, a statesman, philosopher, and correspondent of Tocqueville's, compared *Democracy* to the *Politics* of Aristotle and Montesquieu's *Spirit of the Laws*.[8] We know that Tocqueville was classically educated and that he wrote *Democracy* with a library of political thought at his side—from Plato, Aristotle, and Cicero to Tacitus and Plutarch to Machiavelli, Descartes, Pascal, Hobbes, Locke, Montesquieu, and Rousseau.[9] From the way he lived with these great minds and applied their thought to the problems of his present and future, it is evident that Tocqueville himself possessed an intellect of uncommon independence and depth. As a political philosopher, he was thrilled by the opportunity America presented to observe the workings of a political and social system hitherto unknown to humanity (28ff), and in seizing this opportunity he left us with an invaluable guide to understanding how the treasures of philosophic thought bear on the whole picture of modern democracy.

The second defense of Tocqueville's relevance is that his very distance from us helps us constructively to question our assumptions as modern democratic citizens. When he published *Democracy* Tocqueville had been a foreigner in America and was an aristocrat in what he called democratic times (14, 247).[10] He wrote as an outsider, but also as a friend to democracy (666). Unlike other prominent thinkers of the modern age, Tocqueville was not hostile to or dismissive of liberal democracy,[11] but he was able to look at democracy dispassionately and see its flaws and dangers as well as its great promise. Even more importantly, he was willing to call attention to these dangers even at the risk of offending modern readers (400). It is easy to dismiss Tocqueville's criticisms as the murmurs of a dispossessed aristocrat, and accept only what is congenial to us. It is much more useful, however, to remain open to the possibility that Tocqueville is a real but "hard friend" of democracy[12] whose criticisms may be sound medicine for what ails us.

In this spirit, the present volume will undertake a study of Tocqueville's political thought, especially as found in *Democracy*. Though this ground has been covered before, we shall attempt to demonstrate that there is yet more to be gleaned from careful attention to the concept of democracy as Tocqueville defines it, and the distinctive political philosophy informing his judgment of and advice to modern democracy. Through a close reading of *Democracy* and related documents, we shall attempt to grasp the core ethical, psychological, and even metaphysical principles of Tocqueville's thought,[13] and to identify important continuities and discontinuities between his thought and that of authors by whom he was influenced. In doing so, we hope to illustrate Tocqueville's own contention that a great book is not one that dogmatically prescribes to us what we ought to think, but rather one that leads us to think more deeply about the problems we must face for ourselves.[14]

Why Individualism?

Tocqueville numbered himself "among those who believe that there is almost never any absolute good in the laws," and his exploration of the merits and flaws of democracy reflects his view that democracy in itself is not an absolute good (13, 52). Democracy can have many meanings, but the primary meaning Tocqueville ascribed to it was a society founded on the perception of equality among citizens (45ff). One of the chief proclivities Tocqueville attributed to modern democratic citizens was a sort of love affair with equality, to the point that we cannot find fault with it and seek it above all other things (189, 479ff). This tendency can be witnessed in the way we often speak of democracy as if it were the one thing necessary for order and happiness, of equality as if it applied to all spheres of life, and of discrimination as if it were always an evil rather than a frequently necessary skill. Of course, upon deeper reflection it is hard to miss that this is not the case. Who will deny that it is good to discriminate between right and wrong, or that lives must be organized in accordance with the diverse talents and interests of unique individuals? Most tellingly, who would actually be willing to live under the government of pure democracy, where all matters are decided by the majority whatever its views?

What we usually mean to praise when we praise democracy is liberal democracy, a hybrid form of government, associated with a distinct political culture, in which the concept of liberty is at least as important as that of democracy.[15] In fact, most if not all advocates of liberal democracy place liberty above democracy when the two conflict. Take for instance Thomas Jefferson (1743-1826), whom Tocqueville calls "the most powerful apostle that democracy has ever had" (249). In drafting the Declaration of Independence, the birth certificate of our country and the first document in our organic law, Jefferson proclaimed the equality of all men, but he specified that this equality consists in the equal right of all men to liberty. Since equality in liberty means that no one is naturally subject to the jurisdiction of another, it follows that government must be "democratic" in the sense that it is rightfully established only by the consent of the governed. However, all men being equally and naturally free, no one has the right to subject himself or his fellows to a complete loss of natural liberty. Every government has the duty of securing natural rights, and no form of government has the right to abuse them, even with the consent of the governed. The Declaration does not demand that every government be democratic beyond its initial establishment—"any form of government" may in principle be legitimate[16]—but it does demand that every form of government, including popular government, be liberal.

Though the specifics have changed, Americans still seem to regard liberty and democracy in this light. Equality for us is above all equality in liberty. Though equal liberty is significantly expressed in the democratic form of governance—the right to participate in public debate and political processes is a common justification of what we call "civil liberties," for example—we still believe that liberty has a more fundamental meaning that applies even against the will of the majority. This is most evident in the power we have accorded courts to overturn legislation and the acts of elected officials when they are deemed to conflict with our fundamental liberties as Americans or as human beings – especially those liberties enshrined in the Bill of Rights. It is also evident in the way this notion of rights infiltrates almost all of our activities and relationships, prompting us to question and often to rebel against even the most venerable and popular institutions when we are persuaded that they conflict with the equal rights claimed by individuals. In several important cases, such as racial or gender discrimination in public accommodations or the workplace, we even call on the authority of the state to enforce rights in the private sphere.

There are some today who claim that the pursuit of individual liberties and rights has gone too far, that the excessive imposition of "fundamental liberties" by courts erodes democratic governance.[17] This perspective also has its foundations in our civic tradition. Though the Declaration denies government the right to infringe on liberties, it also gives "the people" the ultimate authority to judge when liberties are being violated and what is to be done about it within the limits of prudence. To cede this decision to a handful of "unelected" magistrates may seem illegitimate, imprudent, or both. This objection on behalf of democratic self-governance can itself be rooted in the notion of equal *liberty*, though how this liberty for self-governance squares with the liberty of individual rights favored by present-day courts is another question.

Another objection complains that the notion of rights today is slipping from a focus on negative liberties—the freedom of citizens to act as they please within broad parameters—to an emphasis on equality of outcomes.[18] This view can be accused of pitting one condition of liberty against another, since measures aimed at equalizing "outcomes" (such as affirmative action) are often defended as rectifying circumstances that rob individuals of truly free choices.[19] Though this defense is plausible, so is the view that calling upon judges and administrators to impose their preferred version of liberty on society is ultimately less liberal than allowing citizens to work out liberty's meaning in the private sphere or debate it in the democratic branches of government.

From this two things are evident. First, the nature of modern democracy cannot be grasped without acknowledging the status of liberty as equality's peer in the modern democratic ethos. Second, it is not easy to agree on the precise demands, or even the broad meaning, of liberty. This means that a fundamental—perhaps the fundamental—question we must ask about modern democracy is the nature of liberty and the precise relationship it has to the other leading principle of our society: equality.

As it happens, this is the very task Tocqueville sets for himself in *Democracy*. Though the title of his book refers to democracy and not liberty, Tocqueville's chief argument about democracy, understood as equality of social conditions, is that it will increasingly dominate the modern age, and that it will result in one of two prospects for modern civilization: equality in liberty or equality in servitude (52, 640). Throughout the book, Tocqueville passionately denounces the forms tyranny can and might take in a society dominated by the equality of citizens (243ff, 410, 663). At the same time, he proclaims himself a devotee of liberty and strives to call forth a figurative army to make liberty prevail in modern times (11ff, 643, 666). Like us, Tocqueville insists that equality must be equality in liberty. This agreement might lull us into believing that Tocqueville's analysis of liberal democracy differs from our own only in the eloquence of his accompanying observations. Were this so, Tocqueville's aristocratic perspective and classical education would be mere window dressing on a presentation of democracy that is essentially American.

This study shall argue instead that Tocqueville's foreignness runs deeper, extending to a view of liberty and its nature, goodness, and limitations that differs significantly from, whether or not it conflicts with, that embodied in dominant strains of American political thought. Though Tocqueville had great respect for the principles and practices of American government and political culture, he subtly but forcefully locates key components of our intellectual lineage in philosophic and theological concepts of liberty that he believes to be mistaken and dangerous to society (403ff). Even while frequently using America as a model of how a democratic society can successfully combat its own worst tendencies, Tocqueville indicates that, by the Jacksonian age, Americans had not fully grasped the character of the dangers they were facing or even the solutions they themselves had employed (502).[20] Though he aims these lessons at his French audience, the insights Tocqueville intends to convey can also be read as contributions to a more profound understanding of the American political experiment, an experiment our founders and greatest statesmen understood to be indicative of whether liberal democracy could "long endure" anywhere on earth.[21] And though his approach is rhetorically subtle, Tocqueville seeks to contribute nothing less to this experiment than a new sense of what liberty is and how it ought to guide and limit the concept of equality.

What does Tocqueville have to teach us about liberty? This question can be answered in terms of what liberty is, and in terms of what it is not. Tocqueville's focus in *Democracy* appears to be on the latter point. He is at pains to enumerate the threats democracy poses to liberty, and foremost among these is a phenomenon he labels "individualism." Individualism in the sense Tocqueville employs is a more (*moeur*)—an idea connected to certain habits and sentiments, or a habit connected to certain sentiments and ideas (275). The scope of this more is very broad, and we shall see that its implications run throughout the text of *Democracy*, even in those passages not explicitly referencing the term. The essence of individualism is the willingness of each citizen to withdraw into the private sphere, and neither to act nor desire to act in relation to matters of public concern (482ff). Tocqueville sees individualism as a mistake inasmuch as it conflicts with the nature of human happiness and undermines all political institutions save those of despotism (484ff). He sees it as a particularly dangerous mistake because of its immense allure to human beings formed by the conditions of democratic society (643). In brief, Tocqueville sees individualism as a profound misunderstanding of liberty whose acceptance by democratic citizens will allow them to believe themselves free while they are in fact succumbing to a new and chilling form of despotic control (661ff).

Tocqueville does not exaggerate when he says that his principal goal in writing *Democracy* is to combat individualism (643). Accordingly, this study of Tocqueville's thought will seek to demonstrate and explain the centrality of individualism to his analysis of modern democracy. For this reason our focus may appear rather gloomy. Individualism as Tocqueville describes it is both an error and the natural tendency of democratic societies, features that lend an air of fatality to Tocqueville's frequently somber predictions of the troubles democracy will encounter. Yet these difficulties must be looked at in the proper context. Tocqueville does not think that democracy is alone in being misguided about the path to human flourishing. Rather, his political science emphasizes the proneness of all forms of government and political cultures to prejudice and passion (28). Human nature has such difficulty in "firmly grasping the true and the just," Tocqueville reasons, that political leadership must always strive to mitigate the falsehoods and injustices that are congenital to a given political society and therefore inescapable, though not unmanageable (39, 241, 518).

Despite these theses, Tocqueville's perspective is anything but hopeless. Though he doubts there is usually "absolute good in the laws," he does believe in an absolute good that can be sought with the assistance of laws, however imperfectly adaptable those laws are to the task. By "absolute good," Tocqueville refers to the final end or purpose of a given activity, that for the sake of which everything else is done (221). In classical political philosophy, the end of human life was said to be happiness, which consists in virtue understood as the perfection of the highest faculties of human nature.[22] Although Tocqueville never declares himself to be a proponent of such classical views, there is ample reason to believe that these concepts are indispensible for understanding his thought.[23] In *Democracy*, Tocqueville calls for the intellectual leaders of modern democracy—among whom he is certainly foremost—to become "perfect master[s]" of Greek and Latin literature (452). In an 1852 speech to the Academy of Moral and Political Sciences, of which he was then the president, Tocqueville insisted that the greatest question facing political science in modern times was the proper understanding, comparison, and evaluation of the relative merits of ancient versus modern political thought (1991, 1220-21).

Though he was well aware that modern political philosophers—by some of whom he was profoundly influenced[24]—denied the possibility or goodness of classical virtue or happiness, Tocqueville repeatedly comes back to these (or similar) notions in *Democracy* and uses them directly or implicitly to judge the potentialities of liberal democracy. In a matter no less closely connected to liberty than that of rights, for example, Tocqueville defines rights as virtue applied to the political realm, and defines virtue as that which renders a human being great (227). Greatness and happiness are Tocqueville's favored terms for the highest or most precious goods human beings seek individually and through political institutions, and though he fears these terms will sound strange to modern democratic ears, Tocqueville insists on using them at crucial junctures in his analysis (52, 509, 517, 675). Moreover, Tocqueville defines human greatness in terms of the intellectual and moral association of the individual in what he calls "the admirable order of all things," an expression akin to the ancient Greek κόσμος. Though Tocqueville did harbor certain important reservations about the adequacy of ancient political philosophy, careful consideration of the distinctive notion of liberty animating his critique of individualism will reveal the debt that Tocqueville's "different kind" of liberalism owes to Socratic thought.[25]

For Tocqueville, genuine liberty is both a source of human greatness and itself a form of greatness (11, 52).[26] Since the virtue at which liberty aims is in some sense the opposite of individualism, one can understand why Tocqueville sees individualism as a threat to genuine liberty. Yet virtue, as the perfection of the human being, also involves a sort of "manly independence" (247), so that it might aptly be called "good individualism" or "individualism well-understood."[27] As Jack Lively notes, Tocqueville did not "believe in the sanctity of private values" (1962, 222). He deplored both the tyranny of the majority over the thought of individual minds, and the withdrawal of individuals from engagement with public affairs. The individual Tocqueville exalted above society was not the private individualist but rather the exemplar of human perfection whose virtues provide a model for the common good of society itself. Though politics cannot directly produce such greatness and the happiness it makes possible, which require the free assent of each human being (1957, 117), the existence or non-existence of such virtue is a matter of public as well as private concern. Moreover, laws and mores can assist individuals in seeking virtue by mitigating their worst tendencies and encouraging their best (518). In so doing political society can provide a space in which virtue is likely or at least able to grow and flourish. This, for Tocqueville, is the absolute good at which politics ought always to aim. In order to understand Tocqueville's "new political science," then, it is necessary to explore what he means by virtue and how it can serve as a standard for delimiting the scope and nature of democratic liberty.

Tocqueville's enterprise is one of hope because he believes that he can identify in our nature not only a proneness to error but also a love of truth, not only a vulnerability to selfish passions but also a disinterested willingness to sacrifice for an objective moral order (433ff, 502). Though perfection cannot be demanded of any society, improvement always has the assistance of the better angels of our nature (89).[28] In fact, the greatest strength of democracy for Tocqueville lies in its highest promise, the promise to liberate virtue or human greatness from the artificial constraints of conventional hierarchy and prejudice. While fully endorsing this grand promise, Tocqueville warns that the concepts of equality and liberty, in distorted form, can themselves become obstacles to the realization of human potential. In declaring ourselves "more than kings," he fears, we might unwittingly render ourselves "less than men" (665). In his characteristically paradoxical way, Tocqueville foretells that the promise of democracy might well be broken unless we prove ourselves willing to admit, and combat, democracy's perils.

This study will attempt to unpack Tocqueville's hopes and fears for modern democracy by focusing on the promise of democracy and the threat of individualism. Our first part, "More than Kings," focuses on the concepts of democracy, liberty, and individualism themselves, and on the political science Tocqueville employs to study them. Chapter 1 explains what Tocqueville means by democracy, why he saw its rise as irreversible, what he saw as its peculiar promise, and why he feared it would nonetheless prove destructive of human happiness unless properly directed. Chapter 2 explores Tocqueville's model for a well regulated democracy, one capable of fostering a virtuous liberty through the cultivation of a healthy moral order under the guidance of leaders practicing what Tocqueville calls "the legislative art." Chapter 3 indicates why Tocqueville saw this model as difficult to maintain in modern times, and why he feared that the failure of his legislative art would leave democratic peoples susceptible to an extreme form of individualism paving the way for what he called "administrative despotism." Our second part, "Less than Men?," examines more specifically the means Tocqueville saw as actually or potentially regulating democracy in modern times. Chapter 4 explores the ways in which civic engagement, founded on but tempering individual self-interest, served to combat individualism and foster virtue in Jacksonian America. Chapter 5 considers the role of nineteenth century American Christianity, and the particular moral order it proffered, in doing the same. Chapter 6 recounts the fate of these salutary forces in the century and a half since Tocqueville, and measures the extent to which the decline of Tocquevillian approaches to politics has allowed individualism to become the problem he feared it would. The book concludes with a discussion of how Tocqueville's legislative art might be applied to combat individualism in our own time, and to promote genuine liberty instead.

Notes

1. Unless otherwise specified, parenthetical references are to Tocqueville (2000a). I have occasionally modified the translation, consulting Tocqueville (1961, 1981), e.g. using "liberty" for "*liberté*," "fellows" for "*sembables*," and "pride" for "*orgueil*."

2. For the political-philosophic importance of this claim, see Robert Eden (1990).

3. For a penetrating account of these challenges to the nation-state, and what they mean for democratic governance, see Pierre Manent (2006).

4. André Jardin (1988, 225ff).

5. Harvey Mansfield and Delba Winthrop (Tocqueville 2000a, xvii).

6. See J. P. Mayer (1966).

7. A major exception is Rogers M. Smith (1993), who faults Tocqueville for missing the extent to which inequality has played a role in American history. Smith admits that this critique applies more to certain epigones of Tocqueville than to Tocqueville himself. As our study will show, equality is one of several powerful causes to which Tocqueville's political science appeals in describing American political society, though he clearly sees it as dominant in modern times, and for defensible reasons.

8. Mansfield and Winthrop (Tocqueville 2000a, xxxiii).

9. Jardin (1988, 56ff); Tocqueville (1977, 130-131: letter to Beaumont, April 22, 1838).

10. On Tocqueville's foreignness, see Joshua Mitchell (1995, 1ff).

11. James Ceaser (1990, 15).

12. See Friedrich Nietzsche (1954, 169): "Compassion for the friend should conceal itself under a hard shell, and you should break a tooth on it. That way it will have delicacy and sweetness."

13. Though Tocqueville once likened metaphysics to self-torture, he saw metaphysical opinions as exerting a powerful force on human affairs, and later admitted that he had always sought to achieve the goals of metaphysics through "good sense" (1985, 64, 320: letters to Charles Stoffels of October 22, 1831, and to Francisque de Corcelle of October 16, 1855). Compare Xenophon (1994, I.i).

14. Tocqueville (1985, 294: letter to Corcelle, September 17, 1853); quoted by Eden (1986).

15. Ceaser (1990, 6ff).

16. Martin Diamond (1975).

17. See Robert Bork (1990), Mary Ann Glendon (1991, 1ff), and Antonin Scalia (1997). Compare Franklin Roosevelt (1937).

18. This is the libertarian view, espoused by scholars such as Robert Nozick (1974).

19. Thus John Rawls argues that justice, including significant state intervention in the lives of citizens, is fairness, granting equal chances of happiness to all citizens (2001).

20. Tocqueville ascribes great wisdom to the Puritans and Federalists, whom he sees as having laid the foundations for a self-regulating democracy in America (31ff, 107, 143ff, 168-69, 486-87). Yet as we shall see in chapter two, Tocqueville draws lessons from the Puritans inconsistent with their self-understanding, and uses those lessons to supplement deficiencies in the Federalist account. Compare Ceaser (1990, 14ff).

21. Abraham Lincoln, *Gettysburg Address* (2001).

22. See, above all, Aristotle (2002).

23. Others who have noted this tendency in Tocqueville include Robert Kraynak (1987, 1181ff), George Pierson (1959, 463, 455), André Jardin (1998, 253), James Muller (1975, 40ff), and Albert Salomon (1935, 424). Those who have denied or doubted it include Jack Lively (1962, 13, 222ff), Marvin Zetterbaum (1967, 34, 38, 41), John Koritansky (1986, 9ff, 97ff), Winthrop (1986, 248, 251; 1993, 217), Mansfield and Winthrop (Tocqueville 2000a, xxiiiff, xxxvii), and Manent (1996, 39), though all of the latter acknowledge Tocqueville's concern for human greatness, and some see glimpses of the connection for Tocqueville between greatness and justice.

24. Notably Montesquieu and Rousseau. See Mansfield and Winthrop (Tocqueville 2000a, xxx), and Tocqueville's Letter to Louis de Kergorlay, November 12, 1836 (1977, 418). The third author Tocqueville mentions "living with every day" is Pascal, a profound critic of modernity. Scholars who take Tocqueville to be fundamentally Rousseauian include Allan Bloom (1990) and Koritansky (1986). Those who emphasize the

influence of Montesquieu include Raymond Aron (1965), Ceaser (1990), and Paul Carrese (2003). Tocqueville's connection to Pascal is given more weight by Peter Lawler (1993), Bruce Frohnen (1993a), and Mansfield and Winthrop (Tocqueville 2000a). Ceaser, Carrese, and Mansfield and Winthrop note some parallels between Tocqueville's thought and that of classical political philosophy, while James Muller (1975), Eden (1990), Steven Salkever (1990), and Thomas Pangle (2004) take this point farther. This diversity of influences reveals itself in the plethora of allusions to authors ancient and modern in *Democracy*, references which are often partly admiring and partly critical, demonstrating the breadth and independence of Tocqueville's mind. As Michael Palmer pointed out to me, no one who genuinely combined the insights of Montesquieu, Rousseau, and Pascal is likely to have fit squarely within the thought of any of those three eminent authors.

25. Tocqueville characterized himself as a "liberal of a different kind" (1985, 29: letter to Eugène Stoffels of September 16, 1823).

26. See Tocqueville (1955, Preface). Several insightful scholars have accused Tocqueville of painting liberty in rhetorically sublime colors while failing to define its transcendent qualities. They conclude that liberty for Tocqueville is ultimately negative, signifying the absence of constraint, and thus not coherently connected to any idea of virtue or human greatness. See Jack Lively (1962, 10-11), Zetterbaum (1967, 27-28), Edward Banfield (1991, 42-43), Sanford Kessler (1994, 58), and Pierre Manent (1996, 18-19). This study will attempt to prove otherwise, especially in chapter 2.

27. "Now, is not all the grandeur of man in the grandeur of the individual and not in the grandeur of society, which is an ideal being produced by the spirit of man? Society is made for the individual and not the individual for society. By what strange reversal of things does one arrive at sacrificing the individual in view of favoring society?" (Tocqueville 1990b, 277; compare Mansfield and Winthrop, in Tocqueville 2000a, xxxvii).

28. For Tocqueville's contrast between the beast and angel within human beings, see his discussion in *Democracy* (521) and his letter to Kergorlay (quoted in 1959a, 28).

Part I
More than Kings: The Rise of Democratic Individualism

Chapter 1
Democracy, Political Science, and Human Nature

According to a tradition of classical writing, the key to any great work is in its beginning.[1] Tocqueville, whose college years were steeped in the study and imitation of Cicero and Demosthenes,[2] illustrates this maxim well. He tells us that the key to almost his whole work is in its second chapter, an account of the founding of America (29). The roots of that chapter, however, lie in the preceding chapter and the Introduction he affixed to the first volume of *Democracy*. This study of Tocqueville will not be able to maintain a line-by-line analysis of his great work, but it will begin by following Tocqueville's beginning as closely as possible. This will allow us to grasp the main concepts and modes of thinking that will undergird subsequent discussions. The present chapter will unpack Tocqueville's Introduction, wherein he introduces the concepts of democracy, which he says is conquering "the Christian universe"; of a "new political science" whose teachings ought to guide the leaders of democracy if the latter is to benefit humankind; and of human nature, whose capacity for moral greatness, need for liberty, and dependence upon moral order define the standards by which political science can contribute to democratic governance. Our next chapter will examine the additional concepts, lessons, and model Tocqueville presents in the first and second chapters of *Democracy*. Together, these reflections will prepare us to understand the cause and character of the threat of individualism as Tocqueville sees it, the means by which he seeks to combat it in his writings, and the relevance of those writings to our own time.

The Origins of Democracy

Let us begin with democracy. As noted, Tocqueville is writing for a European audience divided between parties for whom democracy is a radically polarizing concept. Tocqueville agrees with these parties as to the importance of the subject—he does not attempt to see differently than they do, but further (15). By seeing further, Tocqueville explicitly refers to his concern for the long-term future of democracy over and above the more ephemeral career of politicians, platforms, and even dynasties. And yet the beginning of *Democracy*—its introduction and first two chapters—indicate two other meanings of the claim to see further. First, Tocqueville seeks to understand the present and future of democracy by tracing its history, both in Europe (in his introduction) and America (in the first two chapters of volume 1, part 1). Second, he explores the relationship between democracy and human nature, a factor he takes as determinative in understanding what has fuelled the rise of this new social and political order, what its duration and effects are likely to be, and what responses to it are either prudent or imprudent in light of this analysis. Thus Tocqueville attempts to see further into the future as well as the past, and further into the causes of events as well as their outward forms (29).

In seeking Tocqueville's understanding of democracy and its relation to human nature, we must bear in mind that it is not his practice always to spell out the meaning of his analytical concepts. The greatest books, he once wrote, are those in which the author sets the minds of readers "on the road leading to truths [but] has made them find these truths for themselves."[3] This maxim goes back at least as far as Plato, who claimed that a serious man's most serious works are not written, but in his mind.[4] In other words, the true value of philosophic texts lies less in their explicit arguments and more in their ability to frame key issues in a way that inspires profound thought about them. Plato's Protagoras even claims that the poets of old were, in this sense, philosophers in disguise.[5]

If the writing of philosophy can be so artful, then we require a corresponding art of reading the works of philosophers, whose deepest thoughts are not spelled out as such.[6] Of late, the notion of "esoteric writing" has become controversial, but it need not be understood in a sinister light. It can be explained by reference to the phenomena themselves with which great writers deal. Wisdom, insofar as it consists not only in the grasping of general ideas but also in their true application to human life, cannot be stated abstractly (411ff).[7] To be of genuine use, philosophic writing must reveal the contours of reality in all their complexity, requiring the reader—with the author's assistance—to develop wisdom by searching for answers, or at least understanding. This is precisely what Tocqueville does in *Democracy*, which he tells us is organized around a "mother idea" that connects all of its parts, an idea he leaves to his readers to discover (14). In examining the parts of *Democracy* we must be on the search for the key idea or ideas accounting for its whole, an activity that ought to enhance our ability to grasp the realities of democracy and humanity around and within us.

Tocqueville's concepts of democracy and human nature unfold together in his Introduction and beyond. Tocqueville never gives us a definition of democracy—for which he is often faulted—but in his very first lines he identifies it with "equality of conditions," a social phenomenon related to but distinct and even separable from what he calls "the government of democracy" (3, 187ff).[8] A people can be "democratic" without having a democratic system of government because citizens can be equal without governing themselves. Under a totalitarian government, for instance, every citizen and every institution must bend to the will of the state; all are equally subject to it. This perversion of democracy will attempt to justify itself by appealing to the equality of citizens and even to the equality or relativity of moral values, as did Mussolini (1883-1945).[9] It will also show its dependence on the popular will by striving mightily to manipulate it through an intensive and relentless stream of propaganda.[10] A milder but more prevalent threat is what Tocqueville styles "administrative despotism," a system in which citizens rarely or never participate in the decisions of a government that regulates the smallest details of daily life, guaranteeing equality and well-being at the price of genuine liberty (661ff). In this era of declining "social capital,"[11] it is not hard to see what Tocqueville means when he claims that modern societies will be increasingly democratic in the social sense, though not necessarily in political terms.

Democracy as a social state reaches beyond the public vs. private distinction at the core of democratic liberalism.[12] It describes a set of features in a given society—economic, cultural, and psychological equality—that constrain the actions, habits, and thoughts of individuals and private groups as well as governments. The social state not only affects political mores and laws, but even "creates opinions, gives birth to sentiments, suggests usages, and modifies everything" in the life of private citizens (3). Tocqueville claims that the social state, with its powerful effects on all areas of life, was the first phenomenon he noticed in America. Its prominence in his account of liberal democracy forces us from the outset to question the possibility of human liberty in its political, moral, and intellectual forms. Seeing our susceptibility to the influence of the social state makes us wonder whether human nature is capable of genuine freedom, and this wonder prompts us to study the social state and its influence over us in order to free ourselves of this influence and arrive at an independent judgment of political and social questions.[13]

The threat to liberty posed by a fully developed and unregulated social state is very much a part of Tocqueville's message in *Democracy*, and democracy in America exhibits this dangerous maturity, having "nearly attained its natural limits" (12). In Europe—Tocqueville's primary audience—democracy is less mature but has wreaked more obvious havoc. Tocqueville looks to American democracy in order to anticipate the development of the European democratic revolution still in progress. First, however, he gives us an account of that revolution and why Europe is in need of taking lessons from America.

The first question Tocqueville raises about European democracy is how old it is. "Some consider it a new thing," whereas to others "it seems the most continuous, the oldest, and the most permanent fact known in history." If it is new, it may be accidental and still stoppable; this is what royalist authors like Joseph de Maistre (1994) claimed. If it is the most permanent fact of history, then democracy is not only irresistible but worthy of celebration as a return to reason. This attitude can be seen in the tendency of French and American republicans to adorn democracy with symbols from ancient Greece and Rome rather than from the Middle Ages, the immediate ancestor of the democratic age. This signaled not only a rejection of the darkness associated with Christianity and feudalism, but also a conviction that the democratic spirit is a natural phenomenon transcending space and time.[14] We can see a variation of this perspective in our day in the notion that liberal democracy is the final stage of human history, the perfect satisfaction of the basic human desires that have driven our political and cultural struggles to this point.[15]

On the royalist view, democracy is a faddish imposter on the political stage, without justification in the true needs and wants of humankind. Society, including the people, will only be free when it returns to the masters of old. In the republican view, democracy is so fundamental as to be identified with human nature itself, and liberty means embracing it as fully as possible rather than resisting it in any way. Tocqueville, in tracing the history of democracy, chooses neither of these options. In a move designed to challenge the premises of both royalists and republicans, he locates the origins of democracy in twelfth century Europe (4). This implies that democracy in its modern form is nowhere near as ancient or natural as its devotees claim. What we call ancient democracies were not democratic at all in the modern sense, having been based on a social order in which the vast majority of the population were slaves or servants and not free citizens (450). What makes modern democracy possible is of more recent vintage, and cannot so easily be equated with human nature. Nonetheless, democracy is more venerable than royalists would like to think, and therefore reveals more about human nature that they would readily admit. This middle-agedness of democracy signals Tocqueville's view that democracy can neither be thrown off as an accident of history nor blindly embraced, both options representing an oversimplification of human nature and its demands.

Tocqueville's brief history of democracy enables us to see how it obtained its purchase on the minds and hearts of those whose descendents would become modern citizens, revealing both the source of its appeal and any limitations it might have. The story begins in feudal France, whose social and political order was defined by the possession of land, the acquisition or transference of which took place mainly by force (4). Those who owned the land by dint of military ascendency also had "the right of command" over its inhabitants, an arrangement that seemed literally to illustrate the view that "might makes right." Initially, this reign of force was tempered primarily by the rule of inheritance. A man's progeny did not have to fight their father for possession of his estate, as would anyone else.[16] Though we may take the principle of inheritance for granted, there are many ways a society can arrange inheritance, and how it does so says much about it. Tocqueville faults political writers, "ancient and modern," for neglecting the influence of estate laws on the course of history (47ff). Changes in estate laws were a pivotal development in the history of democracy, and it behooves us to look more closely at their forms and effects before and after democracy began its rise.

In feudal times, estate law was founded on primogeniture, meaning that the owner of an estate—a manor or manors, the surrounding land, and governance over the land's inhabitants—was not permitted to sell the family's property or to choose his heir. The estate had to be passed down to the eldest (usually male) heir, to whom it was "entailed." The result was that what Tocqueville calls "family spirit . . . in a way materialized in the land" (48). Land belonged to a family more than to any individual. The family saw itself in the land and saw itself as representing the land, and since the land itself (including governmental power) remained the same from generation to generation, the family perceived itself as existing stably over wide swathes of history. Compared to the family, then, each member and his personal interests seemed small. The general effect of this family spirit on individuals was to subsume their personal selfishness and lead them to act in the interests of the family instead of their own—or even to identify their own interests with those of the family.

The abolition of primogeniture changes this situation dramatically, and it makes little difference whether inheritance becomes elective or a citizen is required to divide his possessions according to some prescribed legal formula. In either case, one knows ahead of time that no estate will remain intact from one generation to the next, and it becomes difficult or impossible to predict what will become of a given family arrangement (including the family's social-political status) over time. Thus the spirit of the family disintegrates, and the members of the family are left to the pursuit of their individual interests (48). This is not wholly a bad thing. Tocqueville later relates how this revolution has transformed the family from a realm of stiff formality and duty to one of sweet love and friendship (558ff). All the same, love and friendship often exact less of us than do formal duties and long-term interests. As a consequence, the tendency for members of modern families is to treat their bonds as they would treat any other personal relationships, coming and going as they please, and keeping or leaving their inheritance (property and social-political stations) according to perceived individual interests. Home sweet home may be sweeter than before, but the place one calls home more frequently changes, and the lives and habits of individuals become much more their own, for better or worse.

What does this teach us about human nature and its relation to law? Tocqueville describes the family spirit and its power as "an *illusion* of individual selfishness. One seeks to perpetuate and in a way *immortalize* oneself in one's remote posterity. Whenever the spirit of family ends, individual selfishness reenters into the *reality* of its penchants" (49, emphasis added). Tocqueville's words reveal his fundamental ambivalence toward the change, which in turn points to his complex view of human nature.[17] On the one hand, the turn to individual selfishness seems to be a liberation from constraints that are arbitrary because they are based in something unreal, artificial, and exaggerated. The family as tied to an estate is not truly eternal, and the attempt to grasp at immortality through the family is ultimately an illusion. There is something much more realistic about a "selfishness" that gives up on such pretensions and looks for ways to make the family serve the interests of its living members.[18]

Yet this transition is not fully satisfactory either to Tocqueville or to actual human societies. Even in democratic countries where the laws of landed property have ceased to support this spirit of the family, many citizens will seek to perpetuate their family "by other means" (49). In fact, the very existence of wills (and trust funds) demonstrates that human beings continue to care about "immortalizing" themselves through their posterity, even when it is much more difficult to do so. By rendering this attempt onerous, the law can encourage citizens to pursue other goods, but it cannot extirpate their natural longing for the good that is glimpsed in familial continuity. Illusory as this good may ultimately be, its appeal demonstrates a fact of human nature to which Tocqueville will constantly return: human beings are naturally motivated not only by individual selfishness but also by a longing to associate with an order of things greater and more enduring than their individual selves (504, 510). By shaping the environment in which we live, the law can favor the development of one human tendency or the other—individualism or the spirit of membership within a greater order—but it cannot uproot either of them from the human heart, which is naturally divided between them (520).

This example also teaches us that the law must sometimes take sides when it comes to this inner conflict of human nature. Leaving citizens free to choose their way in a given sphere, such as inheritance law, is not the same as neutrality. In fact, the freedom to choose along one dimension—the selection of heirs—can itself be a constraint along another dimension of choice—individualism vs. family spirit. A citizen cannot effectively choose to live in relation to his posterity if he and his posterity are free to dispose of their possessions at will. Only a constraint on individual choice—the law of entail—frees him and his descendents to govern their mutual relations in accordance with an common interest greater than their individual desires. To the extent that seeking such a common purpose is natural and beneficial, a law that appears progressive in its multiplication of choices may actually initiate a "work of destruction" with respect to an important element of human happiness (49). Though liberating in some respects, such a law contributes to the erosion of social bonds and tendency toward extreme individualism whose effects Tocqueville dreads (50, 482ff, 643). His analysis therefore points to both the power of legislation and the responsibility of the legislator to wield that power for the genuine good of humanity and not merely for the maximization of liberty abstractly defined.

Returning to the history of democracy, the interest of feudal lords in "immortality" by way of the family helps us to understand the first transition on the way to democracy: the founding and growth of "the political power of the clergy" (4). Christianity proclaims that the gates of Heaven are open to all, poor and rich alike. If anything, the poor seem to have the advantage insofar as it is easier for them to set their hearts on the treasures above rather than on those of the earth.[19] In this and other respects, the teachings of Christianity are quite at odds with the feudal order, which assigned superiority to whomever conquered or inherited land. As Tocqueville knows, this divergence is not the whole picture, and later he identifies key features of Christianity as "aristocratic" by comparison to the spirit of modern democracy (519). Nonetheless, Tocqueville seeks to correct both the reactionary opponents of democracy and its anticlerical votaries by locating the first seed of democracy in the late medieval strengthening of Church power. Like the laws of entail, this power reveals a willingness to regulate worldly goods with an eye to an enduring order that is first imagined and not seen, but is then—through such regulation—realized (at least partly) in political affairs. By offering an immortality not tied to the familial relationships defining socio-political life at that time, the Church was able to influence the aristocracy while organizing its own hierarchy on a much more egalitarian basis. In Tocqueville's words, it placed former serfs in the midst of nobles and even occasionally rendered them more powerful than kings. Thus did a chink appear in the chain binding status to birth and strength.

From this point on, democracy grows as "new routes for coming to power are discovered" (4). The Church moderates the nobility, fostering civilization and stability, which in turn generate a need for civil law and the jurists to formulate and implement it. The rule of law allows commerce to flourish, opening the way to power through success in trade and finance. As piety, legal acumen, and commercial savvy become means of rising in society, the relative "value of birth is seen to decline." "The mind becomes an element in success" for those whose intellectual or moral skills the nobles require; and this in turn opens the door for those who can satisfy the taste for the literature and arts of these newly risen citizens. The pattern is clear: the needs of those in power give status to those who can satisfy those needs; these newcomers in turn have needs that empower others who satisfy them. Eventually the multiplicity of needs establishes such a multiplicity of opportunities for success that the ascendency of no particular group—the nobility included—can be taken for granted. Democracy as a social state emerges from this gradual but ultimately radical destabilization of the feudal order.

This is not the end of democracy's story, but it is a very significant stage, and we must pause here to see what lessons Tocqueville draws from it. Democracy emerges from the diminishment of the class or caste system and the growth of what we would call equality of opportunity. Tocqueville's terms are less prosaic and indicate what he sees as the promise and peril of democracy so understood. "Once works of the intellect had become sources of force and wealth," he writes, advancement was open to all on the basis of talent (5). "Poetry, eloquence, memory, the graces of the mind, the fires of the imagination, depth of thought . . . profited democracy . . . by putting into relief the natural greatness of man." What Tocqueville means by equality and democracy here must be precisely understood. Equality signifies the lack of any artificial or conventional barrier to the emergence of the natural talents possessed unequally by human beings. Since Heaven distributes these gifts at random, as Tocqueville puts it, they cannot be assigned to any pre-ordained social class. Still, the natural expression of these talents is a society in which some citizens succeed and are admired more than others.

This stage of democracy corresponds to the hope of men like Thomas Jefferson that democracy, by providing equality of opportunity, would facilitate the emergence of a "natural aristocracy" based on talents and virtue, as opposed to the conventional one that had been based on force and prejudice (50).[20] Tocqueville clearly sympathizes with this hope, which regards equality not simply as good (or just) in itself, but also as good for facilitating those accomplishments that constitute human happiness. In fact, it is precisely in democracy's ability to facilitate the recognition and rise of a "natural aristocracy," and to break down arbitrary barriers to human flourishing, that Tocqueville locates the power, promise, and justice of modern democracy (compare 52, 383, 413). Yet Tocqueville is less sanguine than Jefferson about the prospects of democracy fulfilling this great promise.[21] Several features of the new democratic order emerging from the ruins of the old feudal society combine to fill Tocqueville with a "religious terror" at the thought of what the democratic revolution might still do to European society if allowed to continue without direction (6).

The virtues and vices of democracy stem from the same root: the distribution of favor and power according to the satisfaction of human needs or desires. When a conventional aristocracy is firmly in place, power belongs only to it and to those who meet its demands. Thus the resources of society—the material and moral support society lends to the development of human talents—are distributed according to the peculiar needs or tastes of this class. Those talents the nobility recognizes are likely to flourish, and those it despises or deplores will tend to languish. Insofar as the nobility's whims disagree with the natural character of human greatness, this dynamic stifles general happiness. Democracy liberates humankind from the whims of the conventional aristocracy, and raises the possibility of a distribution of rank in accordance with natural talent. This is the promise of democracy as Tocqueville sees it. Of course, some means must remain for selecting which talents will be supported and which will be ignored. Ironically, the very selection process by which democracy liberates us from the choices of the old nobility threatens, without further regulation, to betray the promise of democracy and to stifle human achievement in a different, but no less arbitrary, way.

Democracy drowns out the influence of the aristocracy by multiplying the needs whose fulfillment brings success. The trouble is that success is thereby tied to the satisfaction of "the most superficial passions of the human heart as well as the most profound" (5). Democracy in itself cannot guarantee that those who aim at satisfying the better desires of men will prosper more than those who aim at gratifying our baser nature, or even that the latter will not end up over-whelming the former with their success. Thus democracy cannot guarantee that it will, on balance, give more encouragement to the good use of human talents rather than to their misuse. In fact, Tocqueville sees a distinct danger that democracy will *naturally* tend toward the latter effect. Plato's Socrates brought out this flaw in democracy by likening it to a group of children asked to choose between a physician who would provide them with healthy but bland fare and a cook whose tasty treats would bring them a pleasant malnourishment.[22]

It may seem unfair to compare democratic citizens to children, but the parallel is at least plausible when it is a question of promoting human greatness and happiness. By definition, greatness is a rare and difficult thing. Although we can all recognize and admire it, it is easier for both the potentially great and their admirers to settle for the satisfaction of mundane necessities and superficial or even harmful pleasures rather than to sustain the extraordinary efforts and make the painful sacrifices needed to cultivate genuine virtue. This danger is manifest in our commercial society today. In a democratic or "free market" environment, one can amass more wealth by making soap than by producing great literature, and one can sell more soap by patronizing soap operas than by supporting budding Shakespeares. Worse yet, one can sell more wares of almost any kind through advertisements suffused with sophisticated but callous appeals to selfish and unregulated passions. Even the U.S. Army has stooped to peddling itself as "an army of one."[23] Finally, one can profit immensely by selling pornography or deadly narcotics even in a legal environment that attempts without full success to restrict or ban these "products." Although free choice can and sometimes does support the excellent use of human talents, it also can and does provide immense stimulation for what is least impressive in our nature. Only adherence to some standard beyond equal choice itself can solve this dilemma.

Though Tocqueville finds no reason to conclude that the very worst desires will become the norm in democratic societies—he predicts that violence and brutality will be less prevalent than apathy and mediocrity (567ff, 674)—he is under no illusion that the liberation of human talent through the mass liberation of human desire will automatically make for the flourishing of genuine human greatness. Instead, for reasons we shall explore later, Tocqueville considers this liberation, all by itself, more likely to drive humanity into a state of decline, one that is tolerable to most of us but incompatible with the grand promise of happiness that made democracy seem so fair in the first place—unless something extraordinary is done to direct democracy's course.

This threat of mediocrity, which alone is enough to sadden and chill Tocqueville as he considers democracy's future (674), is not the end of democracy's dangers. Democracy brings noble and serf, rich and poor closer and closer to one another even as it throws into doubt the standards that once governed their relations (6). More precisely, it replaces any fixed standard of relations with that of subjective interest or desire. This begs the question of why those who end up with less in such a system—less money or less honor—ought to respect that outcome. It raises the question of why, "after having destroyed feudalism and vanquished kings, democracy will recoil before the bourgeoisie and the rich." As opportunities are equalized through the reign of individual desire, the abstract idea of equality becomes increasingly attractive to the human heart. This attraction is enhanced by two powerful and seemingly contrary inclinations of the human psyche. First, human beings have a tendency to respect or even worship what appears to be most powerful, and as equality is seen to dethrone authority after authority it tends to grow in moral clout for this reason (479ff). Second, human beings tend to resent others with more power or status than themselves, and equality becomes attractive as a rhetorical weapon by which the advantages of the talented can be made to appear unjust (189). The result is that measures to combat inequality and with it the natural talents that are its cause will gain increasing appeal in a democratic society.

In this light consider the work of John Rawls (2001), perhaps the most influential political theorist today. His main principle is that inequality is intolerable unless it demonstrably serves to benefit those who are worst off. The term benefit is highly subjective, since in the "original position"—the imaginary condition from which Rawls insists one must deliberate about constitutional matters—one does not know the ends to which anyone will employ the "basic goods" distributed by society. Thus, for the sake of "justice," a philosopher might have to give up goods that would otherwise secure his leisure to philosophize so that another citizen may have more time to pursue his special interest, counting blades of grass! Though Rawls does not demand absolute equality, and though he subjects the idea of equality to that of the good in principle, it seems evident that his standard tends, by abstracting from the nature of the good to which equality is directed, to draw the strong (in Tocqueville's words) to the level of the weak rather than elevating the small to the rank of the great (52). This blending of subjectivism and egalitarianism may account for why Rawls has been more successful than those who embrace only one or the other, such as libertarians (who tend to maximize individual choice regardless of outcomes, or to attribute all good outcomes to the maximization of free choice) and Marxists (who reject "formal" in favor of substantive equality, and hence call for an absolute leveling of goods).

Tocqueville teaches that equality is legitimate when and only when it seeks to make all men great (52). Since this goal is not strictly achievable, equality is only legitimate when it accepts certain significant limits on its aspirations. In this, Tocqueville shares an affinity with Alexander Hamilton (1755-1804), who wrote that "the first object of government" is "the protection of different and *unequal* faculties of acquiring property" (Publius 1996, emphasis added). It is important to note, however, that while Tocqueville approves of Hamilton's guardedness toward equality (168-69), Tocqueville is unwilling to reduce unequal talents to facility at material acquisition, and thereby to abstract from the question of what constitutes a good life (506ff).

On Tocqueville's view, democracy is in danger of being caught between two dismaying options. Option one is a "laissez-faire" system in which talent is rewarded for its abuse or neglect as much or more than for its full development. Option two is a system that stifles talent altogether in the pursuit of an equal and uniform distribution of goods. Tocqueville's evident interest in the promotion of human greatness—the healthy and complete flourishing of human talent— causes him to fear both possibilities. Still, Tocqueville does not believe either tendency of modern democracy can be completely avoided. Instead, he addresses his fears by developing a "new political science" that is able to come to terms with the fact of modern equality, seeking to direct democracy as much as possible toward the realization of its promise—the liberation of natural talent— and the minimization of its perils, chief among which is ignorance of or apathy toward the existence of human greatness itself (7ff, 518-19, 661ff).

Political Science and the Pursuit of Moral Order

Tocqueville has come to be seen as the prophet of democracy.[24] In part this is because of the perceived accuracy of his predictions concerning the character of modern societies.[25] No doubt he also invites this designation by frequently employing religious language to explain the dominance of equality in modern times. In his Introduction, Tocqueville claims that the democratic revolution is victorious throughout "the Christian universe" (6). He famously refers to it as "a providential fact," citing its universality, its duration, and its uncanny ability to profit even from those who oppose it. Democracy's "gradual and progressive development" gives it "the sacred character of the sovereign master's will," making it appear that those who want to stop democracy are daring "to struggle against God himself" (7). It would almost seem that, after having rejected the republican notion that democracy is the absolute good determined by nature, Tocqueville has now come to the same conclusion on supernatural grounds. In the face of democracy, he suggests, nations have nothing more to do than "to accommodate themselves to the social state that Providence imposes upon them." Has Tocqueville avoided the blind worship of democracy in one form only to embrace it in another?[26]

We see immediately that this is not the case, for Tocqueville goes on to decry the "frightening spectacle" of "Christian peoples" who are allowing themselves to be swept away by the torrent of democracy (7). It is possible, he warns, that the current of democracy will plunge them into an abyss, but if so, it would be their own fault for failing to realize that "their fate is in their [own] hands." The leaders of Christian nations in Tocqueville's day had divided into two camps, one completely opposing democracy and the other wholly embracing it. This left countries like France to vacillate between two extremes: when democracy took power, "it was adored as the image of force; when afterwards it was weakened by its own excesses, legislators conceived the imprudent project of destroying it." What no one had tried, and what Tocqueville recommends, is for "those who direct society" to "take hold of [democracy] so as to direct it." Likening democracy to a child, Tocqueville calls upon "the most powerful, the most intelligent, and most moral classes of the nation"—the natural aristocracy—"to instruct" democracy and even to "correct it" where that is necessary, but not to cast it out into the street. Since democracy will inherit power despite all opposition, it must not be neglected and left to "its savage instincts," but instead given an education rendering it capable of governing as well as possible. To outline this education, to show its necessity and its possibility, is the goal of Tocqueville's "new political science."

Tocqueville presents democracy in two seemingly opposite lights: on the one hand, as an inevitable decree of Divine Providence; and on the other, as a project to be perfected through human knowledge and will. This presentation foreshadows his later pronouncement that Providence has left us partly free and partly bound, tracing a "fatal circle" within which we are free to choose (676). Equality of conditions is inescapable, but it depends on us whether equality leads "to servitude or freedom, to enlightenment or barbarism, to prosperity or misery." It is the task of political science to describe to us our social condition and the limits it places on our political choices, as well as to illuminate the choices we have by instructing us in "the science of affairs," in the "true interests" of humanity, and in the means of adapting government "to time and place," "to circumstances and men" (7).

In teaching us how to work within the social state, political science is not silent about what we should think of the social state itself. Tocqueville insists that political science depict the social state and its main features in such a way as to persuade citizens of their divine origin. For political science is charged with instructing society not only for the sake of enhancing its knowledge of affairs, but also so as "to purify its mores" and "if possible to reanimate its beliefs" (7). The logic pointing to this commission is simple but rich with implications. Tocqueville holds that no social state is absolutely good when left to its own tendencies (240ff). Every socio-political order is in need of moderation, and such moderation is most effective when it takes the form of deliberate and habitual self-restraint. This is provided by mores, the moral and intellectual habits of a people, which Tocqueville considers more important than the laws themselves for explaining the success or failure of nations (292ff). Mores in turn are formed by multiple causes, including certain influential laws (e.g. laws of inheritance supporting or dissolving the spirit of the family) and the social state itself. Tocqueville also contends, however, that mores cannot be founded without beliefs (11). Indeed, due to the centrality of beliefs to the economy of the human action (417), what citizens believe about the connection of their social state to the divine will must have a powerful effect on the mores they form, including those by which the excesses of the social state itself is moderated.

Beliefs about the social state are central to the formation of mores for three reasons. First, the social state is the dominant factor in the life of any society, the "generative fact" from which all other features of life flow, or by which they are modified (3). For example, the family exists in both aristocratic and democratic societies, but its structure and relationship to individuals and laws is drastically different in each. Second, human beings tend to revere what seems most powerful and irresistible in their lives, imbuing it with cosmic moral significance. This tendency is essential to what Tocqueville calls the human soul, which is degraded not by "the use of power or the habit of obedience," but by the use of illegitimate power or obedience to usurped and oppressive power (8). When forced to submit to a given rule, one can hope to escape degradation by finding it to be legitimate. Therefore it is tempting to believe, even contrary to other evidence, that a power to which everything else submits—and such a power is the social state—is the touchstone of legitimacy (479ff).

From this follows the third cause of the social state's prominence: the tendency of citizens to identify the defining principle of their social state with the requirements of universal justice. In aristocratic times, Tocqueville observes, the human mind is possessed by the fact of inequality and finds it next to impossible to conceive of the notion that two beings might be or be treated as equal. Hierarchy and difference are seen even where they do not exist or are not justified (420-21). In democratic times, the opposite effect is felt. The more conditions are made equal, the more residual inequalities or differences strike the eye as unusual and offend it as unjust (640ff). As equality increases, toleration of inequality lessens, and the zeal for equality and uniformity increases. This zeal becomes a blind passion, increasingly impervious to any rational criteria of discrimination.

Tocqueville does not believe that the first two effects of the social state—its dominance or the reverence it thereby inspires—can be avoided. Those who still seek to defeat democracy will themselves be defeated, and any rebellion it may continue to provoke in the hearts of citizens will result at best in sterile if honest attempts to preserve aristocratic institutions or ideas (675). Most citizens will therefore accept democracy as the actual and legitimate foundation for social and political order. The key for Tocqueville is in the third effect—the deification of the social state itself. The way in which the social state is revered makes all the difference for a society, and is variable enough that political science may here seek to exert a beneficent influence.

The variable in question comes to light when we contrast Tocqueville's account of democracy's providential character with his description of democracy's blind devotees. The latter worship democracy "as the image of force" (7). In response to its power, they treat it like a god and therefore tolerate no limits to it. Tocqueville, in a subtle but significantly different phrase, describes democracy as the will of the Creator and "sovereign master" of nature.[27] By calling democracy the will of God, Tocqueville hopes to persuade citizens that to oppose it is immoral as well as futile,[28] and to paint their submission to it legitimate and therefore not degrading. By refusing to identify democracy as itself a god, Tocqueville leaves room for the possibility that God expects us to embrace democracy in a reasoned, critical, moderate, and liberal fashion. He compares democracy to the stars of heaven, which the Bible insists are signs of God's grandeur and not beings to be worshipped. Thus Tocqueville makes clear that modern man, however fundamental he considers democracy to be, must conceive of it as existing within a moral order, rather than itself constituting a sufficient moral order.

This attempt to place democracy within a theological-moral order is an essential feature of Tocqueville's political science, and the remainder of his Introduction presents us with its justification and initial application to American democracy. The justification emerges from Tocqueville's brief account of the moral order and its effects in former times, "when royal power, leaning on the aristocracy, peacefully governed the peoples of Europe" (8). Though he admits that feudal society was in some ways miserable compared to modern society, Tocqueville also contends that it enjoyed "several kinds of happiness one can conceive and appreciate only with difficulty in our day." The causes of such happiness appear to be two. First was the division of power among the king and nobles, which "raised insurmountable barriers against the tyranny of the prince." Of course, this did not prevent the king and nobles combined from oppressing the people. Thus, the second cause is of even greater importance—and that cause is nothing but the moral order itself.

Tocqueville depicts the effect of moral order on three distinct classes within the feudal order: kings, nobles, and people (8). In each case, the moral order places a check on the will of the group in question without degrading souls. Kings, though "vested in the eyes of the crowd with an almost divine character," were conscious of receiving this respect from the people and reluctant to abuse it.[29] The nobles possessed an even greater legitimacy than kings: their authority was seen as "a trust placed by Providence in their hands." The social-political hierarchy of aristocratic times appeared as providential as does democracy in democratic times, but the aristocracy regarded their authority as borrowed from a higher power who expected them to use it well. Thus, "without seeing in the poor their equal," they "nevertheless took the sort of benevolent and tranquil interest" in their lot "that the shepherd accords to his flock." The people, for their part, acted without baseness even when they resigned themselves to the injustices of their chiefs, because they regarded these iniquities as "inevitable evils sent by the arm of God." Of course, they loved their superiors more when they were lenient and just, and in this judgment they were supported by usages and mores that, inspired by a moral order transcending the social state, placed boundaries on the otherwise arbitrary power of the nobility.

Although Tocqueville's brief portrait of the feudal order is somewhat (and deliberately) idealized, it does not pretend to represent the ideal condition of humanity. Tyranny is moderated and not eradicated; leisure, luxury and refinements among the few exist side by side with labor, coarseness, and ignorance among the many. As Tocqueville's previous history of democracy has shown, these divisions were not made purely in accordance with natural talent or desert (8). Yet we should never forget that for Tocqueville "there is almost never any absolute good in the laws" (13). For him, the moderation of tyranny is a tremendous achievement, as are the positive fruits this moderation bore in medieval Europe: the cultivation of the mind and arts by the nobility, and of "generous sentiments, profound beliefs, and savage virtues" in the people (8). Tocqueville's political science seeks to emulate this model in order to apply a similar check to the tyrannical tendencies of democracy. The people, like the aristocracy of old, must be persuaded to wield their authority as a providential trust and not as an absolute empowerment. Those who benefit from democratic favor must, like the kings of old, seek to merit that favor. And those at risk of ill-treatment by democracy must be protected by usages and mores if possible or, if not, at least saved from degradation by an understanding and acceptance of the providential necessity of their fate. Through this appeal to an overarching moral order, Tocqueville seeks to regulate the concept of equality and promote those virtues compatible with modern democratic society (675-76).

Democracy, Moral Order, and Human Nature

Tocqueville's Introduction to *Democracy* presents not one but two models for the desired democratic moral order. The first model, while attractive to many of Tocqueville's readers, and even similar to positions he embraces in the rest of his book, proves fundamentally inadequate, requiring Tocqueville to press further in his search for an order that will attenuate democracy's vices and bring out its natural advantages (7-8). Examining this model's promises and flaws will prepare us to see what Tocqueville is after and why he has chosen to pursue it through a book focused on democracy *in America*.

This first attempt at a democratic moral order emerges when Tocqueville follows his account of the historical feudal order with a hypothetical description of its democratic counterpart (8-9). The premise of this hypothesis is that social ranks have become confused, land has been divided, power has been partitioned, intelligence has been equalized, and social equality has generally prevailed without opposition, so that "the empire of democracy is peacefully established over institutions and mores." In this "empire of democracy" we see an idealized depiction of the means by which democracy might regulate and moderate itself without appeal to principles foreign to democracy itself. Thus Tocqueville makes clear that the government in this society has no divine character, the citizens feel no special pride and have no lofty ambitions, and do not consciously choose to make great sacrifices for the common good. Government works because the people consider it necessary, regard its laws as their own works, insist on their rights as a matter of reciprocity, associate with one another as the necessary price of freedom, and even stumble into heroic acts in the course of defending the common good in which they all share. In such a society mediocrity prevails, but an order is sustained in which rights are respected, license is checked, and government works for the benefit of all.

Readers of *Democracy* will no doubt be struck by the resonance between this portrait and many passages of the book that follows, and a true measure of its significance requires us to see precisely how this hypothetical model compares to the reality of democracy as Tocqueville observed it in America. America both vindicates and vitiates this model, depending on the depth of one's analysis. On the one hand, Tocqueville describes America as a political society in which the people regard themselves as like God: the origin and end of all things (55). Naturally, this lessens their disposition to revere any mind or will other than their own (404). Nevertheless, they obey the law because it is their own and respect the rights of others so that their own may be respected (229ff, 227ff). They frequently abandon their usual absorption in private affairs to see to public business, conscious that their private affairs depend upon it (500). Though they do not study philosophy, Americans are nearly perfect Cartesians, passing most ideas and customs before the bar of individual reason, and employing their reason to calculate how things private and public can profit them individually (403ff). It almost seems as if America is simply the embodiment of the "empire of democracy" from Tocqueville's Introduction.

Yet Tocqueville's complete analysis of the American soul paints a far more complex picture. He presents the United States as a country founded as much on the religious zeal of the Puritans as on worldly self-interest, and claims that certain dogmas and mores of Christianity still possess unquestioned authority in America, so much so that Christianity is its first political institution (31ff, 406, 280). He speaks of a trajectory of civic involvement by which Americans only begin to participate in political life for reasons of calculated self-interest. Once they have satisfied themselves that seeing to the public good is rational in this sense, Americans often become wholly absorbed in public affairs (63ff, 488ff). They come to consider politics half their life and cherish their political freedoms as good in themselves, not only as means to private prosperity (228). They even grow to identify themselves with their country so viscerally that they cannot bear to hear strangers criticize its climate or soil (227). They willingly sacrifice their own good for that of the public, moved by genuinely disinterested passions, and suspend their business enterprises for an entire day every week in order to contemplate a divine order of magnificence and virtue (502, 517). Even in America, where democracy developed peacefully along with mores and laws, the empire of democracy does not reign without bowing to goods that transcend the horizon of democracy itself. These transcendent goods reveal what is missing from the "empire of democracy," and in doing so reinforce the importance of measuring one's model of moral order against the standard of human nature.

Tocqueville's assertion that there is almost never any absolute good in the laws gives him a characteristic impartiality when it comes to the social state. He insists that one not judge democracy by the standards of aristocracy, or vice versa, even describing these two social states as distinct humanities (675). This last expression is clearly hyperbolic, though, for Tocqueville is constantly judging both of these social states, not by the standards of the other, but by the standard of humanity itself. Though human nature is always found in one social context or another, and though a major feature of human nature is the need to accept the legitimacy of the prevailing social order, human nature has needs that do not derive from the social state (510), and no social state perfectly captures the complexity of human nature and its needs (223, 518). Aristocracy aims at glory and greatness while ignoring the haphazard distribution of talents and the natural right to liberty of all men (234-35, 413). Democracy formally recognizes the liberty of all, but offers little support to great talents and even threatens to stifle intellectual and moral greatness in the pursuit of absolute equality and uniformity (52, 189, 480ff, 645ff). These defects account for Tocqueville's view that the law rarely embodies the absolute good—for Tocqueville measures the absolute good in terms of the perfection of human nature, and not the perfection of the goals of the social state, at which laws typically aim. What is absent from the empire of democracy but present in America is an understanding that the ultimate purpose of life transcends, without repudiating, the order defined by equality, and hence a willingness to embrace laws and customs that moderate the flaws of democracy despite its regnancy.

This glance at American democracy helps us to understand why Tocqueville holds that "everything [is] not good and useful in an order of things like" the empire of democracy he describes in his Introduction (9). Though this empire represents "all the goods [democracy] can offer" to humanity, democracy itself is not in command of all or even of the greatest goods humanity craves. What democracy needs, and what Tocqueville's political science is intended to provide, is a moral order both suited to its particular character, and determined to compensate for its peculiar limitations. This, and not the empire of democracy pure and simple, is what Tocqueville goes on to recommend to the Europeans of his day, and it is the lesson he hopes to teach through the example of American democracy. It is a lesson pointing to the necessity of a firm grasp of human nature and the absolute good that perfects it—of an "elevated ground" from which legislators and other leaders may survey democracy, judge it, and guide it away from misery and toward happiness (702, note XXII).

The remainder of Tocqueville's Introduction demonstrates the need for an intellectual leadership of democracy, based in such an understanding of human nature, that respects the necessary limits posed by the democratic social state while transcending those limits in thought and mitigating their consequences in deed. In keeping with his view that great books assist the reader in discovering the most important truths rather than stating them outright, Tocqueville demonstrates the centrality of human nature and its good in this Introduction without trumpeting his own view of the subject. The reader must be alert for clues to be found in countless passages of *Democracy*, but most of all to the "sum of ideas," the "general impression," and the "mass of reasons" presented by the work as a whole (14-15).[30] The first clues are to be found in the final passages of his Introduction, in his articulation of the problems democracy faces and in the character of those citizens he calls to help solve them.

The problems of democracy emerge in Tocqueville's account of the issues plaguing France in his day, issues which are partly practical (10). The government has inherited all the prerogatives of the nobility, leaving no one to check its power. Without a fixed notion of rights, the wealthy and poor can only relate to one another by means of fear and force. Self-interest has replaced virtue, but without a science of interest it cannot be well-directed. The greatest practical problem, however, stems from the centrality of moral order in human affairs. Society is tranquil not from a sense of well-being, but from the inability or unwillingness of citizens to make efforts toward well-being. As Tocqueville later explains, almost every human action is born from the idea we have of God, our own nature, and the duties and rights they impart to us (417). Each individual requires fixed ideas of these things in order to live well, and every society relies upon a common understanding of them to harness the collective action of its members. In the absence of such a moral order, citizens lack "the courage and energy needed to seek something better" (10, compare 86ff). A democracy so limited will halt amidst the ruins of aristocracy without being able to build its own civilization.

Any of these practical problems might be addressed by building an "empire of democracy," or a moral order in which democracy itself is the guiding principle. Yet Tocqueville's enumeration of problems French democracy faces does not end with these. He finds the problems "in the intellectual world no less deplorable" than the practical ones, and even believes that the former should evoke more sadness and pity than the latter (10-11). By the intellectual world, Tocqueville refers to the complex interrelation between human sentiments and ideas that defines us as human beings. He claims that "the natural bond that unites opinions to tastes and actions to beliefs has been broken" in the heat of the battle for and against democracy, and that each of the parties has taken up "a language that corresponds poorly to [its] true sentiments and secret instincts." In the account that follows, Tocqueville seeks to demonstrate the inner contradiction in the positions taken by both opponents and proponents of democracy, and to persuade his contemporaries to take up more coherent views. Though he aims at forming a coalition in favor of democracy, however, Tocqueville does not attempt to unite all parties into one camp. Instead, he declares certain figures to be usurpers of democratic leadership and calls for their expulsion and replacement by others. Far from cooling the heat of prior battles, Tocqueville rallies a new army and prepares it for a coup d'état. After discussing the democratic revolution in general, and the French Revolution in particular, Tocqueville stages a revolution of his own. His motives for doing so help us to understand his own view of human nature and why it impels him to write a book to combat democratic individualism.

For Tocqueville, sentiments and ideas are naturally bound to one another by what he calls "the laws of moral analogy" (10).[31] Although he does not spell out the provisions of these laws, his discussion implies that language, through which we form and express ideas, beliefs, and opinions, must be harmonized with sentiments, instincts, and tastes. Actions should then follow from this union. This does not imply that all sentiments are created equal, and that authenticity or sincerity in the expression of one's true feelings is the essence of the good life. Rather, Tocqueville believes that some sentiments and their corresponding ideas are naturally high because they correspond to objects that are naturally high, and others are naturally low on account of their corresponding objects (456). The problem of democracy in France has been that its core idea—that of equal liberty for all—has been seized upon by "base and servile souls," "men without patriotism and morality," and interpreted according to their low instincts (12). "Noble and generous spirits," on the other hand, and "honest and enlightened citizens," have opposed democratic liberty, largely for its association with the venal spirits Tocqueville condemns. Democracy itself is inevitable, but it will flourish if and only if provided with a worthy moral order, and a moral order worthy of human nature can only come from the leadership of souls able to take hold of democracy's central doctrines and direct them in terms of what is truly and naturally good for human beings.

Tocqueville's book is not aimed at reconciling all parties to democracy so much as to the formation of a new generation of leaders reconciled to democracy and willing to strive against all opposition in the cause of ennobling it. These leaders need not all approach democracy from the same perspective, yet Tocqueville does not welcome all perspectives into the coalition he forms. Rather, he reaches out to what he will later call the "natural aristocracy," to those "virtuous and peaceful men whose pure mores, tranquil habits, ease, and enlightenment naturally place them at the head of the populations that surround them" (50, 11). Whom he includes and excludes from this aristocracy tells us much about Tocqueville's views on what is naturally high and low, naturally good and bad, and thus sets the stage for his more detailed exploration of this moral terrain in *Democracy* as a whole.

Tocqueville calls upon three groups to unite their efforts on behalf of democracy (11). The first are "Christians . . . full of zeal, whose religious souls love to nourish themselves from the truths of the other life"; the second are earthly men, "partisans of liberty" who see in it not only "the origin of the noblest virtues" but "above all . . . the source of the greatest goods"; the third are "naturally proud and noble men" with "independent minds and generous hearts," who appreciate "what is holy and great in" liberty. These groups are divided when it comes to the absolute good for human beings. Some place it in this life, and others in the next. Some see it in the virtues or goods liberty produces, others in liberty as something virtuous and good in itself. All are potentially in agreement that liberty is part of a complex of human goods including virtue and earthly prosperity and must therefore be embraced as the guiding principle of modern civilization. To reach this point, Christians must only reflect that human liberty is the source of all moral greatness; partisans of liberty must see the dependency of liberty on mores and of mores on religious beliefs; and independent minds must see the necessary connection between democratic liberty and the noble and proud liberty they possess. Tocqueville's political science aims at persuading each of these groups to join this consensus on the merits of democratic liberty well understood, which he styles "the holy cult of liberty" (12).

Whether Tocqueville's view of the good corresponds to one of these groups, or is something else entirely, remains to be seen. Our first clue comes from looking at those he excludes from this aristocracy: all those "who, in the name of progress, striving to make man into matter, want to find the useful without occupying themselves with the just,[32] to find science far from beliefs, and well-being separated from virtue" (11). It is true that Tocqueville does not simply exclude from his coalition those who are skeptical or even disbelieving with regard to religion and virtue. "Materialists," who look to the earthly benefits of democratic liberty, may join Tocqueville's coalition provided that they understand the benefits of both religion and virtue for democracy.[33] Nonetheless, Tocqueville's own criterion for democratic leadership is centered on an idea of virtue as an immaterial or transcendent good grounded in nature (456). In fact, Tocqueville holds that the peril facing democratic society is found in the prospect of humanity losing the use of its most sublime faculties, "not elsewhere" (519). For Tocqueville, virtue is not a means to gain material goods, but vice versa.[34]

Tocqueville is therefore firm in his rejection of those who would embrace the "empire of democracy" without qualification. Rather, he insists that democracy preserve in its citizens those elements of human life that transcend our narrowly individualistic and materialistic preoccupations. The pursuit of private interests must be accompanied by a love of justice or the common good. Knowledge of affairs must be joined to beliefs about the greater purpose of human life. The desire for material well-being must be moderated by the ability to master one's own desires through the practice of virtue. Democracy demands a moral order transcending democracy itself because human nature requires us to live in relation to an order transcending the human individual (417, 502-21), not a merely conventional order that is reducible to the aggregate of individual wants (240). The individualism Tocqueville writes to combat is therefore best understood as the antithesis of the sort of virtue he calls upon his readers to cultivate in democratic society (643, 675).

Tocqueville's Introduction gives us an account of the origins of democracy, the responsibility of political science to outline a moral order capable of embracing yet directing democracy, and the relation of that moral order to the demands of human nature. In the Introduction itself, all of this comes in highly compact form, and serves to prepare the way for the more extensive and detailed examination of these topics in *Democracy* proper. Through the example of American democracy—which he constantly compares to other political orders, modern, medieval, and ancient—Tocqueville develops his ideas of the trajectory of democratic social change, the options political science faces in responding to such change, and the broader implications of this change and response for human happiness. In America, Tocqueville sees an image of democracy itself, and is therefore able to use America to make generalizations about what all modern democratic peoples will face (13). In America he also finds a democratic system that has neither been stifled by reactionaries nor simply left to its blind instincts, but rather hedged in with laws and mores suitable to a healthy democratic society (12). Tocqueville is therefore able to use America as a basis for reflection on what regulations and directives are possible and beneficial for democratic peoples in general. He is neither uncritical of all features of American democracy nor naïve enough to believe that what is good in America can simply be transplanted to other places (12-13). Yet America is an ideal setting for him to develop a political science that can guide or at least enlighten the inhabitant of any modern democratic society. It is to the details of that setting and that science that we now turn our attention.

Notes

1. Plato (1968, 377a); Aristotle (2002, 1098b); Cicero (1948, II.lxxix).
2. Jardin (1988, 59-60).
3. Tocqueville (1985, 294: letter to Corcelle, September 17, 1853).
4. Plato (1942, 344c). Plato goes on to say that truth is kindled in the soul "as a result of much being together concerning the matter itself and from much living together," and once kindled, "nourish[es] itself" (translation from Plato 2007, 7). Tocqueville speaks of "living a little every day" with Rousseau, Montesquieu, and Pascal, and of the

soul's desire for truth "nourishing itself" and fuelling an ascent toward "mother ideas" (435). Tocqueville may have borrowed this concept of living together from Plato, from Plutarch (1932, 293-94), or from both. Compare Tocqueville (1970).

5. *Protagoras*, (2004, 316d-e). Plato's Socrates provisionally denies this in the *Republic* (1968, 595a-607e), but conditionally affirms its possibility in *Phaedrus* (2003, 278a-d).

6. For an influential—though still to some minds scandalous—contemporary account, see Strauss (1952).

7. On the need for experience of human affairs to grasp political science, see Aristotle (2002, 1095b).

8. See Lively (1962, 50); Aron (1965, 187); Ceaser (1990, 26ff); and Manent (1996, 1-12).

9. In a 1921 speech (1951-63).

10. See Denis de Rougemont (1941), Aron Gurwitsch (1945), and Hannah Arendt (1956).

11. See Putnam (2001), and our discussion in chapter 6.

12. Ceaser (1990, 17).

13. Allan Bloom (1987, 246).

14. Compare Tocqueville's criticism of the Americans for naming their seat of legislation the "Capitol" (444). Tocqueville acknowledges the continued relevance of ancient modes of thought, but not on account of any continuity with modern democracy – rather the contrary (450ff).

15. Francis Fukuyama (1992).

16. This opened the door to another peaceful route to acquisition—marriage. Fealty was of course another means of acquisition, though the possession it gave was indirect and, in its breach, it became another source of contention.

17. Tocqueville experienced the conflict between these two notions of family in his own life. He eventually married a woman of lower social status against the express wishes of his family (Jardin 1988, 232ff).

18. Thomas Jefferson, a key figure in the abolition of laws of entail in America, famously wrote that the earth belongs to the living (2004: letter to James Madison, September 6, 1789).

19. Matthew 6, 19ff; 19, 16ff; Luke 12, 16ff.

20. Jefferson (1979, 75ff: letter to Adams, October 28, 1813).

21. In Jefferson's defense, it should be noted that he envisioned this natural aristocracy as being cultivated in large part through the local or ward-based democracy, which America never adopted, and on the foundation of an agrarian economy, which gave way before the forces of industrialization (see note 20 above). In a sense, however, this means that Jefferson's hopes for democracy were based on an underestimation of its potential to transform the world.

22. Plato (2007, 521d-522a). See also Plato (2004, 313d-e).

23. The Army once advertised on the basis of Uncle Sam's needs, an appeal to duty. For some time, its motto was "Be all that you can be," an appeal to virtuous self-interest. Its current campaign is a textbook case of extreme individualism, including the element of self-conscious or "ironic" fantasy.

24. J. P. Mayer (1966).

25. Ceaser (1990, 29) discusses the most significant of these.

26. Marvin Zetterbaum contends that Tocqueville makes this claim because he is an unqualified proponent of democracy seeking to eliminate resistance to it (1967). I offer a different account of Tocqueville's motives here.

27. On the importance of God as Creator, see Joshua Mitchell (1995, 99).

28. Tellingly, Tocqueville seems to consider some adherence to aristocratic institutions "honest," if sterile and misguided (675).

29. Consider the night-roaming of Shakespeare's Henry V before the battle of Agincourt (1961).

30. Seymour Drescher (2003, 630) argues that the two volumes of *Democracy* (published five years apart) are distinct books representing fundamentally different understandings of democracy itself. Tocqueville, while admitting to differences in subject and minor changes of mind from one volume to the next, unambiguously asserts that "the two parts [of *Democracy*] complete one another and form a single work" (399). This study tends to uphold the veracity of Tocqueville's claim.

31. See Ralph Hancock (2002).

32. This insistence that justice transcends utility is traced back to Socrates by Cicero in his *Laws*, I.xii (1928, 333).

33. This embracing of religion is a point on which Tocqueville and John Stuart Mill, despite their affinity in many other things, parted ways. See Jardin (1988, 274-75).

34. Tocqueville seems to regard religion as instrumental to virtue naturally defined (278, 284, 419, 519). This would leave him in the category of what he calls "independent minds" rather than "Christians full of zeal." On Tocqueville's religious beliefs, which are generally taken to be vague but genuine, see Doris Goldstein (1960, 379-93), Kraynak (1995), Jardin (1988, 528-33), Lawler (1993, 87, 92), Lively (1962, 183-84). With Kessler (1994), I credit Tocqueville's admission to Gobineau: "I am not a believer." See Chapter 5.

Chapter 2
Liberty, Rights, and Justice
in the New World

"There is nothing more unproductive for the human mind than an abstract idea. Therefore I hurry to run toward the facts" (590). This sentiment helps us to grasp why Tocqueville presents his most profound thoughts about political society in the course of describing a real political system: the United States of America. Despite his disdain for purely abstract ideas, however, Tocqueville insists on the obligation of an author to "push each of his ideas to all its theoretical consequences and often to the limits of the false and impractical" (15). By his own account, Tocqueville took an "impassioned pleasure" in "regarding the affairs of men by wholes," and took little interest in particulars in themselves.[1] Hence no example could deeply interest Tocqueville unless it contained lessons on what he called "the greatest problems human destiny presents" (418). For him, the theoretical consequences of American democratic principles stretch far beyond the practical limits of the colonial, Revolutionary, and Jacksonian periods on which his text focuses. In presenting the history and functioning of American political society Tocqueville confesses that he saw in America much more than America. America held his gaze long enough to inspire *Democracy* because Tocqueville saw in America "an image of democracy itself" (13)—an image with which he might depict both the problems inherent in democracy's relation to human nature and the possible solutions to those problems.

As our analysis of Tocqueville's Introduction has shown, Tocqueville saw the central challenge of democracy to be its placement within a moral order capable of moderating democracy and making it live in relation to those transcendent goods required by human beings as such. In Tocqueville's France, by his own assessment, proponents of democracy tended toward materialism, and defenders of the transcendent tended to oppose democracy. French democracy was therefore lacking the moral education necessary to render its rule beneficial to humanity. America presented a different picture. There, democracy was born and raised in an atmosphere resonant with "biblical perfume," and with a "real

39

. . . political life" like that of ancient Athens (33, 40). Nineteenth-century American mores were demonstrably compatible with democracy, and yet they did not exclude civic virtue and religion, making America an outstanding test case and model for Tocqueville's notion of a moral order capable of directing modern democratic societies.

His criticisms of American democracy and its Puritan founders notwithstanding, this study will argue that Tocqueville uses his account of the development of American political institutions from colonial times to the age of Jackson as a platform for those ideas he believes capable of bringing the best out of democracy. These ideas—liberty, rights, and justice—are naturally congenial to democratic societies, but also vulnerable to an excessively individualistic interpretation that undermines their true merits. Tocqueville gives them a unique content by insisting that they be placed within a moral order that is both rooted in the mores of a particular people and informed by standards drawn from humanity itself, a placement that can only be achieved through the artful balancing of social forces by legislators and other leaders of society. In this chapter we shall consider how Tocqueville explores the need for and nature of this political art in the first two chapters of *Democracy*.

National Character and the Influence of Mores

Tocqueville informs us that the second chapter of *Democracy* contains "the seed of what is to follow and the key to almost the whole work" (29). Its topic is America's "point of departure and its importance for the future of the Anglo-Americans." This chapter is striking in many ways. It is here that Tocqueville introduces his thesis that the Puritans were the true founders of America, crediting them with the establishment and promulgation of the "principal ideas that today form the bases of the social theory of the United States" (31). It is here that he announces the necessity of blending the "spirit of liberty" with the "spirit of religion," and begins to sing the praises of township government or participatory as opposed to representative democracy. He also begins the chapter with a curious account of when "the seed of the vices and virtues of his mature age" can first be seen in a man, extending this by analogy to the national character of peoples. If the beginning is half the whole,[2] we must pay close attention to the seeds Tocqueville is planting in this chapter, in order to unlock the guiding principles of his entire work.

Tocqueville signals the significance of this chapter to the universal concerns of political science by rejoicing in the opportunity to examine the origins and development of American political society. America, he claims, is the only country whose point of departure is not shrouded in the darkness of ignorance or mythology,[3] and in which the influence exerted by a people's original condition on subsequent development can therefore be measured. This enables Tocqueville and his readers to "see much further into human events" than past observers have been able to do. Providence, he says, has placed a torch within our reach whose light allows us to see more clearly than anyone before the "first causes" of the "destiny of nations" (28-29). Hence Tocqueville's account of the American point of departure is meant to have implications for the study of all polities, democratic and otherwise.

Tocqueville's exploration of the first causes of national destiny is almost entirely focused on what he calls "national character": the prejudices, habits, and dominant passions shared by members of a given political society (28). National character is nothing other than the subset of mores—habits of the mind and heart (274-75)—characteristic of a certain political society. By calling it a first cause, Tocqueville signals that his political science will treat mores as central to political life. It is not that Tocqueville ignores what he calls physical causes such as geography or even economics. It is rather that he understands these factors, which some might regard as overwhelmingly determinative of how human beings live, as far less influential than they are commonly thought to be.[4] The reason that physical causes loom larger in the opinions of many than they do in Tocqueville's political science relates to the very content of national character itself. Since a certain set of prejudices, habits, and passions defines the horizons in which most of us think most of the time, its relevance to our individual and collective lives is practically invisible, unless one is willing to engage in the sort of political-philosophic introspection underlying Tocqueville's initial chapters.

National character is crucial because of the tremendous if invisible influence it exerts over individuals and societies. To grasp Tocqueville's view of the extent of this influence, we need only review the content of his first chapter: "External Configuration of North America." Here, Tocqueville examines the geography of North America and the natives or "Indians" who lived there when Europeans first arrived. In painting this scene, Tocqueville reveals the extent to which moral causes shape our relations with the physical environment, and therefore help determine the character of human life as a whole. This in turn raises questions about the nature of genuine human liberty and means by which political society can pursue it.

The influence of mores is indicated by as simple an act as naming a river. Tocqueville notes that the great Mississippi, which divides the United States and gives its soil an immense fertility, takes its name from the Indians' "pompous language," and means "Father of Waters." The French called the same river St. Louis, "in memory of their absent fatherland [*patrie*]." This tells us that both societies share a patriarchal identification of power with fatherhood, though one reveres nature as the greatest father, while the other sees nature as a sign of the still greater fatherhood of a political and religious order supporting sovereignty and sainthood. The Anglo-Americans, as we know, gave no name of their own to the river; instead they constructed 300-ton ships to navigate its waters (20). This signifies a society in which nature is revered neither for itself nor with reference to political-religious hierarchy, but rather treated as a resource to be exploited for the comfort of human life.[5] Thus, far from determining culture by themselves, natural or physical facts are interpreted in radically divergent ways

by political societies with varying moral perspectives, or different national characters.

The power of mores does not stop at rivers but extends to the way in which
peoples regard nature or the given world as a whole. Tocqueville goes out of his
way to contrast the experiences of those Europeans who landed in the West In-
dies and South America with those of the English who landed in North America.
The former "believed themselves transported to the fabulous regions that poets
had celebrated,"[6] and became enamored of a realm in which everything "seemed
prepared for the needs of man or calculated for his pleasures." In regarding nature as a paradise, they did not notice that "death was hidden beneath that brilliant cloak." The English colonists, who settled on "the inhospitable coast" to
the North, had no such illusions. To them, nature presented a grave face, dis-
playing not only a melancholy foliage, but also the debris of a death which
struck relentlessly to the silent indifference of nature herself. The English re-
sponded by focusing their intellectual energies on industry, or the taming of nature, a habit that became so ingrained that Tocqueville will later accuse the
Americans of never pausing to consider the grandeur of the continent they are
laboring to conquer (461). Lest we think geography is itself the cause of these
differing mores, however, Tocqueville notes that the enterprising Anglo-
Americans also met "a few small tribes" of Indians wandering amidst the forests
and prairies, making no more effort than the plants themselves to change the
face of nature (22-23). Again, national character is seen to determine a group's
relation to nature, rather than vice versa.

Tocqueville's presentation of these three societies is, of course, oversimpli-
fied. His account focuses on certain salient features of the groups he is compar-
ing. Tocqueville chooses to emphasize those features that provoke evaluation
because he is inviting the reader to rise above the standards of a given society
and attempt to judge societies themselves by a higher standard. Each of the three
ways of life he depicts in this chapter presents us with a different set of goods
and evils, achievements and failures. As political philosophers have long known,
the confrontation with what we would call cultural diversity frequently inspires
one of two errors: either an instinctive rejection of what is alien to our own way
of life, or an easy conclusion that no way of life is better or worse than another.[7]
For Tocqueville, each of these responses obscures the real question posed by the
conflict of human customs: does one way of life correspond better or worse than
another to what human beings need and desire by nature?

Tocqueville's political science makes no pretense of neutrality on the question of how human beings ought to live. Instead, Tocqueville considers the highest aim of political science to be the knowledge of that "fact" whose features
allow us to measure or evaluate human "values" themselves: our unchanging
human nature.[8] We may usefully designate this standard as "natural right": "a
standard of right and wrong independent of positive right" and "discernable to
human reason."[9] If such a thing exists, knowledge of it cannot help but transform our approach to every particular "culture" or national character. Even if no
society can simply change its way of life at will, only such a universal standard

could serve as a basis for purposeful reform of a political culture, or for the liberal education of leaders within that culture. Tocqueville's opening chapter is a sort of training in how to make such judgments, paving the way for his evaluation of America from its first foundations onward.

When we begin to evaluate the groups as Tocqueville depicts them, we find that the appreciation for beauty of the Southern Europeans seems marred by a narcissistic naiveté: they love nature only by falsely believing it to be their adoring servant. This error is contemptible in itself, and also dooms them to relative weakness. The English hostility to nature, by contrast, is virtuous in a Machiavellian sense: it promises to make them masters of North America one day. Yet it involves a double depravation of consciousness: esthetic and philosophic. If there is no time to consider the beauty of nature as it falls under one's axe, then one also misses the truth that the success of one's labors depends on the prior provision of a suitable work environment (21).[10] Resting in a false sense of independence, the mind never strives to grasp the objective order of things, treating all external objects, other human beings included, as resources for practical enterprises, rather than as features of a greater order or cosmos (compare 505). This excessive industriousness, being contrary to the full expression of human nature, has both social and psychological costs, which Tocqueville will later discuss at length (506ff, 530ff).

Tellingly, Tocqueville indicates that both European societies have rendered themselves unhappy by distorting nature in opposite ways—one seeking to enjoy it uninterruptedly without labor, the other seeking to master it completely through labor. Of the three groups here treated, only the Indians appear to be satisfied with nature as it is. Does this satisfaction render them happy? Promisingly, Tocqueville goes on to describe the natives as profoundly uncorrupt, perfectly "equal and free," and generally "philosophical" in their beliefs (24-26). It should not escape our notice that the Indians seem to possess precisely those virtues to which a democratizing and enlightened Europe aspires without the civilizational edifice through which the latter seeks to cultivate those virtues. In fact, the perfect equality, liberty, and philosophy of the Indians are rooted in their being "all ignorant and poor" by European standards. The validity of these standards is called into question by the possibility that Indians are freer and happier in their ignorance and poverty than are Europeans in their learning and wealth. The Indians seem to have fulfilled their human nature by living in harmony with nature as a whole, and in doing so proved that human nature is apolitical, thriving most in the absence of that elaborate coercive and artificial political structure Tocqueville calls civilization.[11]

Tocqueville reinforces this suspicion by noting that in "orderly (*policées*) countries"—that is, countries where an unequal social order is defended by coercive authority—the ignorant and poor are coarsened by their resentment of the "enlightened and wealthy." The former are both angry that some of their fellows are happier than they are, and fearful of those on whom they depend. They see no way of bettering their condition, and the consequent desperation disturbs their "internal state of soul," rendering them more "insolent and base" than their material conditions alone would make them (24). By contrast, it almost appears as if the Indians are truly free because the moral order by which they live corresponds to nature itself, and as if the nature to which it corresponds mandates a complete and almost anarchical equality among human beings.

Before exploring this possibility further, it is worth emphasizing that the effect of social inequality on souls, while it demonstrates that economics can influence mores, ultimately proves the primacy of mores over economics. However damaging social inequality in itself may be, its effect is exacerbated by a society's reversion to barbarism, when the coarseness of the people becomes "profound corruption" (24). So long as moral order prevails over political society, however, some degree of coarseness in the people may be combined with energy, generosity, beliefs, and virtues, and souls may avoid degradation (8). Even if political society in itself were responsible for corrupting human beings, then, the most fitting remedy might be a moral order capable of mitigating this corruption, rather than a return to nature, per impossible.[12]

The power of mores over economic influences is driven home as well by the Indians' imperviousness to money as a result of their moral purity. Tocqueville ironically describes the Indian as "ignorant of the value of wealth," going on to describe his conscious indifference "to the well-being that civilized man acquires with it." Not only did the Indian "kn[o]w how to live without needs," standing therefore in little need of wealth; he was also willing to "expose himself to die of hunger in order to assist the stranger who knocked at the door of his hut in the night."[13] The Indian's contempt for material comforts and distinctions appeared to make him the perfect embodiment of those virtues celebrated in European traditions. Not only was he free, independent, and content with the goods provided by nature, he was also as charitable as a Christian saint and as brave in the defense of his tribe as were citizens of "the most famous ancient republics" (25). Tocqueville completes this picture by repeating a story from the French explorer Charlevoix about the "contrast in the mores of the Europeans and those of the savages": the Hurons were "scandalized" when their French allies stooped so low as to loot the corpses of their mutual foes, the Iroquois (680).

This account exposes the conventionality of the economic goods that frequently define the relationships constitutive of political society, and thereby underscores the primacy of mores within politics. It seems that the combination of liberty and morality that is a pious wish of Western civilization was a reality among the savage tribes of North America, and that such a reality was both made possible by and itself made possible the absence of a robust political order. Were these impressions the whole of the story, the lesson would seem to be that such a primitive state is the definitive condition of human happiness, and that civilization as we know it represents the decline of man.

Yet whatever admiration Tocqueville has aroused in his readers with this account of native life is abruptly dashed when he goes on to relate why the French were in turn horrified by the behavior of their Huron allies. However much the Hurons deplored the French treatment of the Iroquois dead, the French were at least as shocked by the Huron treatment of an Iroquois prisoner: having tortured him to death, they proceeded to devour him (in the words of Charlevoix) "like ferocious beasts" (680).

Tocqueville makes no attempt to defend cannibalism or discredit the revulsion it is likely to inspire in his readers. For him the condemnation of Charlevoix is an invitation to reflect on the enigma of the mixture of great virtues and great vices in the life of the American Indian. Unlike his source, however, Tocqueville uses this example not in order to decry the supposed bestiality of the Indians, but in order to teach the reader something about our common humanity. For Tocqueville unequivocally regards the American natives as "members of the great human family" and understands their ferocity, however deplorable, as no less human than their virtues. Later in *Democracy* he notes the similarity he finds between the mores of the Indians and the ancient Germanic tribes from whom Europeans descended, leading him to remark that, "in the midst of the apparent diversity of human things, it is not impossible to find a few generative facts from which all the rest flow" (315). In this first chapter, Tocqueville finds such a generative fact in the connection he sees between the intense courage and generosity of the native and his astounding pitilessness: namely, his limitless pride (25-26). For Tocqueville, such pride is in fact a constituent part of our humanity, for better and for worse (604), and its management is crucial in determining the vices and virtues exhibited by a given society. From this root of Indian virtue and vice we learn something about ourselves that helps explain both the necessity of political society and the nature of the immensely difficult role it must play in our lives. In other words, we begin to glimpse the connection between natural right and the conventional moral order.

Contra Charlevoix, Indian ferocity can only be explained by the potentialities of our distinctly human nature. Essential to our nature is a desire to transcend the physical conditions of our lives in some fashion. Even the Indian, who seemed perfectly content in his "ignorance and poverty," was not without a sense of transcendent order. He believed in God and "the existence of a better world," and these beliefs confirmed and greatly magnified his sense of self-importance. "There is no Indian so miserable," Tocqueville observes, "who, in his bark hut, does not entertain a proud idea of his individual worth," scorning any activity save hunting and war as beneath his manhood (314). Moved by such beliefs, the Indian fought with courage for his own honor and that of his tribe. When torturing an enemy, he accused him of the other's tribe's crimes against his own, and consumed him as a symbol of justified vengeance. This sense of justice and the competing claims to it of various tribes—a moral order—defined his very existence (compare 314ff). Such pride fueled the native's self-sacrifice as well as his cruelty, and colored every aspect of his life. He forewent material advantages, not out of simple contentment with necessities, but for the sake of an honor based in a peculiar notion of moral order. Not even his rest or domestic pleasures remained untouched by this order and its demands, as we see in the sequel to Charlevoix's tale. When sleeping after a battle, the Hurons dreamt that the enemy pursued them and ran the rest of the way home. Upon the warriors' arrival, the women ran out to celebrate victory by donning the bloody scalps of the enemy (680).[14]

Far from accepting nature as it is or living in true independence from social constraints, Tocqueville suggests, the Indian was keenly pained by the harshness of his "impoverished" life: "all the music of the savages is somewhat lugubrious," he quotes Charlevoix as saying, though the latter could not have explained this sadness (680). The Indian braved this harshness, not by seeking material comforts, but by consciously eschewing them in order to devote himself to an all-consuming cycle of tribal conflict. This conflict was rooted in an unshakable sense of self-importance and an implacable need for self-distinction within a moral order defined by mores very much akin to what Tocqueville calls "national character." In fact, the tribal mentality of the Indian appears to be more intense than the national character of the Europeans and Americans with which Tocqueville juxtaposes it, and therefore potentially more arbitrary or contrary to nature than the latter. Having seen the whole of Tocqueville's portrait, we are left to wonder whether the Indian is not more but less free than his civilized brothers, due to his greater immersion in an artificial moral order.

Natural Right and Political Society

What lesson may we draw from this account? The hope that Tocqueville raises, and dashes, in the example of the Indians is that of a correspondence between national character or mores and nature. In other words, Tocqueville suggests that genuine liberty and happiness would result from a conventional or political order grounded in natural right. Judging by this standard, Tocqueville's account seems to confirm his prior statement that the absolute good is seldom found in actual laws (13): none of the societies he describes is capable of accepting nature—the truth about man and his physical, social, and psychological needs—without distortion. Tocqueville's presentation therefore begs the question of what such a correspondence between nature and politics would look like, or whether it is even possible. Though Tocqueville nowhere answers this question explicitly and in abstract terms, it nonetheless constitutes the central question of his political science. In outlining that science, he recommends that we search the annals of political philosophy for alternative positions on such fundamental questions, paying special attention to the difference between ancient and modern political thought (1991). Following Tocqueville's advice, we can piece together his thoughts on the application of natural right to society by juxtaposing his writing with key modern and classical theories.

Tocqueville's view of the junction of political and natural right can best be glimpsed by examining two models of political life. Both models would structure political life on the basis of the demands of nature, or natural right, though each conceives of nature differently. According to the first model, which we may call materialism, human life should be organized around the provision of natural necessities, and relations among men should be regulated by their more or less equal and similar material needs and abilities to provide for them. So long as men remained content with the satisfaction of what this model calls their true needs, occasions of contention would be kept to a minimum, and social authority could likewise be minimal.

In Plato's *Republic*, Socrates and Adeimantus construct a similar order in their quest for a just city in speech, only to have it knocked down by the imperial demands of Glaucon, whose erotic and spirited nature cannot abide the notion of such materialistic mediocrity. To him, our first model is nothing but "a city of sows." A crucial question for interpreting classical political thought is why Socrates, who considers Glaucon's taste for luxuries and honors to be a type of sickness, so readily allows Glaucon to re-found their "just" city. The answer seems to be that Socrates, though he considers the particular objects of Glaucon's desire to be harmful and unnatural, regards the origin of these desires as eminently natural. For Socrates, the human soul longs for a good transcending the order of material things. The possession of this transcendent good is impossible without virtue, or the perfection of personal character. Since such perfection is rare and difficult, most human beings fail to fulfill their own nature, and hence remain fundamentally unhappy. In ignorance of virtue, or fear of its strenuous demands, they seek to mitigate their unhappiness by the fruitless pursuit of superfluous external goods, such as material pleasures and comforts, political power and social prestige, and the like.[15]

On this Socratic view of human nature, it is senseless to envision a social order that is internally harmonious because its members live in placid enjoyment of their physical environment. Human nature, with its longing for a transcendent good, renders such a solution impossible. Tocqueville, who also holds that the human soul cannot rest content with material things without doing violence to itself (11, 34ff, 284, 431ff, 510ff, 601ff, 663ff), teaches this lesson from the beginning of *Democracy* by emphasizing first the allurements, and then the disappointments, of Indian life. The very pride that causes the Indians to rise above the materialistic model of man (e.g. through self-sacrificing generosity) or to fall below it (e.g. through cruelty and cannibalism) is symptomatic of an irrepressible human longing for what Tocqueville calls the sublime or "high" (510, 456). The same can be said about the virtues (poetry, industriousness) and vices (naiveté and hostility to nature) defining the national characters of "orderly countries." Man's transcendent desire causes him always to become something better than or worse than—but never the same as—the other animals.[16] And for Tocqueville as for Socrates, this inability to rest content with material things is a result of man's possession of a rational soul (431-37, 504-5).

This Socratic-Tocquevillian critique of our first model for a politics of "nature" leaves us with a new question: how, if possible, to construct a second model, one that harmonizes politics with nature as a whole, including both external nature and a human nature longing to transcend it? The answer, of course, depends on the precise character of this transcendent desire. For what does man long, and can he achieve it by political means?

For many centuries now, the thrust of modern political thought has been to deny any reality to the object(s) of our transcendent longings. As Thomas Hobbes put it, there is no *summum bonum* (greatest good) or happiness. Though man longs for an eternal or lasting satisfaction, the pursuit of any imagined good capable of satisfying this desire constitutes vainglory and the greatest threat to political order. Men must remain content with improving their individual and collective abilities to satisfy their material needs, and forget about anything grander. Their reward for doing so will be a peaceful and prosperous society capable of providing for all such limited desires until death becomes unavoidable. The major difference between Hobbes's political model and the *Republic*'s "city of sows" is that Hobbes's sovereign must combat human vainglory (including that of the Glaucons and Socrateses of the world) by means of a political science delegitimizing and a political authority punishing any attempt to speak or act in terms of higher goods.[17] Thus we might call this modern view a modified or neo-materialism.

Tocqueville's critiques of materialism in general, and of American materialism in particular, make it clear enough that he rejects this Hobbesian approach. In fact, Tocqueville's greatest fear for modern democratic society is that it will issue in an administrative despotism enforcing such a neo-materialistic model of social order on a henceforth degraded citizenry (661ff). As we shall see in our next chapter, Tocqueville's war against individualism is explained by his view that individualism may be the cause of man's definitive abandonment of the sublime goods constitutive of his humanity. In order to comprehend the intention of Tocqueville's thought, then, we must discern his distinctive vision of the transcendent good that renders human happiness possible, and his model for its pursuit by means of political authority.

Once again, it is useful to begin with the Socratic response to this question. In the *Republic* and elsewhere, Socrates links human flourishing to a manner of life harmonizing two distinct but interconnected orders: man and the cosmos, or internal and external nature. That human being is happy whose soul is well-ordered, with its higher or nobler faculty ruling over its lower powers. That faculty of the soul is highest which is capable of apprehending the natural order of beings and of goods. For Plato's Socrates, this means that the philosophic life, or life of contemplative reason, is the life of supreme virtue and happiness. As we shall soon see, however, the achievement of this good by political society—the harmonizing of national character with the order of things, or the philosophizing of a people—is impossible in the classical view.[18] Only the individual of rare virtue fulfils human nature through the relentless pursuit of wisdom. Since politics is the preeminent means by which human beings order their pursuit of the good,[19] politics according to its own standards must be informed by the Socratic view of the good, if the latter is true. Yet if politics cannot simply achieve this good on the communal level, political society's ability to promote the "absolute good" becomes significantly problematic.

Tocqueville, who maintains that absolute good is almost never found in the law while insisting that law be measured by the absolute good of man (compare

13 with 221, 518, 665), is an heir to this Socratic tradition. Subsequent chapters will show that Tocqueville is not uncritical of classical political thought, but on at least one fundamental point Tocqueville seems to regard ancient philosophy as superior to its modern counterpart: its concern for the soul. This is revealed most clearly in a later chapter of *Democracy* in which Tocqueville discusses the effect of religion on the souls of Americans. In the midst of this account, Tocqueville denounces the doctrines of materialists as not only pernicious but contradictory. Materialists believe "they have sufficiently established that they are only brutes," but having proved this "they show themselves as proud as if they had demonstrated they were gods" (519). Tocqueville reminds us of the innate transcendent desire of man stemming from his possession of a soul, which causes him to need to grasp and relate himself to a meaningful cosmos or moral order (510, 417). The significance of materialism for Tocqueville is its denial of the soul's existence, and hence of any cardinal distinction between man and beast. Of course, materialists do not deny that man possesses a faculty of reasoning surpassing that of animals, but the modern critique of ancient thought does deny that reason is an ordering principle of the soul, pointing to a higher order in light of which the rational animal naturally longs to live. Machiavelli, "the greatest captain of modern times" (627),[20] never used the word "soul" in his political writings, and described reason as an instrument for the satisfaction of desire rather than a faculty capable of directing desire to its proper end.[21]

Were Machiavelli correct, Tocqueville contends, man should at least adopt "a modest idea of himself"—living, for instance, in peaceful contentment with minimal material goods. Several centuries of waxing materialism had by Tocqueville's time indicated otherwise. Materialism had not so much convinced men to abandon the idea of God altogether, as to believe that they could and should take God's place. Our next chapter will explore the costs Tocqueville sees as consequent to this "dangerous malady of the human mind"—materialism—in democratic times. Our point here is that Tocqueville considers it to be a malady or disorder, a distortion of the truth about ourselves. In the remainder of the chapter he elaborates his own belief in the soul, "the divine principle contained in man," the superior "portion of our nature" the very belief in which "is so necessary to the greatness of man." "Socrates and his school" gave philosophy a "sublime spark" by acknowledging the superiority of the soul to the body (519-20). That Tocqueville's own use of the term soul is Socratic to a significant degree can be seen in his assertions that there exists an order of things transcending matter (456), that human beings can in principle both contemplate this order (505) and act in accordance with it (417), and that human happiness depends upon the achievement or approximation of a genuine "association" with this "admirable order of all things" (505, 509, 518ff).[22]

These reflections prepare us to see how Tocqueville measures the potential of political society, through its various arrangements or by its absence, to help or hinder the achievement of natural right or the absolute good. Tocqueville's first chapter reveals to us the danger posed to our apprehension of the true order of things—the basis of natural right—by our proud insistence on distorting its features to suit our own sense of self-importance. At first we suspect that this pride exists only within political societies, which seek to uphold certain views of reality not only through their laws and institutions but above all through their national characters. On second glance, it appears that the truthful apprehension of nature is even more threatened by the absence of political society, which abandons human beings to an uninhibitedly proud insistence on their own centrality within the universe.[23]

If neither the presence nor the absence of political society leads us to truth and happiness, what hope can there be for humankind? The answer lies once more in Tocqueville's reminder that the law rarely if ever gives us the "absolute good" at which it must aim. Due to the difficulty of both its discovery and dissemination, the whole truth about the defining features of natural right—"God and human nature"—cannot penetrate national character deeply enough to serve without qualification as the common platform for political and social action (407ff). Yet it by no means follows that some societies, through their national characters, do not approximate the truth more closely. Nor does it follow that some societies are not better at producing and preserving the conditions in which individuals are free to strive for a better command of the truth. Nor does this difficulty prevent those who possess such a command—those Tocqueville calls the "natural aristocracy" (50, 247)—from contributing to the reform of political society in order to render it friendlier to natural right or the true moral order. In Tocqueville's complex political model—our second model for the joining of politics and natural right—the pursuit of natural right must remain a problem or challenge even for the best of political societies, but this challenge need not be unmanageable. The most fundamental of all political problems is nothing less than the challenge of harnessing, bridling, and directing toward the true or absolute good, that noble but proud desire residing in the hearts of all human beings to live in association with the order of things.

That no political society simply adopts a truthful relationship to the natural world is driven home by Tocqueville's opening words in chapter two:

> Go back; examine the infant even in the arms of his mother; see the external world reflected for the first time in the still-obscure mirror of his intelligence; contemplate the first examples that strike his eye; listen to the first words that awaken the sleeping powers of his thought; finally, attend the first struggles that he has to sustain; and only then will you understand where the prejudices, habits, and passions that are going to dominate his life come from (27-28).

In the arms of his mother the infant's intelligence is still obscure, because it possesses no means of self-expression, and yet it already has the potential to reflect the natural world like a mirror. Thought or cognitive capacity, whose ultimate aim is the contemplation of truth, is an innate faculty of man (compare 431, 435). Paradoxically, the means by which this capacity comes to fruition—the learning of language—is highly conventional. The language we employ to grasp reality is embedded in a culture whose usages will inevitably color our view of the truth, perhaps even obscuring it entirely on some points (593). Likewise, the personal struggles we undergo before the age of reason excite the distorting influence of pride, prompting us to form attachments and antipathies contrary to the objective value of things. Neither of these unfortunate influences is dispensable: the intellect does not grow in a void, and must be situated in a given culture and personality if it is to grow at all. Yet as a result of this situation, character formation all too predictably begins with the potential for truth (and hence genuine liberty) but culminates in the dominance of prejudice, habit, and passion.

Two lessons follow from this account. First, enlightenment or true learning must begin with subjects already immersed in a set of beliefs, habits, and passions, some of which will inevitably be false or misleading. Education for virtue must therefore aim more or less at the recovery of one's natural potential, which is both supported and hindered by one's national and personal character. Higher education is therefore essentially a matter of personal liberation and must take place individually and subsequent to an initial period of moral formation (compare 50, 247, 410, 417, 431, 435-37, 452, 613-15, 663). This is not to say that education in groups is impossible, only that it must be carefully aimed at the conversion of individual souls toward the truth, as Plato puts it.[24] Second, it follows that national character—whose content must be accessible to the bulk of society's members—will never be completely liberated from prejudice, habit, and passion, which necessarily intrude upon our collective lives. Extraordinary efforts to apprehend and disseminate the truth may succeed at reforming national character, and imbuing it with significant elements of wisdom, but these elements will never be unmixed with error. In practice, every society is riddled with opinions that distort the truth about such fundamental issues as liberty, justice, and happiness (223, 240, 407). The best one can hope for is not a national character that is perfectly wise, but one open to the existence and influence of those who strive to see nature more clearly (11-12, 50, 247).

The culminating lesson of these reflections is that society must be judged by the standard of truth, but not too rigidly. Instead of demanding that a given society be without error, it must be evaluated by its relative openness to the truth or to the influence of those who seek it. Considering "the weakness of our nature, which, incapable of firmly grasping the true and the just, is most often reduced to choosing between two excesses" (39), one may even praise a society for being less hostile to truth than it might otherwise be. The question for Tocqueville's political science is not, as some Enlightenment thinkers might have it, how prejudice can be replaced with knowledge society-wide (compare 179). The question is rather how the weaknesses of human nature can best be moderated, producing the conditions in which personal enlightenment and sound political leadership are most likely to occur.

Tocqueville's opening chapters teach us something vital about the necessary conditions for human liberty: namely, that it is insufficient to leave man "to the savage independence of his nature" (24). The example of the Indian proves that man naturally grasps for a moral order capable of giving his life meaning and inspiring virtue, but also tends to bend this moral order to justify the excesses of an inherently limitless pride. If the seed of human virtue is to grow into a mature organism capable of seeking truth without distortion, contrary growths must be pruned. In particular, human pride must be tamed. Ultimately, men must be made to acknowledge something of their individual nothingness so that they may be freed to seek meaning outside of themselves, in the objective "order of all things" that can be grasped by the mind rather than in the presumed dominance of oneself and one's kin, which are mere assertions of the will (504-505). The tendency of individuals to make themselves the center of things must be checked by something that stands between them and nature as a whole. The tribe is insufficient for this purpose, as it is too closely bound to the individual. A greater order is necessary, one capable of overawing the individual and complicating his relation to the universal order.

This intermediary object is what we often call civilization, a social order embodying a larger[25] and somewhat stable system of unequal human relationships. Another word for this phenomenon is political society. Without it, Tocqueville implies, human nature shines in some respects but ultimately languishes in "ignorance and pride." "National character" as Tocqueville uses the term attaches men to political society, whose moderating effect on human pride eventually opens the door to "the spirit of analysis" or the scientific study of human affairs by certain of its members (28). In this light it is telling that Tocqueville depicts native Americans as generally ignorant of their own past and incurious about or disdainful of the Europeans taking over their continent (26, 313), while building his own account mainly on the reports of French and American authors, politicians, and scientists. As corrupt as they often are, more civilized societies encourage or at least allow some of their members (Tocqueville and some of his sources being examples) to transcend the limits of national character and seek knowledge of nature itself, a possibility that the pure and robust mores of Indian society do not seem as ready to allow.

This tremendous advantage of civilization explains why Tocqueville ends his first chapter by proclaiming the justice of the Anglo-American conquest of North America, despite his later detailing of the many injustices committed by the colonists against the Indians (26-27, 320ff). Though the Europeans' crimes against the natives cannot be excused, Tocqueville implies that justice could not ultimately have been served by leaving souls in the grip of tribal morality.[26] Orderly (*policées*) societies may corrupt souls inasmuch as the inequalities they enforce do not actually or seemingly correspond to natural differences; but they are also *polite* societies, societies in which individual and tribal wills are trained to give way to an idea of right or justice surpassing the individual and his immediate kin. This training liberates man from the absolute claims of his own ego while binding him to a social order that still seeks to justify itself in relation to a higher order of things, opening the door to further questioning by those inquisitive spirits who do not accept every feature of the conventional version of this order. If man's sense of justice and purpose is to transcend individual and tribal pride and grasp the natural order itself, it must be disciplined by the intermediate orders of civilization, political society, and "national character."

As the intermediary role of national character suggests, Tocqueville does not hold that political society can or ought to use it to abolish human pride altogether. For him, the pride that government must tame contains a promise as well as a threat: man's desire to transcend nature marks him as the only being within nature capable of understanding nature and mirroring it in his mind (27-28, compare 604). If this desire is never simply met through national character or conventional moral order, there is still a great difference between a national character open to deeper reflection on the true character of the teachings it imparts, and one closed to such reflection. National character must be dogmatic and it must connect the particular members of a society to a concrete moral order. Yet it ought also to remind citizens that the order of things to which they are connected possesses features not determined by their own wills. Furthermore, it ought to suggest that some of these features will best be understood only by those capable and willing of devoting themselves to higher studies. By both appealing to and regulating particular pride, national character can habituate men to the influence of leaders whose qualifications ought to be talent and virtue (50), opening up the possibility of both individual truth-seeking, and an enlightened leadership seeking to bring the mores on which society is based into closer harmony with the truth pursued by individuals of rare ability.

It follows that national character can misfire in two ways. In the first place it will err by becoming excessively rigid. As the encrustation of opinions, whether their origins be philosophic or otherwise, national character is a potential obstacle to truth and virtue, and its influence must be measured if the search for truth is to take place freely within society. At the same time, national character will err by becoming excessively slack. Erroneous mores are not simply erroneous. They represent at the very least the human aspiration to know the truth about nature and happiness. And even when they contain distortions of nature, they also contain elements of truth, elements the moralist attempting to reform political society would be imprudent to discard. National character comprises the first encounter of each human being with the innate desire to know the nature of things, and could not practically be abandoned without suppressing the very instinct that defines our humanity (compare 13, 665). This is precisely the danger Tocqueville glimpses in modern democratic individualism, which, by plunging men into the pursuit of comfortable self-preservation, threatens to distract entire societies from any meaningful relation to the elemental notions of cosmic order: God and human nature (417ff, compare 10ff).

In Tocqueville's view, national character is something that political science ought neither to reject nor embrace without criticism. The alternative for societies is not national character versus natural right, but rather states of national character more or less beneficial to the virtuous pursuit of genuine moral order. The problem of politics becomes how to sustain national character or a popular conception of moral order while simultaneously moderating its potentially stifling effect on genuine human liberty. Rather than dealing with this problem in purely abstract terms, Tocqueville examines it in light of a concrete example: the American founding, which he takes to have occurred with the New England Puritans. Tocqueville's chapter on the American point of departure is a study of the development of American national character. Through it he enables us to see in specific terms how national character can be strong enough to found and sustain a thriving civilization and simultaneously moderated enough to promote human liberty. This lesson in the political "art of being free" is the deepest sense in which this chapter constitutes the key to the teaching of *Democracy*.

Liberty and Moral Order in Colonial New England

Human nature is in need of liberation. National character is both the thing from which it frequently must be liberated, and an expression of that which makes such liberation possible: the desire for truth. For the sake of politics and the goods it provides to all citizens, this desire, which burns to some degree in all human hearts, must begin within the limits of national character, but for the sake of truth society must allow minds to transcend national character. The mores that direct a people's activities must be robust enough to structure individual lives around a conventional moral order and flexible enough to encourage or allow critical thought about this order. Striking this balance is a difficult feat in any society, but Tocqueville focuses on the peculiar difficulties posed by democratic society, which tends to reject any ordering principle save that of equality. Without the mediating influence of other ideas, equality's effect is to erode any national character centered on the influences of particular authorities and replace it with unreflecting adherence to public opinion or the mass mind (403ff). This threat, which we shall examine in our next chapter, means nothing less to Tocqueville than the loss of moral order altogether.

In Tocqueville's view, the absence of national character is more damaging to the development of genuine liberty than even an overly restrictive national character would be. In the absence of an orientation toward an order transcending itself, the dominant portion of any society is able to exert more force over minds than when its rule is connected to ideas the mind can question. In democratic times, a public opinion unconstrained by national character can be expected to lead citizens down the path of materialism, conformity, and mediocrity (508ff, 661ff). Tocqueville's quest for a democratic moral order can only be accomplished through the cultivation of a national character that, while necessarily varying from one society to the next, must be both compatible with democracy and open to the ascent of the mind toward truth. Tocqueville finds such mores—real if imperfect—in America, and locates their origins in colonial New England. His account of these origins shows us the possibilities and limits of moral order, and hence those of liberty itself, in democratic times.

It may seem odd that Tocqueville attempts to ground his case for a liberal national character on the New England Puritans, a group whose name is synonymous with fanaticism and repression. Tocqueville's intentions will become clearer if we consider another term for the Puritans used frequently today, but with a very different resonance: the Pilgrims, whom we think of as coming to the New World in search of freedom, prosperity, and peace. The different connotations of these names reveals that our very memory of these early settlers is bifurcated between their zeal for religion on the one hand and for liberty on the other. Tocqueville seizes upon both elements of early New England life and argues that, despite their seeming opposition, both were necessary for the founding of a great democratic republic like America. The Puritans' balancing of the spirits of religion and of liberty (43), though certainly not ideal in all of its particulars, represents for Tocqueville a rare accomplishment without which liberal democratic civilization has little hope of fulfilling its human potential.

The very name Puritan suggests a rigid moral code closed to realities it does not anticipate—a suspicion that is partly confirmed in the account that follows. Indeed, Tocqueville readily admits that the Puritans went too far in their policing of mores and intolerance of faiths other than their own. Their laws were often "bizarre and tyrannical," "austere," and (of course) "puritanical." Yet Tocqueville reminds us that the Puritans were almost as political as they were religious, and their politics were radically republican. Even their most repressive laws "were voted by the free concurrence of all the interested persons," whose mores were yet more austere than the laws (39). Though Puritan society rigidly excluded those who would not adopt its ways, its operations depended on the voluntary adoption of those ways by all or most of its members. Quoting the Mayflower Compact, Tocqueville notes that the New Englanders, "without denying the supremacy" of the motherland, "constituted themselves" in the New World, and governed themselves, "as if they came under God alone" (35-37). Somehow, the Puritans combined a robust moral order with political liberty and equality, a feat Tocqueville's political science seeks to replicate, though in a gentler form, in the democracies of a later day.

This correspondence between Tocqueville's goals and the accomplishment of the Puritans explains why he finds "nothing . . . more singular and more instructive than the legislation of this period," without which one could not understand "the great social enigma that the United States presents to the world in our day" (37). This enigma refers first of all to the combination of political liberty and religious zeal still noticeable in Jacksonian America, even if the religious element had become more tolerant and less dominant by the 1830s. It also refers to the continued vibrancy of participatory political institutions and mores in the midst of a successful federal Union. In Tocqueville's view, both enigmas were central to the success of American democracy, not only in the sense of its endurance, but above all in the sense that they supported a moral order capable of moderating certain excesses of equality without repudiating the government of democracy. Tocqueville thus saw New England as responsible for both the combination and dissemination of "the two or three principles that today form the bases of the social theory of the United States" (31). Without the Puritans, there would be no America, and hence no *Democracy in America*. In order to understand Tocqueville's book, we must look for the "two or three" principal lessons he draws from the Puritans' success at establishing and disseminating these social principles.

Tocqueville's first lesson emerges by way of contrast. He begins by describing the "family resemblance" shared by all Anglo-American settlers before distinguishing the "strong nuances" that made the Puritans so influential. A certain blend of political liberty and religious formation was common to all Englishmen of the period, and yet it did not always bear fruit as with the Puritans. Educated in the "rough school" of partisan conflict, the English had embraced "more notions of rights [and] more principles of true liberty" than other Europeans, including "township government, that fertile seed of free institutions." "Religious quarrels" had led to the "more profound cultivation" of the mind in order to defend and challenge beliefs, in which cause mores had also become purer (29). Another feature shared by all English colonists was democracy: immigration tends to have an equalizing effect in the lives of immigrants, and the "rebellious land" of the American coast would not produce enough goods to support both master and serf. English America was thus destined to be a realm of equal liberty, one where each citizen had to be made interested in the execution of his own business and that of the community if these affairs were to be handled well (30).

It is the ability to cultivate and sustain such interest, and thus to found a flourishing political order on the soil of democratic liberty, that Tocqueville admires in the Puritans. This ability is not to be taken for granted. One might expect that the protection of private property is sufficient to interest citizens in their own affairs, and that the guarantee of political rights suffices to involve them in the common good. Yet the study of human affairs convinced Tocqueville that it is, in fact, exceedingly difficult to motivate men to take good care of their own business, not to mention that of the public (86, compare 31). This difficulty plagued the other Anglo-Americans settlements. The Virginia colonies saw several waves of settlers, including those seeking (and failing) to find gold or merely wanting to escape from personal troubles in the motherland. Neither group was able to survive the rough conditions of settlement. After a time, industrialists and farmers came ready to earn their living in the New World; only this last group, a "moral and tranquil race," had any success at all. Yet Tocqueville is at pains to point out that their tranquil morality was incapable of founding a great civilization, for it was "elevated in almost no points above" the common level; they possessed "no noble thought, no immaterial scheme" on which to found their new colony (31). As a result, they were quickly tempted to embrace the institution of slavery, a move that slackened their industriousness and enervated their intellects, establishing an order contrary to the "social theory of the United States," and one that Tocqueville saw as posing a threat to the continued existence of the Union in his day (346).

The founding of New England, by contrast, offers us the "singular and original" spectacle of a social order founded on "a purely intellectual need." The Puritans, "perhaps without a single exception, had received a quite advanced

education" in the motherland, and would have been successful there if their beliefs had not rendered such a life repugnant to them. As it was, they tore themselves from a comfortable position and endured hardship, separation from loved
ones, and a terrifying likelihood of death, all "to make *an idea* triumph"
(Tocqueville's emphasis). It is this idea that Tocqueville unfolds over the next
several pages, quoting from Puritan speeches, letters, and laws, and from sympathetic historians, and admixing his own analysis. The Puritan idea was religious
in nature, but "blended at several points with the most absolute and democratic
republican theories"; it was an idea almost as political as it was religious; an
idea Tocqueville summarizes as wanting "to live . . . in their manner and pray to
God in liberty" (32-35). In other words, it was an idea that brought the developing English concept of political liberty to life by rooting it in the soil of religious
belief and communal life: a robust national character.

Tocqueville begins to unfold the Puritan idea by citing Nathaniel Morton, a
contemporary historian, who echoes the Puritans' belief that they were instruments in the hands of God. Though distancing himself from this claim to supernatural aid, Tocqueville notes the elevating effect it has on the reader "despite
oneself" (33). A sense of divine mission is a powerful impetus to great achievements. Tocqueville calls "true and profound" the thoughts of another historian,
Cotton Mather, whom he (mis)translates as writing that the New England colonies succeeded due to a *belief* in the aid of Providence (686).[27] Why are such
beliefs so important? Reflecting on the veneration shown throughout the United
States for fragments of Plymouth Rock—"a stone that the feet of some miserable persons touched for an instant"—Tocqueville concludes that "the power and
greatness of man is wholly in his soul" (34). The soul is that part of us which
connects us to the idea of moral order, and when it is fully engaged by such an
idea it enables us to rise above material constraints and accomplish great things
(510, 520). The idea of moral order possessing the Puritans was so vivid that it
was capable of inspiring even Tocqueville's jaded French readers, not to mention the Pilgrims' fellow Anglo-Americans. This ability to inspire souls gave
Puritan efforts an effect far outlasting the lives of a few poor settlers. Ironically,
the very secret of American commercial prosperity was a national character that
strictly subordinated commercial interests to overarching religious and political
ideals.

The wisdom (or fortune) of the Puritans was to have seen (or stumbled
upon[28]) a certain truth: that "man is so made that he prefers standing still to
marching without independence toward a goal of which he is ignorant" (87). In
order to flourish, society requires the free cooperation of individuals. If "independence" simply divides men, they will fail to form a society capable of repli-
cating itself, and thus lose their independence. If social order is based on force
alone, however, free cooperation will fail and government will be rendered sterile at first, and altogether powerless in the end. Liberty and stable order are
permanent requirements of a healthy political society, but how are the two to be
combined? Tocqueville concludes that "there is nothing in the world but patriotism or religion that can make the universality of citizens advance for long

toward the same goal" (89). Only religion and patriotism—understood as an active concern for God and country respectively—are capable of eliciting the free cooperation of citizens in a shared life; only they are capable of defining a moral order that can support and sustain liberty by attaching it to a durable political structure.

Patriotism and religion hold such power because they connect daily affairs and the human institutions that regulate them to a moral order in which particular acts come to light as meaningful (compare 417). In so doing they form a bridge between social-political life and the deepest longings of human nature. It is necessary to form such a bridge because man's natural desire for meaning renders him indifferent at best to a political order that is not tied to some such greater cause, while the objects of religion and active patriotism—God and country—often seem obscure or remote from the concerns of ordinary life. Religion and patriotism therefore depend upon two elements: a "social theory" or set of ideas by which daily affairs are connected to a higher order; and daily rituals or observances to remind their adherents of that connection (64). A society that fails to define a moral order or bring it to bear on daily life will either fail to establish itself, or, if it has inherited its success from past generations, dry up the well of energy on which it lives (89).

The genius of the Puritans was to connect both patriotism and religion to the daily lives of citizens in such a way as to secure the free and deep devotion of citizens to a more or less liberal democratic order. "More or less" is a necessary qualifier here because Tocqueville's analysis points to the conclusion that liberal democracy must be founded and secured in ways that do not sit comfortably with what we would consider a "purely" liberal democratic perspective. In our day as in Tocqueville's, liberalism is frequently defined by the aim of privatizing morality or divorcing it from public order. Tocqueville speaks of those who would promote utility without justice, or replace religion with doctrines of self-interest (11, 282); we can think of those who insist on excluding "comprehensive doctrines" from the public realm.[29] Tocqueville not only rejected this view but actually declared a rhetorical "war" upon it. Not only did he insist that every society, liberal democracy included, requires moral order; he went so far as to claim that the weakness of external authorities in democratic society made it especially dependent on strong mores (282). For Tocqueville, a liberty not rooted in mores is ineffectual, and mores not grounded in religious beliefs are impotent. Hence religion and patriotism are indispensable foundations of liberal democracy. This view, which made Tocqueville a self-professed "liberal of a different kind,"[30] helps to explain the importance for him of the Puritan roots of American national character.

As fundamental as this teaching is to Tocqueville's political thought, it does not entirely resolve the problem of national character. The kind of liberty we have seen in Puritan life—the free assent of the human soul to a certain idea of moral order embodied in a given way of life—is hardly equivalent to the true or philosophic liberty discussed earlier. Tocqueville admits that Puritan legislation was frequently "bizarre and tyrannical" as well as instructive. He also makes clear that the moral order upon which political society depends need not and ultimately cannot simply be true, and that the costs of false and even dangerous public beliefs have to be weighed against their benefits, which may be more weighty (278, 419). Yet genuine liberty, in Tocqueville's view, aims at the apprehension of truth by virtuous individuals. The question remains, therefore, how a society that inspires free assent to an inspiring ideal—thus instilling its citizens with a sense of conventional moral order—can simultaneously remain open to the pursuit of a true moral order that may conflict with the conventional one. This question leads to the second and third lessons of Tocqueville's account of the Puritans: the necessity of the idea of rights and of a higher justice expressed by means of what he calls the "art of the legislator."

The Idea of Rights as "Virtue [in] the Political World"

Tocqueville claims that Puritan New England embodied all "the general principles on which modern constitutions rest," principles that include religious liberty,[31] representative government, and individual liberty (39). He goes on to show not only that these principles were modified by practices and beliefs that emphasized religious sectarianism, active participation, and collective (township) liberty, but that this modification of modern principles was precisely what made the Puritans able to lay the foundations for a thriving liberal democratic society: the United States of America. Far from vindicating modern political principles per se, the success of democracy in America reveals their inherent limits and establishes the wisdom of a *new* political science willing to depart from a purely modern approach to politics for the sake of sustaining a politics that is both healthy in absolute terms and viable in the modern age.

This "new" politics can be seen in the Puritan notion of civic rights. The Puritans believed in human liberty and expressed it through a radical version of popular sovereignty. So jealous were they of the right of all interested persons to participate in making the laws that they insisted on having common affairs "treated in the public square and within the general assembly of citizens, as at [ancient] Athens." This practice diminished the force not only of representative government, but also of personal liberty understood in an individualistic or private sense.[32] The New England citizen was free to participate in the making of laws, but those laws came from and sustained a tight-knit society in which religion and morality were strictly policed; citizens were obliged to serve their country (e.g. through militia service); and society was obliged to look after the needs of its members, from poverty and transportation to inheritances and public education. The net result was "a real, active, altogether democratic and republican political life reigning" "in the heart of the [New England] township." "Interests, passions, duties, and rights," while belonging to citizens who freely participated in public affairs, "came to be grouped around the township's individuality" rather than around private life (40-41). In this way the national character of the Puritans was able to bring about the free concurrence of wills in an order that was, with modifications, applicable to an evolving American democratic society.

In the early New England township we see confirmation of Tocqueville's famous claim that no one is less independent than the free citizen.[33] Along with Jean-Jacques Rousseau, a man whose ideas he "lived with" every day,[34] Tocqueville believes that genuine liberty requires that the individual see himself as part of a larger order to which he freely belongs.[35] Tocqueville's account of township government is perhaps the most Rousseauian part of his writings, and it leads us to wonder just how much Tocqueville shares with Rousseau. Some have feared that Tocqueville's connection to this radical philosopher signifies his agreement with Rousseau's teaching that man is by nature asocial; that political society is wholly artificial; and that political freedom is the product of a radical denaturing of man as opposed to the realization of natural rights.[36] Tocqueville's puzzling silence on the Declaration of Independence, with its language of natural rights, and his emphasis on the religious and cultural roots of American liberty, to the apparent exclusion of its Lockean philosophic heritage, are indications that this fear points to some truth about him. If it were the whole truth, then we could not expect the sort of civic virtue Tocqueville admires to connect citizens to any moral order existing outside of political conventions. Political morality would not only be distinct from the whole truth about nature, but actually contrary to it.

However influenced Tocqueville was by Rousseau, it is clear that he departed significantly from his master's thought. We have already observed Tocqueville's contention that man's natural condition is characterized by a savage pride that must be tamed by political society. Far from being asocial, however, man as Tocqueville describes him longs to live in a moral order structuring his relationship to people and things—"savagery" being merely one expression of this human need. In Tocqueville's view, the integration of citizens into a political order does not require denaturing but rather the cultivation and direction of a natural instinct toward a certain end (89). Also, though Tocqueville expects the particular moral order that guides a society to contain mixtures of truth and falsehood, he judges it according to its ability to create the conditions in which individual souls may turn toward the whole truth, not by its success in denaturing citizens or robbing them of any sense of their own nature in terms of which they might question the sufficiency of the reigning moral and political order. Individualism for Tocqueville is an intellectual and moral error, not a dangerous truth to be hidden or buried in salutary myths (482). Tocqueville shares Rousseau's disdain for an Enlightenment that would eradicate belief and champion reason as the sole bond of political society, but he does not view belief as entirely unreasonable; to the contrary, he regards it as a necessary and potentially healthy stage in the ascent of the mind toward truth (179).

For all these reasons, Tocqueville rejects Rousseau's concept of a general will to which the will of individual citizens must be subordinated (410).[37] For Tocqueville, the idea of the will of the community completely dominating polit-

ical life is both fantastic and unjust. It is fantastic because it presupposes a government whose will encompasses the genuine interests of all citizens, whereas
all actual governments are dominated by a group whose will tends to ignore or
violate the interests of other groups (223).[38] It is unjust because justice demands
the fulfillment of the needs of our common humanity, and even the interests of
an entire people are unjust when they conflict with this universal standard of
human affairs (240). The common good at which citizens ought to aim is not
defined by any political process, but rather by nature itself, and seeking it therefore requires an act of intellectual and moral transcendence that can never be
embodied in laws and customs alone. Its best regular political expression is
found, not in the will of one class or even of the generality of citizens, but in the
mutual dialogue and compromise of diverse classes held together by a common
idea of natural right transcending them all.[39]

The liberty of the Puritans is exemplary by Tocqueville's standards because,
while expressing itself routinely in the will of the majority, it is rooted in a higher idea transcending even the general will of all citizens: the idea of justice, understood as grounded in nature and divine revelation and applicable to all human
beings. Puritan mores preserved liberty by both engaging citizens' wills in the
regulation of daily affairs and subordinating their wills to a larger order knowa-
ble by and binding upon but not created by human beings, and thereby preventing any one group—the majority included—from imposing its will unless that
will could be justified with reference to this higher standard.

The functioning of Puritan liberty within its moral order can be glimpsed in
a scenario Tocqueville briefly recreates for us. John Winthrop, the great colonial
leader, had been accused of arbitrary acts as a magistrate. After giving a speech
in his own defense, Winthrop was acquitted "and from then on he was always
reelected governor of" Massachusetts. In the course of his defense, Winthrop
made the following statement, which Tocqueville refers to as "this beautiful
definition of liberty":

> Let us not deceive ourselves about what we understand by our independence.
> There is, in fact, a sort of corrupt liberty, whose usage is common to animal and
> man, and which consists in doing all that one pleases. This liberty is the enemy
> of all authority; it suffers impatiently all rules; with it, we become inferior to
> ourselves; it is the enemy of truth and peace; and God believed it necessary to
> rise against it! But it is a civil and moral liberty that finds its force in union, and
> which it is the mission of power to protect: this is the liberty to do without fear
> all that is just and good. This holy liberty we ought to defend through all ha-
> zards, and expose for it, if necessary, our very lives (42).[40]

As usual, Tocqueville's quotation is modified to suit his particular intentions,
and thus we can take its details as a key to unlocking Tocqueville's own view of
the way in which national character ought to mediate a society's understanding
of the core political notions of liberty, rights, and justice.

To begin with, the speech makes clear that liberty cannot be defined in
terms of desire or pleasure. It is beneath the dignity of man to base his life on

what he shares with the other animals. Here Winthrop—and Tocqueville through him—is referring to the classical notion of virtue as the specific excellence of a thing. Human virtue is defined in terms of what distinguishes the human species from others: rational speech and the way of life it makes possible, including both knowledge and intelligent society.[41] Thus nature serves as a standard for measuring human perfection; when we fall short of this standard, "we become inferior to ourselves."

This statement helps us to unlock Tocqueville's approach to politics because it explains not only why political liberty must be defined in terms of virtue, but also why it cannot simply be identified with virtue. For Tocqueville, virtue is the greatest good for man, and virtue is the free (*libre*) choice of what is good.[42] On the one hand this means that liberty without virtue is bad or corrupt, and that genuine liberty must take its bearings from virtue or lose its legitimacy. On the other hand, the good represented by liberty cannot be divorced from the potential for abuse without destroying the good itself. In forcing a man to do virtuous deeds one robs his actions of liberty, which is an essential feature of virtue. Compelling someone to do good may sometimes constitute a lesser evil, but it can never produce a virtuous act; hence it is never as good as inspiring him to do it freely. Liberty is bad when abused, but liberty as a good can always be abused. Man requires authoritative constraints to prevent him from straying from virtue—for example, a national character connecting him to a conventional moral order—but those constraints must be loose enough to allow him to pursue virtue of his own free will. Authority must encourage virtue without being able to guarantee its achievement.

The key to a genuinely liberal politics must therefore be something between perfect liberty or virtue on the one hand and corrupt liberty or vice on the other—something capable of directing the latter toward the former, without being able to transform the one into the other. For Tocqueville, this mediating thing is nothing but "the idea of rights." "After the general idea of virtue," he says, I know of none more beautiful than that of rights." "There are no great men without virtue," and Tocqueville evidently considers virtue or individual greatness the most beautiful idea we can know. Yet the notion of rights is a close second, since it is "intermingled" with that of virtue: "The idea of rights is nothing other than the idea of virtue introduced into the political world" (227). If virtue makes individual men great, respect for rights renders a people great. This makes two things clear. First, Tocqueville considers individual greatness to be superior to collective greatness. Human perfection is a rare accomplishment that cannot be replicated throughout a society, but remains the standard against which collective life must be judged. Second, Tocqueville believes that a lesser but genuine form of virtue is possible for societies, and is achieved through respect for rights rather than the full-fledged practice of virtue itself.

What does Tocqueville mean by a respect for rights? Just as virtue, for Tocqueville, requires the pursuit of the whole truth about nature, so do rights, virtue's lesser cousin, enjoin adherence to the shadow of truth on which political society is based: the conventional moral order. "It is with the idea of rights," he continues, "that men have defined what license and tyranny are." The idea of rights is that subset of mores that enlightens a man as to when he is or is not required to obey authority. With it, he can instinctively judge his own conduct and that of others, and respond accordingly. Thus he can "show himself independent without arrogance and submissive without baseness" (227).

Here Tocqueville echoes his past statement that both the use of power and obedience to it deprave men only when they are considered illegitimate (8). The idea of rights is what legitimizes both phenomena; it teaches man to recognize "the right to command" in some of his fellows, while placing limits on that right. When those limits are observed, the citizen who obeys "raises himself in a way above the very one who commands him" (227). This is possible because the citizen is not obeying man at all but rather an overarching idea to which both ruled and ruler are bound. Thus the idea of rights authorizes both obedience and resistance to those in authority depending on the correspondence of their commands to that idea, by whose authority they command. In principle, respect for rights introduces virtue into the political world by providing a standard by which citizens may pursue virtue by their own lights in most cases, but defer to the judgment of leaders in others. To the extent that this notion of rights approximates the true idea of virtue, or natural right—from which the idea of rights is importantly distinct[43]—authority is thereby strong enough to oppose or support those human tendencies most clearly contrary or conducive to virtue, while leaving citizens free to work out the details of virtue for themselves.

This model of liberty grounded in a notion of rights itself grounded in the idea of virtue is illustrated by the story of Winthrop related above. The people of Massachusetts had accused Winthrop of committing arbitrary acts as magistrate. Clearly they believed he had violated some objective standard without which he possessed no authority; they, as a community, had the right to resist any such usurpation. Winthrop's response is to dispute the people's conclusion but not their premise. He accepts the grounds on which the people had accused him and uses the same grounds to construct his defense. Winthrop reminds the people that their independence pertains only to "all that is just and good," and that the just and good include civil and divine authority; theirs is "a civil and moral liberty that finds its force in union." Winthrop admits that he is bound by the same standard as they are—for "it is the mission of power to protect" such liberty (42)—but he is bound in a different way, a way that requires him sometimes to issue commands, even when unpopular, to suppress abuses of liberty. In a controversy whose details Tocqueville wisely leaves to our imagination,[44] Winthrop persuades the people that he was using his authority to protect their genuine rights, rooted in virtuous liberty rather than license, prompting them to obey him not only voluntarily but enthusiastically from then on.

Though Tocqueville shows us an example of this Puritan model presumably working in favor of the common good, he does not consider it flawless. Tocqueville's language and examples remind us that this model assumes a fundamental inequality among men, by which some are ultimately better suited to command and others to obey. The notion of rights can legitimize such inequality, and even qualify it by limiting the cases to which it applies and by requiring a meaningful interchange between leaders and citizens before authority can be exercised. Yet these measures cannot finally erase that inequality. In order to be legitimate, authority must be guided by objective criteria: "the just and the good." When authority departs from these criteria, the people can or must resist it; and when the people depart from it, their leaders can and must resist them. Yet if the people were as capable as their leaders of discerning the just and the good, they would not need to be commanded (or persuaded) in such matters; and if leaders were always right in their judgments, the need for scrutiny on the part of the people would be far less urgent. The injustices embraced by Winthrop himself raise the perennial problem of who will watch the watchmen, a question that the "respect for rights" solves only partially by requiring peoples and their leaders to engage in serious discourse about the justice and goodness of their actions, in light of conventional beliefs about what is just and good. If, in early New England, injustices were mostly limited to those motivated by the collective intolerance of all citizens, this was a substantial feat, but one falling short of justice *simpliciter*.

By nature leadership belongs to those who firmly grasp the just and good, to the "natural aristocracy that flows from enlightenment and virtue" (50). In practice, of course, those who possess or seek to possess power are by no means limited to the enlightened and virtuous. Nature renders some more deserving of rule without providing any guarantee that they will prevail. The idea of rights as Tocqueville presents it addresses this deficiency of nature by authorizing the people to police their leaders as well as to be policed by them. Yet this solution assumes that the people will possess an idea of rights radiant enough to enable them to discern virtue and vice in their leaders and to treat them accordingly, even though the people will not discern virtue itself clearly enough to live without the authority of virtuous leaders. The idea of rights, which renders liberty compatible with moral authority, is a popular idea standing between knowledge and ignorance of virtue, and its tenuous nature defines both the promise and the limits of liberal politics in Tocqueville's view. In order to ensure that the promise is fulfilled and the perils skirted as much as possible, the institution and cultivation of an idea of rights capable of sustaining liberal democratic order requires a further art whose nature constitutes the final lesson discernable in Tocqueville's account of the Puritans.

Justice and the Art of the Legislator

To describe rights as a mean between knowledge and ignorance of virtue is reminiscent of the Platonic notion of opinion, which also stands between knowledge and ignorance. According to Plato's Socrates, philosophy is the only activity capable of bridging the gap between opinion and knowledge, and political affairs will never be in good order unless philosophers rule or rulers philosophize. Even in Socrates' "ideal" city-in-speech, however, the ideas of the good and the just cannot be grasped by the general populace; rather, the philosopher king or kings legislate on the basis of their knowledge of these ideas and the citizens obey on the basis of an opinion that the philosophers know the just and the good. In Socrates' imaginary city this opinion happens to be true, but the citizens do not know it to be true. True opinion is not knowledge and can never be as secure as knowledge. The conjunction between wisdom and power, upon which the good of politics depends, rests on insecure foundations and is therefore coincidental and even paradoxical.[45] Plato, who can be said to have initiated the quest to reconcile politics and virtue understood as the perfection of man as a rational animal, also presents the most profound articulation of the impossibility of any perfect reconciliation between them.

As we have seen, Tocqueville is an heir to this Platonic tradition. This inheritance is once again evident in his chapter focusing on religion's influence over the souls of Americans. In addition to his remarks about the soul itself, Tocqueville here states that "the whole art of the legislator consists in discerning well and in advance [the] natural inclinations of human societies" in order to steer them closer to the "unmoving" goal "toward which the human race should always tend." Without specifying precisely what this goal is, Tocqueville indicates that the peril of democracy is that modern man, while he "takes pleasure in [an] honest and legitimate search for well-being, . . . will finally lose the use of his most sublime faculties." In other words, the danger is that the mores, national character, or idea of rights defining the realm of democratic opinion will definitively lose sight of virtue or the natural standard of human perfection. Tocqueville proclaims it the task of legislators "and all honest and enlightened men" to resist this danger by applying "themselves relentlessly to raising up souls and keeping them turned toward Heaven" (518-19). In a striking departure from modern political thought, Tocqueville indicates that the central task of politics is, as Plato suggested, to care for souls.[46]

This discussion of the legislative art and its concern for the soul prepares us to understand the third and final lesson of Tocqueville's chapter on the Puritans: that the achievement of justice in human affairs requires the application of political science through a political or legislative art directed toward the shaping of mores. The science of politics (focused on unchanging human nature) and art of politics (focused on the variable social state and national character) are both necessary for reasons that can be grasped theoretically and seen in the example of the New England township.

For Tocqueville, justice (like virtue) is higher, better, and more permanent than rights. In fact, his idea of justice is closely tied to that of virtue itself. He defines justice as "a general law . . . that has been made or at least adopted not only by the majority of this or that people, but by the majority of all men." This striking definition is framed in democratic terms, as if justice must be "the will of [some] majority," and it is only a question of determining which one. It also seems to presuppose the practically impossible: a universal assembly of humankind, including all the peoples of the world, past, present, and future. Tocqueville speaks in such terms in order to remind democratic readers that there is something greater than the majority to which they are attached, and thereby to reveal to them the impiousness and detestability of "the maxim that in matters of government the majority of a people has the right to do everything." Yet Tocqueville is not content to appeal from the majority of "this or that people" to the entire community of any nation; he appeals instead to "the sovereignty of the human race" itself (240). In this manner he signifies that justice is rooted not in the actual will of individuals or majorities or even peoples, but in the needs of human nature, which remain the same "at any time and in whatever political condition" (520). In other words, justice (like virtue) is grounded in natural right. In practice, therefore, justice is an idea to be known only through the study of human beings and their permanent needs—that is, through what Tocqueville calls political science.

Political science ascertains what is just and good for human beings and thereby defines the enlightenment and virtue that qualify certain great men to be the leaders of society. That leadership, however, cannot consist in simply proclaiming what they know about justice and virtue. Society is not dominated by reason or science but rather by opinion. Opinion at its worst consists in "coarse commonplaces" or "dangerous [maladies] of the mind"; at best opinion takes the form of "respect for rights" or a more or less accurate sense of the limits of liberty and when to follow those whose grasp of the just and the good appears to be firm. The arguments of virtuous leaders will fall on deaf ears unless the fundamental opinions that dominate a society—its national character and idea of rights—are receptive to those arguments. Winthrop would not have been able to persuade the discontent New Englanders unless they had previously believed in the idea of the just and the good to which he appealed, even though his application of it initially differed from theirs. Nor could any people hold its rulers accountable to such higher standards unless the rulers and governed shared a common respect for them. The institutional operation of politics is dependent on a deeper sort of politics, one that understands and fosters the mores that make a people more receptive to just rule. This deeper politics is what Tocqueville calls the art of the legislator, and it is the essence of the art of politics he seeks to advance in *Democracy*.[47]

The legislative art must be grounded in political science partly because that science ascertains the character of the justice the legislative art attempts to apply to political affairs. Political science is also necessary to grasp the obstacles to such an application. Through the study of politics Tocqueville is able to conclude that societies are essentially factional in the classical sense of that term: defined by opinions or interests inimical to the true good of society. Not only are "the great" and "the people" factions within a certain nation, but every nation is a faction within humanity, whose "universal society" it tends to abuse. In Tocqueville's view, it is not possible to enlighten societies to the point where they simply grasp and observe true justice, nor is it even possible to establish a truly "mixed" government in which various factions would cancel each other out, leaving a pure version of justice behind (240). In practice, every society must be dominated by a particular faction, and therefore also by the opinions that characterize this faction. The art of the legislator is to identify those opinions or habits within a given society that are either good in themselves or capable of restraining the bad opinions or habits of that people. Applying universal justice to a given society, such a legislator can identify a strategy for enhancing its virtues and moderating its vices by use of concepts and practices tailored to the faction dominating that society (518).[48] In other words, the art of the legislator attempts to fashion or sustain an idea of rights best capable of approximating justice in the circumstances of a given political society.

Tocqueville's chapter on the American point of departure is an example of the legislative art in action. It is not that Tocqueville believed the Puritans had mastered this art—his alterations, omissions, and criticisms belie any such impression—but rather that he exhibits this art in his account of the Puritans. Tocqueville studies the origins of American national character in order to find beliefs and habits compatible with democratic society but also running contrary to its dominant prejudices and therefore capable of moderating its worst excesses. The New England spirit of liberty as Tocqueville portrays it is balanced by a spirit of religion that seems to be its contrary: the one eschewing every authority in favor of unfettered experimentation, the other abjuring all doubt and bowing "with respect before truths that it accepts without discussion" (43). By the standard of virtue, such self-contradiction would seem to fall short of the good, but seen through the lens of an art seeking to counterbalance the excesses of materialism and civic apathy besetting modern democratic society, it appears not so much as a contradiction as a salutary balancing act.

From the artful legislator's point of view contradiction can itself be useful, so long as it is confined to the level of national character or opinion.[49] If human nature, "incapable of grasping firmly the true and the just, is most often reduced to choosing between two excesses" (39) the best or least bad choice may often be the juxtaposition of excesses capable of moderating one another. Society by itself will veer toward one particular excess, and the legislator must correct this by promoting the opposite tendency, even if in itself this tendency too can be excessive. Thus Tocqueville admits that in an age of faith and social hierarchy, when souls were held "almost numb in the contemplation of another world," he would have promoted material desires, the excesses of which "would soon disappear in the common physiognomy" of such a society (518). In a democratic and skeptical age tempted to embrace materialism, apathy, and majority tyranny, Tocqueville advocates instead a concerted effort to promote religious unity, civic participation, and respect for authority, trusting that the excesses to which these latter notions can be taken will never redefine modern society. This is why the Puritans, despite their flaws, are Tocqueville's chosen model to illustrate the application of his political science to modern democratic society. It is also why he avoids the identification of America's founding with documents such as the Declaration of Independence, whose proclamations of equal liberty do not easily lend themselves to the emphasis he wants to place on the role of religion and communal life in shaping national character.[50]

The opening chapters of *Democracy* introduce us to the key notions of Tocqueville's political science and political art by way of application rather than abstract enunciation. Political science teaches us about human nature, which is characterized by two contrary but related tendencies: first, the desire and ability to reflect and live in accordance with the truth of things; second, a pride that prompts us to distort the truth in favor of our self-importance as individuals. Political society has the difficult task of both taming that pride and promoting the search for truth and virtue, but the difficulty of that search precludes social mores or a "national character" that simply corresponds with the true moral order. Neither peoples nor their leaders can be relied upon to grasp truth and justice firmly in all cases, and so a healthy politics requires a popularly accessible notion of rights by which peoples and leaders can rule, judge, challenge, and persuade one another in the ever-imperfect quest for natural justice. To shape this notion of rights in the service of genuine virtue is the task of a deeper political or legislative art, which Tocqueville himself exhibits by insisting upon a model of democracy that emphasizes qualities in opposition to the extremes favored by democracy itself. By locating the notions that moderate democratic excesses—especially piety and civic spirit—at the root of a society defined by equality and liberty, Tocqueville has armed his readers with weapons accessible to democratic leaders that can be used to combat those excesses in a political environment otherwise susceptible to embracing opposite extremes. Before considering how he will recommend wielding these weapons, our study will turn to a closer examination of the threat Tocqueville discerns in the unregulated reign of democracy, a threat he sums up in the term "individualism."

Notes

1. Letter to Kergorlay, December 15, 1850 (1985, 252ff).
2. Aristotle (2002, 1098b).
3. Compare George Washington (1988, 240; quoted in Jaffa 2000) and John Locke (1982, § 101).
4. Tocqueville's attention to these issues is partly a result of the influence of Montesquieu, but Tocqueville faults Montesquieu for giving too much weight to physical causes (89, 567).
5. I am indebted to Khalil Habib for this interpretation. My reading of Tocqueville's first chapter is especially influenced by him, though he is not responsible for the mistakes I have no doubt contributed.
6. Tocqueville's more poetic friend, Gustave de Beaumont, helped him to pen these passages of *Democracy*. See Tocqueville (1990a, 21, note f).
7. See Aristotle (2002, I.3, V.3, V.7).
8. Tocqueville's views on political science are explicitly outlined in his "Speech to the Academy of Moral and Political Sciences" (1991). For contemporary critiques of the "fact-value distinction" championed by modern social science, see Leo Strauss (1953), Alasdair McIntyre (1981), and Allen Bloom (1987).

9. Strauss (1953) 4, 9.

10. This seemingly small point has profound implications. See, for instance, Bloom's comment in the introduction to Alexandre Kojève's lectures on Hegel (1980): Hegel's notion of the end of history presupposes that man can definitively conquer nature, which in turn presupposes that nature is something capable of being definitively conquered by man. Bloom points out that Kojève cannot support this last assumption; and were it true, we may add, man's conquering of nature would be a gift given to man from someone or something other than man.

11. Of course, the American natives did possess nations and even federations, but Tocqueville considered them generations away from being fully civilized (313).

12. This is Rousseau's position in *The Social Contract*: "Man was/is born free, and everywhere he is in chains. . . How did this change occur? I do not know. *What can make it legitimate?* I believe I can answer this question." (1978, 46, emphasis added).

13. Compare Luke 11: 5-9, about a man who is *reluctant* to share a loaf of bread with his friend in the middle of the night.

14. This account should be compared to Rousseau's *Discourse on the Origins of Inequality* (1964). Rousseau's natural man is wholly possessed by innocent self-love (*amour de soi-même*) and free from corrupting pride or vanity (*amour-propre*). Tocqueville clearly thinks that the American native is as "natural" as man can be, but describes him as rising above self-love (hence his willingness to suffer and die) in the service of an intense pride (hence his generosity and ferocity). This does not mean that Tocqueville considers self-love (or self-interest, as he styles it) unnatural; but it does suggest that he rejects the notion that pride (and its socializing tendencies) are unnatural historical accretions, à la his master Rousseau.

15. See Plato (1968, II), and Bloom's "Interpretive Essay" in that volume. Tocqueville makes essentially the same argument in *Democracy* (521-22).

16. Compare Aristotle (1984, I.ii.15-16).

17. Hobbes (1994, XI-XII, *et passim*).

18. Plato (1968, 473d-511e, especially 494a, 503b).

19. Aristotle (2002, I.2; 1984, I.1).

20. Tocqueville uses this expression without naming its referent. Mansfield and Winthrop take him to be speaking of Napoleon, but do not find where this famous general stated that "the first condition for conducting war well is to be young." Tocqueville cites Machiavelli's *Prince* explicitly in the same section of *Democracy* (632-33), and Machiavelli in that work argues that virtue consists in conquering fortune and that fortune is conquered by the "young" who are not afraid to "strike her down" (1985, chapter XXV).

21. Machiavelli (1985, especially II, XVIII).

22. Contrast Rousseau (1979, 167) and the views of Descartes, which I have discussed elsewhere (2007).

23. Compare Aristotle's account of primitive man, whom he likens to Homer's apolitical, man-eating, and monocular Cyclopes (1984, 1252b).

24. (1968, 521c). Rousseau, in his *Emile* (1979), considers the possibility of an education that would prevent irrational beliefs from being formed in the first place. Even on Rousseau's own premises—with which Tocqueville disagrees—one has to note the extravagant efforts necessary to produce such an education. Rousseau describes his own liberation from prejudice in his *Confessions* (1995) as taking place through un-learning.

25. Larger than the tribe. For the ancients, the requisite structure was the polis or city, composed of about 30,000 free citizens and 300,000 slaves or servants (450-51). Modern political philosophers tended to favor larger units, from nation-states to global

government, though Tocqueville's mentors Montesquieu (1989) and Rousseau (1978) gave defenses of smaller-scale politics.

26. In his later account of the three races inhabiting North America, Tocqueville details the grave and systematic injustices committed by Anglo-Americans against the natives. He evokes sympathy for all of the afflicted, but is most indignant when it comes to the Cherokees, who had taken up agriculture and cultivated their minds to the point of publishing a newspaper and penning eloquent pleas to the U.S. Government, employing "arguments founded on natural right and on reason" (315-24).

27. Mansfield and Winthrop present Mather's original English, which argues that New England succeeded through "help from God." See Sanford Kessler's abridged edition of *Democracy* (2000b) for a translation of Tocqueville's version.

28. Tocqueville hints several times that he is using the Puritans as vehicles for his own thought. His first hint is in an allusion to an author he had mastered in college: Cicero (Jardin 1988, 59-60). In Cicero's *Republic* (1928), the idea of man being fully formed in his cradle appears in reference to the city of Rome. Scipio, the republican hero whom Cicero uses as his mouthpiece, has finished giving his account of Rome's foundations, and declared that the wisdom of Romulus left Rome fully formed in the cradle. One of his interlocutors observes that Scipio has dissembled, presenting his own ideas on the best political order by attributing them to the legendary founder of Rome. Though Tocqueville stresses that the foundations of American civilization are unique in not being obscured by the darkness of legend, he indicates his willingness to mythologize them nonetheless when he declares that democracy "sprang full-grown and fully armed" from the New England soil (35)—an allusion to the foundational myth of ancient Thebes, cited by Plato (1968, 414b-c) as an example of the sort of "noble lie" that would attach a city's guardians to the regime they must protect. All of this hints that Tocqueville considers himself part of the Socratic tradition according to which no actual political society possesses true justice, a lesson Plato's Socrates taught by finding justice in an imaginary city, and which later Socratics sometimes concealed by exaggerating the justice of actual regimes to which they or their readers had to remain loyal or sought to reform.

29. See Rawls (2001). In principle Rawls excludes from the public square not only opinions appealing to religion and classical virtue, but also those appealing to liberalism as a comprehensive doctrine. Though some might consider the political (as opposed to comprehensive) liberalism Rawls espouses comprehensive enough to vitiate his position, his stance on allegedly non-comprehensive ground raises the question of how liberalism can justify, without reference to comprehensive views, its inevitable censuring of illiberal opinion, no matter how bizarre or tyrannical. In the end, Rawls seems to admit that one comprehensive doctrine can only be refuted by another, since he demands that citizens concede to political liberalism for reasons grounded in their private comprehensive views, and not merely on pragmatic grounds. How it is that a variety of comprehensive doctrines barred from arguing their comprehensive views among themselves can all be expected to concur in this fashion remains, at best, a mystery in Rawls's thought.

30. Letter to Eugène Stoffels, September 16, 1823 (1985, 29; cited in Zetterbaum 1967, 145).

31. Tocqueville does not list religious liberty under this heading, but reminds us immediately prior that in their sectarian zeal the Puritans forgot (and hence recognized) the "great principles of religious liberty" to which they had appealed in England (39).

32. See Benjamin Constant's essay, "The Liberty of the Ancients Compared with that of the Moderns" (1988).

33. Tocqueville (1955, 274ff; see Manent 1996, 121).

34. See Tocqueville (1985, 131: letter to Beaumont, April 22, 1838).

35. See Rousseau (1978), Mansfield and Winthrop (Tocqueville 2000a, lxxxii), and Sheldon Wolin (2001, 5-6), who argues that the chief concern of Tocqueville's writings is to combat the "privatizing" tendencies of modernity and revive "le chose publique"; for Tocqueville, Wolin argues, even liberalism itself was a vehicle for "la politique."

36. See Thomas West (1991) and John Koritansky (1986, 19-28, 148).

37. See Lively (1962, 108, 114, 226-27) and Mansfield and Winthrop (Tocqueville 2000a, lxxii). Bruce Frohnen (1993b, 141-148) demonstrates Tocqueville's intention to unite the private to the public through virtue, rather than to destroy the private and replace it with the public.

38. Tocqueville finds the picture of ancient democracies given by Rousseau in his *Letter to M. D'Alembert on the Theatre* (1960) as fanciful as the city in speech of Plato's *Republic* (Tocqueville 2000a, 538).

39. This dialogical character of the New England national character is discussed in detail by Barbara Allen (2005).

40. I have translated Tocqueville's translation of John Winthrop, which departs in places from the original English, given by Mansfield and (Delba) Winthrop.

41. See Plato (1968, 352b-354a).

42. Tocqueville (1957, 117); see Lively (1962, 13).

43. This distinction between natural right or justice, which is the same for all men at all times and in all places, and the idea of rights, which differs among societies and within one society over time, may explain Tocqueville's reluctance to employ the term "natural rights," which he likely saw as confusing these related but very different concepts.

44. Winthrop was in fact suppressing religious dissenters and political schemes he saw as excessively democratic, actions for which neither Tocqueville nor his readership would likely have much enthusiasm (Mather 1979, 124-27). Yet Tocqueville uses the speech to establish the principle upon which he believes modern liberal democracy must be founded: an equal liberty framed by a robust conception of moral order.

45. See Plato (1968, Books V-VII); Bloom's note 24 (Plato 1968, 463); Pangle's note 5 (Plato 1980, 521); and Strauss (1983, 139). Thus, to paraphrase Machiavelli, Plato teaches that to found on the people is to found on mud. The people must be governed according to standards that, qua people, they will never fully grasp. Machiavelli, by contrast, embraces a political order founded on the satisfaction of desire. In the service of such an order, he expects the philosopher to abandon the notion of truth as knowledge of changeless ideas and embrace a truth that is "effectual" or bounded by becoming (1985, especially III, IX, XV). For Machiavelli, there is no ultimate difference between the goal of the political philosopher and that of the people; the difference is one of "humor" and ability, not knowledge or end.

46. See Plato (1988, 650b).

47. James Ceaser (1990) refers to this as the art of democratic "superintendence."

48. Tocqueville's strategy is essentially the same as that of Aristotle (1984, III.6ff). Wolin finds this approach incoherent since the classics aimed at the common good, but could not identify an agent to realize it. The solution described above—the recourse by the natural aristocracy to the legislative art—aims at the influence of wisdom on the institutions and habits of a society, not on the continual rule of wisdom. This may appear to Wolin as a power grab by theorists (2001, 66, 62). To classical theorists, however, wisdom is the only title to rule that does not ultimately reduce to "sheer bodily ('brachial') force" (Strauss 1983, 129; compare Aristotle 1984, III.10).

Zetterbaum specifically denies that Tocqueville supports the natural aristocracy, arguing that for Tocqueville "the claim of the wise and the good to rule cannot be elevated to an exclusive principle of legitimacy, for no group of men, whatever their talents, can be relied on in all cases to put other men's interests above their own" (1967, 32). Yet this deficiency of humankind is precisely the problem Tocqueville attempts to solve by promoting the indirect influence of the natural aristocracy through the legislative art or superintendence.

49. For the value to statesman of contradictory principles from which a balance can be struck, see Pangle (1992b, 25) and Hillel Fradkin (2000, 92).

50. We will revisit Tocqueville's treatment of the Declaration in chapter 6.

Sicut aspidis surdae, et obturantis aures suas.

Chapter 3
Majority Tyranny, Administrative Despotism, and the Triumph of Individualism

In his account of the origins of modern democracy, Tocqueville reveals his fear that the force by which the democratic revolution has torn down the structures of the *ancien régime* will also prove deadly to humanity itself. Only a new moral order fashioned for a new world can prevent this from happening, and only a new political science can provide the insight needed to build and maintain such a moral order. Tocqueville develops the main tenets of this new political science in his description of pre-colonial America and colonial New England. Here we see in vivid detail and greater depth the reason for Tocqueville's focus on moral order. The intensity of the natural desire to live a meaningful life, combined with the general inability of human beings to grasp the true and the just, requires the mediating influence of political society. The mores definitive of this society must be strong enough to satisfy the human need for meaning while also tempering its extremes, and Tocqueville insists that political society also be open to those who can and will seek the truth about the order of things. This delicate balancing act is only made possible by the influence of great leaders within a society, but society will only accept the influence of such leaders when its mores legitimize that influence.

Tocqueville, who sought to see further into political things than the leaders of his day, strives to develop a legislative art capable of looking after the moral underpinnings of a flourishing modern political order. The chief task of this profoundly political art is to facilitate the influence of those Tocqueville calls the natural aristocracy in their attempt to guide society according to the sovereign dictates of humanity itself, even when these do not accord with the views of the present people or age. A primary concern of Tocqueville's political science is therefore the point of intersection between society and the natural aristocracy.

This chapter will consider the difficulties all societies face in establishing a connection between natural leaders and the general populace, difficulties that are

exacerbated by the advent of popular sovereignty. Later, we shall explore in
detail the solutions Tocqueville proposed for these difficulties in democratic
times. Here our concern will be to detail the consequences he foresaw should
democratic societies fail to take effective measures to limit and direct popular
sovereignty through appropriate mores, definitively cutting themselves off from
the influence of the natural aristocracy. These consequences are revealed in
three famous dangers elaborated in the pages of *Democracy*—majority tyranny,
individualism, and administrative despotism—the dynamic interconnection of
which defines the distinctive challenge of good government in democratic times.

National Character, Social State,
and the Natural Aristocracy

If Tocqueville's second chapter is the key to his whole work (29), his third chapter presents the core problem the second must aid us in solving. Chapter three,
"Social State of the Anglo-Americans," brings Tocqueville's narrative through
the colonial and revolutionary periods to arrive at Jacksonian America. Its title
and opening lines introduce us to the concept of the social state, which corresponds to the "equality of conditions" that loomed so large in Tocqueville's Introduction, as discussed in our first chapter. As before, Tocqueville emphasizes
the immense power of the social state. Though he identifies cases in which laws
can affect and even remake the social state, "once it exists," he tells us, "one can
consider [the social state] as the first cause of most of the laws, customs, and
ideas that regulate the conduct of nations" (45). While consistent with his Introduction, this claim raises doubts about the apparent primacy of national character as elaborated in Tocqueville's second chapter (28ff) and discussed in our
previous chapter. The tension between these two "first causes" sets the stage for
Tocqueville's artful treatment of modern government in *Democracy*.

    The term social state describes the relations of influence and authority that
exist within a society. Though conditions exist between these poles, Tocqueville
usually speaks of the social state as being one of equality or inequality. He does
so not out of a penchant for oversimplification, but because of the relationship
he perceives between the social state and human nature. The same inclination
that causes men to attach themselves to a particular moral order or "national
character"—the desire for meaning—causes them to attach themselves even
more ardently to the principle of the social state itself. By nature we long to live
in relation to the order of things, but the immense intellectual effort required to
ascend toward even a partial understanding of the true nature of things is beyond
the time or capacity of most (417). As a consequence, we look for signs of order
in daily life and are inclined to revere whatever principle seems best to explain
the world in which we live. In any particular age, the social state is the "particular and dominating fact" that is most readily seen; therefore, "this fact almost
always gives rise to a mother idea, or a principal passion, that in the end attracts

and carries along in its course all sentiments and all ideas." Citizens become "obstinately attached" to equality or inequality and comparatively indifferent to "the other goods that society presents to them" (480).

National character is a related but distinct phenomenon. It, too, is born of the human desire for meaning, but unlike the social state, national character is not reducible to abstractions such as equality and inequality. Instead, it regards the particular qualities and habits of a people and its members as they relate, or are thought to relate, to the universal order of things. The degree of equality or inequality that reigns in a society will form a salient feature of national character, but national character as such may include features that qualify or even contradict the social state. This greater particularity and flexibility renders national character a vital means through which the artful legislator can counterbalance the excesses of the social state.

For example, Tocqueville stresses that the social state of the New England colonists was extraordinarily equal: all had come from the same social class in Europe. Yet their equality was modified in crucial ways. To begin with, "all, perhaps without a single exception, had received an advanced education" in England (32). This equally advanced education did not and could not produce equally great results in all of them, however, for "intellectual inequality comes directly from God, and man cannot prevent it from existing always" (51). Instead, this equally high cultivation of the intellect enabled the Puritans to recognize the superior enlightenment and virtue of some among them. As a result of this kind of equality, "the voices of some citizens obtained a power over them that [was almost] aristocratic" (46). John Winthrop illustrates this tendency: his political career was saved by the ability of his fellow citizens to recognize the superiority of his "beautiful definition of liberty" (42), which Tocqueville adopts as an expression of his own vision of virtuous democratic liberty.

Another element of Puritan national character that modified equality of conditions was its intense religious zeal. Though Tocqueville credits Christianity with having introduced the notion of equality into European society (8, 11, 413), he also notes many features of religion that are essentially "aristocratic" or inegalitarian, going so far as to call "any religion whatsoever" "the most precious inheritance" a democratic people may hold "from aristocratic centuries" (519). First, by teaching that God is Creator, religion points to a fundamental inequality in the universe that is in fact offensive to the egalitarian soul—hence the appeal of pantheism in modern times (426). Next, the very basis of religion in divine revelation requires us to believe that God has spoken certain truths directly to some men and not others, an idea fundamentally contrary to the democratic belief that all men possess equal wisdom (408ff). Finally, religion teaches us that we have an eternal soul, which is the superior part of our nature (519ff). This sets up an internal struggle within man between his better and worse instincts; those who win this struggle are virtuous and draw closer to the divine good available to human beings; those who fail become inferior to themselves as well as to the virtuous (520, compare 42). Equal as their social condition was, New Englanders from colonial to Jacksonian times were habituated by their religion as well as by their education "to respect intellectual and moral superiorities and to submit to them without displeasure," a habit that Tocqueville finds to have significantly improved the operation of democracy in that region (191).

The healthy respect for moral and intellectual inequality bequeathed by the Puritans to America is a function of national character rather than the social state. The idea of equality, when it is detached from other goods and rendered an object of blind worship, tends to make any inequality, justified or not, appear offensive (169, 645). This has important implications for the influence of the natural aristocracy over a people. To the degree that the influence of the social state is maximized in democratic society, that society is less likely to revere and more likely to resent intellectual and moral superiorities. An excessively democratic political society is therefore in danger of being cut off from the insights of its most enlightened and virtuous members, undermining the conditions for human flourishing within it.

Thus Tocqueville speaks of the American West as a place where "one can observe democracy reaching its furthest limit." Rather than speaking of what we call "the wild West," or the condition of territories before achieving the degree of law and order requisite for statehood, Tocqueville is here referring to states recently established. He notes that their denizens, whom he refers to as inhabitants rather than citizens, "arrived only yesterday on the soil they occupy" and "hardly know one another." Thus they escape "not only the influence of great names and great wealth, but of that natural aristocracy that flows from enlightenment and virtue." It is not necessarily that no virtuous men exist among them, or that the people have no education to assist them in recognizing virtue. The essential problem is that, the inhabitants not knowing one another, "no one there exercises the respectable power that men accord to the memory of an entire life occupied in doing good before one's eyes." Without the shared sense of a life lived together, the guidance provided by national character cannot be applied to daily affairs, and the natural leaders of society cannot lead. Tocqueville considers this loss so fundamental that he concludes about these Western states that "no society yet exists there" (50, compare 295).

Tocqueville uses the example of the Western states to highlight the centrality of the influence of the natural aristocracy to his evaluation of political societies. That he should use the West to illustrate the "furthest limit" of democracy, though, may seem odd. One would expect him to say that democracy in its mature form is simply not yet established there. Is this not how Americans thought about the West? Tocqueville later notes the zeal with which citizens in long-established states sent religious missionaries to the West in order to solidify the moral conditions necessary to sustain liberal democratic civilization. Their concern to do so magnifies Tocqueville's point. Jacksonian Americans' missionary zeal stems from their belief that "republican institutions" are not self-sustaining, that they require the support offered and limits imposed by religion, i.e. by an authority higher than that of the people itself (280). This belief is a reflection of the American national character—inherited from the Puritans—rather than the democratic social state, which tends to give the people a God-like power over the "political world" and tempt them to believe that "in matters of government the majority of a people has the right to do everything" (55, 240). In America it is the vestiges of Puritanism rather than democracy that, by habituating citizens to obey a higher wisdom, prevents this "impious maxim" from being embraced (280; but compare 641). It was the "aristocratic element" of American national character and not equality of conditions alone that made democracy work in nineteenth century America.

Natural and Conventional Aristocracy

The stress Tocqueville lays on the divergent effects of national character and social state on the influence of the natural aristocracy requires us to probe more deeply into his concept of "aristocracy." Throughout *Democracy*, Tocqueville never lets us forget that the institutionalization of inequality in aristocratic political society is a real and conceptually rich, if historically obsolete, alternative to the embodiment of equality in democratic political society. The reason for Tocqueville's constant reminders about "aristocratic times" will appear from a careful examination of his third chapter.

The importance of aristocracy emerges from Tocqueville's description of the "intellectual influences" that flourished in New England. "One perhaps rightly would have called [the influence of certain citizens] aristocratic," he says, "if it could have been regularly transmitted from father to son" (46). Here we confront Tocqueville's choice to reserve the unqualified term "aristocracy" to refer to the conventional system, dominant in medieval Europe, of according status and authority to the inheritors of large estates. This choice would not be puzzling if Tocqueville believed that aristocracy—Greek for "the rule of the best"—were simply a fiction supported by such conventions. Yet later in this same chapter Tocqueville declares his belief in and concern to promote the influence of "that natural aristocracy that flows from enlightenment and virtue" rather than the whims of estate law. Why then would he abandon the language of aristocracy to convention and not claim it as the property of nature, as did Jefferson, who hoped that democracy would usher in the reign of the natural aristocracy at long last?[1]

Tocqueville's choice of terms is easier to understand when one examines his reasons for not sharing Jefferson's confidence in the selection of democratic leaders. He hints at these reasons when he says that the people of New England "were in the habit of revering certain names as emblems of enlightenment and of virtues" (46). Names and emblems signify reputation, which is not always faithful to reality. Tocqueville later gives an important caution to the reader who would expect too much of "intellectual superiority" in the political realm: "if one casts a glance over the history of the world, one sees that it is much less the force of reasoning than the authority of a name" that holds sway over peoples (613). The extent to which the authority of names overlaps with the force of reasoning depends on two things: an education of the people in the notion of rights or true opinion about what virtues should inspire obedience; and the memory of lives lived well or poorly in the public eye (227, 50). In New England, both of these conditions prevailed to the point that Tocqueville does speak of the people respecting genuine "intellectual and moral superiorities" (191). The chances of sustaining such conditions over time in the democratic social state are another matter entirely.

The first New Englanders were disposed to recognize and respect intellectual superiority because all of them had received an advanced education in Europe. At that time, though equality was progressing in Europe, that society's essential features were still very much aristocratic. The advanced education of the Puritans was therefore also aristocratic in a very crucial sense. In a passage that immediately follows his appeal to the natural aristocracy, Tocqueville describes the effect of the democratic social state on education (51). Simply put, that effect is to promote intellectual mediocrity. The reasons for and consequences of this effect of democracy on education help us to see an important if surprising connection between conventional and natural aristocracy.

A democratic society is dominated by the majority of citizens, who are either poor or not rich—that is, they "need to practice a profession." Hence the ruling element of such societies "requires an apprenticeship," and "can only give the first years of life to the general cultivation of intelligence." When advanced education takes place, its character remains professional: it is directed to "special and lucrative" matters and to "applications [of the sciences] whose present utility is recognized." Those few citizens who become rich will frequently have lost the taste for study by the time they can afford to devote themselves to it. As a consequence, Tocqueville observes that America possesses no "class in which the penchant for intellectual pleasures is transmitted with comfort and inherited leisure, and which holds the works of the intellect in honor." Though "intellectual inequality comes directly from God," an insufficiently educated society will fail to cultivate or respect this natural potential. Minds that might have excelled may be forced into other paths, or minds that do excel may be ignored by a distracted or indifferent populace. This is precisely what Tocqueville sees in Jacksonian America: "the aristocratic element, always weak" in the American environment, is weakened further by the democratic social state, "so that it is difficult to assign it any influence whatsoever in the course of affairs" (51).

This conclusion places conventional aristocracy in a whole new light. Of course, no one could accuse Tocqueville of being an outright defender of such aristocracy. He not only notes the origins of the European aristocracy in force, but explains the necessity of this origin. The permanent elevation of one group of men over others is so "contrary to the nature and the secret instincts of the human heart," so "repugnant to natural equity," that it could only be the daughter of conquest (383).[2] Yet origins are not the same as destinies—else both American and French democracy would have to be condemned from the start because of their treatment of those who stood in the way of their progress (compare 307ff). In order to see why Tocqueville both embraces modern democracy and seeks to instruct it in light of the inequalities of the *ancien régime*, we must consider the ways in which an originally unjust and unnatural inequality can systematically promote the natural and just inequalities that an originally just equality of conditions may threaten, unjustly, to stifle.

One obvious objection to conventional aristocracy is that its membership in no way confers true intellectual or moral superiority, gifts that nature distributes haphazardly and not according to primogeniture (5). When it comes to the cultivation of these haphazard gifts, however, conventional aristocracy has much better potential. We have already noted the immense influence Tocqueville attributes to inheritance laws over the human psyche. By regulating inheritance so as to preserve estates over time, the aristocratic regime creates the illusion of familial immortality and thus fosters a "spirit of the family" to which individual egos are subsumed. By co-opting the lives of individuals in this way, the illusion of the family becomes something of a reality. In somewhat hyperbolic language, Tocqueville claims that when the land represents the family in this way, "it perpetuates its name, its origin, its glory, its power, its virtues" (48). While conventional aristocracy cannot truly presuppose the existence of virtue in its members, apparently it can cultivate and perpetuate virtue in unique ways. To understand how it does so is to understand why the demise of the conventional aristocracy represents a real loss to humanity in Tocqueville's view.

Two things are necessary for the cultivation of virtue: natural talent and lifelong practice. The first condition is beyond the control of man altogether, but the second is a human choice shared by societies and individuals. Only the individual can ultimately decide to practice virtue, and thus no society, aristocracy included, can guarantee that its members will either be able or willing to practice it. No individual is completely free to choose to practice virtue, however, in the absence of social support. When it comes to "the general cultivation of the intellect," for instance, one needs not only native intelligence and the taste for study, but also the leisure for it. A society that drives all of its members into endeavors of "present utility" discourages (if it does not prevent) minds from rising to the "more elevated grounds" without which one cannot possess the judgment to guide society aright (compare 702). A civilized aristocracy, on the other hand, grants not only wealth and leisure, but also the taste for and duty to promote "works of the intellect" (51). Since the noble may either cultivate these himself or patronize the efforts of talented commoners, a decently disposed aristocracy might well provide ampler opportunities for the fruition of great talents than would a narrowly egalitarian democracy.[3]

Of course, not all aristocracies are decently disposed. Tocqueville acknowledges that the European aristocracy, from which he was himself descended, began in conquest and ended in corruption, with a middle phase including both virtues and vices.[4] Nor does the cultivation of great talents alone necessarily outweigh the injustices inherent in aristocratic order. The point of Tocqueville's references to aristocracy in these beginning chapters is to underline the danger he glimpses in the ascendency of democracy. This danger is well stated by Tocqueville himself in a summary he once made of *Democracy*'s theme:

> I had become aware that [democracy was] giving birth to a number of quite dangerous tendencies, [which], if left . . . unchecked, would produce . . . *a steady lowering of the intellectual level of society* with no conceivable limit, and this would bring in its train the mores of materialism and, finally, universal slavery. . . . I viewed the prospect with terror. . . . My aim in writing . . . [was] to teach democracy to know itself, and thereby to direct itself and contain itself (emphasis added).[5]

The problem of democracy for Tocqueville is defined by the difficulty of preserving the influence of the natural aristocracy over the general "intellectual level of society," a task that had been hitherto accomplished, however imperfectly, with the resources held and distributed by a conventional aristocracy. Tocqueville by no means despairs of finding resources for the cultivation of virtue in democratic times, as his praise of American national character attests. In chapters 4 and 5 we shall consider in detail the means by which he thinks democracy can direct itself away from the dangers mentioned here. In the remainder of this chapter, we shall explore precisely why Tocqueville regarded the threat of intellectual and moral decline as both real and terrifying.

Majority Tyranny and the Decline of Leadership

Tocqueville holds that intellectual inequality comes directly from God or nature.[6] Aristocracies at their worst violate this truth by conflating intellectual superiority with good birth; at their best, they assist nature by giving a profound cultivation to superior intellects. Democracies, on the other hand, embrace this truth about nature by denying the importance of birth; at their best, one might expect them to embrace what we call meritocracy or what Tocqueville calls the influence of the natural aristocracy in their midst. Thus, what we have called the promise of democracy entails its embrace of natural inequality. Tocqueville's doubts about democracy's ability or willingness to fulfill this promise are encapsulated in his subtle but incisive critique of popular sovereignty and his famous theory of the tyranny of the majority. Tocqueville's assessment of political society dominated by the will of the majority convinces him that a certain dynamic inimical to great leadership is virtually inevitable in such societies. The resulting decline in genuine leadership creates a void all too easily filled by bad leadership or demagoguery, resulting in an even worse and more general degradation of political and civil life. Our next two sections will examine the causes and worst-case consequences of this dynamic.

After discussing the social state of the Americans Tocqueville proceeds to their political laws, which he cannot explain without reference to their source in the sovereignty of the American people. Tocqueville does more than examine the fact or principle of popular sovereignty, however; instead he focuses on "the dogma of the sovereignty of the people." By dogma, Tocqueville refers to an opinion received on trust without discussion or critical thought (407).[7] In

Tocqueville's view, the principle of popular sovereignty "is always more or less at the foundation of almost all human institutions," inasmuch as whoever rules does so (sincerely or not) in the name of the people ruled.[8] In most ages, intriguers and despots largely abuse the concept of "national will" to justify their exploits, relying on the fact of obedience to buttress their right to command. Only in democratic society does this principle reach its "final consequences," however, the right of the people to approve or reject its governors being recognized by mores and proclaimed by the laws. Tocqueville thus directs us to America so that we may "appreciate the dogma of the sovereignty of the people at its just value" and "judge its advantages and its dangers" (53).

One would expect the liberation of the principle of popular sovereignty to constitute a liberation of humanity, and to some extent this is true. Tocqueville later admits that even the best-intentioned of aristocracies has a natural tendency to concentrate social advantages in its own hands, and therefore cannot be said to aim at the good of the whole people (224). The government of democracy, though it can be mistaken, never has interests contrary to the good of the greatest number, and it is therefore very useful, he argues, to place the government of society in the hands of the majority (222). We must recall, however, that Tocqueville strongly deplores those who seek the useful without the just (11). Justice is not reducible to utility or material prosperity (compare 224),[9] and the interests of the majority are equivalent neither to the interests of society as a whole nor to the universal needs of humankind (223, 240).[10] While Tocqueville's judgment of the dogma of popular sovereignty is not wholly negative, this dogma nonetheless comes to light in his analysis as a blind adherence to a principle that by itself cannot guarantee true justice. Rigid adherence to this principle therefore paves the way for actual injustices which it is the duty of statesmen and enlightened citizens to strive to prevent.

Tocqueville hints at the danger as well as the promise of popular sovereignty in his initial treatment of the political consequences of the democratic social state. First, he notes that men will not long accept equality in some areas, such as economics or civil society, and inequality in others, such as politics. As the role of the bourgeoisie in fomenting the French Revolution attests, citizens equal on some points will eventually insist on being equal on all points. In politics, Tocqueville continues, there are but two modes of universal equality: "rights must be given to each citizen or to none." Political equality can mean equality in liberty or equality in servitude, and the democratic social state per se "lends itself almost as readily to the one as to the other of its two consequences." If a democratic society wishes to escape the clutches of outright despotism, then, it can do so only by strenuously cultivating the equal liberty of all citizens. Popular sovereignty comes to light as the solution to the problem of modern democracy (52-53).[11]

As we shall see in our next chapter, popular sovereignty well understood—what Tocqueville calls "the government of democracy," and we will often refer to as "self-government"—is a major component of Tocqueville's strategy to prevent the democratic social state from reaching its worst fate. From the beginning, however, Tocqueville signals the highly problematic nature of the solution he adopts. In the very words he uses to introduce and recommend popular sovereignty we see the standards to which Tocqueville will hold it—standards which he does not expect it easily to meet.

In delineating the difference between equality in liberty and equality in servitude, Tocqueville makes clear that the legitimacy of the desire for equality hinges, in his view, on the acceptance of a liberty tied to human greatness. In his words,

> [The] manly and legitimate passion for equality . . . incites men to want all to be strong and esteemed. This passion tends to elevate the small to the rank of the great; but one also encounters a depraved taste for equality in the human heart that brings the weak to want to draw the strong to their level and that reduces men to preferring equality in servitude to inequality in liberty (52).

The implications of this passage become evident when we consider that Tocqueville does not believe (per impossible) in the equal potential of all men for greatness. A legitimate passion for equality that grants citizens the liberty to achieve their best must be content with the unequal results that will follow. In other words, equality is a legitimate goal only insofar as one is willing to balance it with other and greater goods. The depravity by which one would actually prefer equality in servitude is therefore sadly easy to understand: given that liberty will issue in inequality, the heart possessed by an "eternal love" for equality (compare 52, 189, 480, 645) must eventually conclude that it can achieve its desire only by the eradication of liberty itself.

In embracing equality under the guise of popular sovereignty, then, Tocqueville understands himself to be embracing liberty, greatness, and therefore inequality, even if he paints them in democratic terms. Genuine democratic liberty, in Tocqueville's usage, is not purely democratic; it must tend to "elevate the small to the rank of the great."[12] This elevation presupposes and can never eradicate the distinction between small and great. The notion of rights by which a free people rules itself ought also to tell it when to obey a higher authority; in this sense rights will constitute "virtue introduced into the political world," and render the people great (227)—but only in the way that a people can be great. "Genuine dignity," Tocqueville implies, consists in knowing "one's place" in society and in the scheme of things (579). The place of any given people is not to exercise absolute sovereignty or legislate as it pleases, but rather, like a jury, to apply a universal law derived from the "universal society" of the human race (240). The preservation of "independence and dignity" in "the democratic times we are in" therefore requires a special effort on the part of "true friends of liberty and greatness" to befriend equality in order to lead it toward justice. Yet these friends of equality "must constantly remain on their feet and ready to prevent the social power from lightly sacrificing" these higher goods (666, 670). This is as much to say that equality will be legitimate and issue in greatness when it is enjoyed by a populace that is free and self-governing but also modest enough to accept the corrective guidance of wise and just leaders (compare 241).

Is such modesty in the people likely to be found in democratic times? As we have seen, Tocqueville looks to democracy in America precisely because American mores or national character had succeeded in moderating the influence of the social state and limiting or directing the will of the majority in healthy ways. Were such a feat impossible, Tocqueville claims, he would have given up writing his book in despair (672). Much of *Democracy* is focused on the way in which democracy can be so regulated. Yet this possibility should not give us a false sense of security. Tocqueville also stresses that those successes the Americans have enjoyed are threatened by an environment that is increasingly hostile to anything that challenges the dominance of equality itself—as liberty and greatness inevitably will—and likely to become more hostile with time (235ff). In America one sees not only the possibility of educating and directing democracy, but also the intense desire of a democratic people to break free from such education and direction. This tendency to shake itself loose from salutary constraints is the first principle of democracy's undoing according to Tocqueville (compare 7ff, 248ff), and it underlies his memorable and crucial discussion of majority tyranny.

Majority tyranny has its roots in what Tocqueville calls "the omnipotence of the majority," but the two are importantly distinct.[13] Justice, for Tocqueville, consists in obedience to the law of humanity, while tyranny connotes disobedience to this law. Tyranny, then, is the misuse and not the mere possession of power, even when exclusive. In principle, all power is legitimate if well used, and no power is legitimate when abused (242). The omnipotence of the majority is not an inherent evil in Tocqueville's view; he gives examples of its good use, and even claims that the majority in America rarely exercises its power tyrannically. Yet Tocqueville considers this good use and lack of abuse to be accidental: circumstances and mores prevent the people from frequently misusing its influence, but the laws do little to prevent it (245, 242). In the end, Tocqueville considers the unchecked power of the majority "dire and dangerous for the future of democracy," implying that omnipotence will predictably become tyranny without a concerted effort to prevent this transformation (237).

Tocqueville's reasons for fearing majority power are based on a simple premise: "a majority taken collectively" is nothing but "an individual who has opinions and most often tastes contrary to another." We are all disposed to fear the results when "one man [is] vested with omnipotence"—in Lord Acton's phrase, we expect absolute power to corrupt absolutely. Why not expect the same of a majority when it is so vested? Men do not change in character by being united; by becoming stronger, they do not grow more patient. We readily admit that one nation can tyrannize over another; why then not one segment of a nation over another? "Only God . . . can be omnipotent without danger, because his wisdom and justice are always equal to his power" (240-41). Yet "the people reign over the American political world as does God over the universe. They are the cause and end of all things" (55). Can anyone wield such power without abusing it? Tocqueville alludes to American "moralists and philosophers" who claim to know they "are speaking to a people too much above human weakness not to remain always master of itself." "That," Tocqueville retorts, "is the language of a slave" (247-48, 240).

Here Tocqueville is taking particular aim at what he calls "the moral empire of the majority" in democratic times, an expression that ought to remind us of the "empire of democracy" he examines and rejects in his Introduction. This "moral empire" constitutes the generally accepted rationale for the legitimacy of majority rule, and it has two principal foundations. The first is "the idea that there is more enlightenment and wisdom in many men united than in one alone"; this is "the theory of equality applied to intellects." The second is "the principle that the interests of the greatest number ought to be preferred to those of the few" (236-37). Tocqueville's account of tyranny and justice explodes both of these ideas. The interests of the greatest number are not legitimate unless they accord with the law of the human race; but intellectual inequality is natural to man and even sacred in character (51, compare 410). Hence the majority must respect inequality or greatness lest its rule become "impious and detestable" (240, compare 227). This potential problem might be averted by arguing, as Tocqueville does, that the "true interests" of the majority lie in maintaining a respect for the natural aristocracy in their midst (compare 7, 11, 50). Yet to have confidence in this resolution, one must believe that the majority is disposed to follow its true interests and use its power wisely, while kings and emperors have so often abused theirs. Tocqueville instead suspects that the majority is at least as likely to be blinded to its own best interests by the power it wields.

Tocqueville's theory of majority tyranny is a variant of his view of all political regimes. The roots of this regime theory are to be found in Aristotle's *Politics* (which is in turn an outgrowth of Plato's *Republic* or *Politeia*). Aristotle defines the regime or *politeia* as the order of ruling offices within a city or *polis*. He subdivides regimes according to two principles: first, by who rules; next, by how they rule. The city may be ruled by one, a few, or the many; and it may be ruled justly (for the common good) or unjustly (for the ruler's selfish interests). As with Tocqueville, Aristotle believes that in principle justice hinges not on who rules but on how they rule. Also like Tocqueville, Aristotle sees that in practice no one can be trusted to rule well without supervision. The good regimes—monarchy, aristocracy, and polity—are largely ideals at which real regimes—tyrannies, oligarchies, and democracies—ought to aim. Individual rulers tend to be tyrants, but ought to strive to be kings; ruling elites tend to be oligarchs, but ought to strive to be aristocrats; ruling majorities tend to degenerate into democracies or ruling mobs, but ought to strive to be polities guided by wisdom and justice.[14]

The political problem deepens when one considers that none of these ruling groups can be expected to strive on its own to be its best self. For Aristotle, every individual or group tends to be biased toward itself, and therefore to confuse its own opinions and interests with the common good or justice. As he optimistically puts it, each group is partly right about justice, but therefore also partly wrong. The effort to grasp justice in its full truth requires what Aristotle calls philosophy.[15] Thus Aristotle echoes Plato's argument that cities will never be well ruled until philosophers rule or rulers philosophize.[16] As Plato well knew, however, there is no realistic possibility of placing philosophers in charge of human societies.[17] The influence of philosophy over politics must be indirect, taking shape especially in the provision of codes of law wisely made to guide society aright.[18] For Plato and Aristotle as well as for Tocqueville, philosophic knowledge of the true human good must be filtered through statesmanship or the legislative art which, without being able to deny power to biased individuals or groups, steers those groups toward a better use of the power they have.

If the essence of Aristotle's solution to political bias is the rule of law, a key function of law in his view is the creation of mixed regimes. Since the law must empower someone to rule, and since there is no way to guarantee true wisdom or philosophy in any one ruler, the law ought to divide and share power among groups and individuals who can be expected to have different biases. If done wisely, this would prevent any one group from simply imposing its biases on the entire polity, and force each group to consult the views of others, modifying its own views in order to cooperate with theirs. Aristotle's political science provides a detailed exploration of what laws and institutions favor the one, the few, or the many, and how such laws and institutions can be mixed to produce a healthy balance of influences in political society. The best practicable regime, which Aristotle simply calls "regime" (*politeia*), is most readily identified by one's inability to say whether it is an oligarchy or a democracy.[19]

This salutary confusion of oligarchic and democratic characteristics is a feature that one can still see in the United States of America. Contra advocates of simpler labels, America is best understood as neither a democracy nor an oligarchy, but as a complex system of power sharing between the rich and the many. In fact, the famed "checks and balances" of our federal system of government—the theory of which Tocqueville so greatly admired—are the inheritance of Aristotelian political science, though not without important modifications. One key difference is indicated by Tocqueville's own denial that mixed government—"in the sense that one gives to this word"—is truly possible. In any political society, Tocqueville contends, "one principle of action . . . dominates all the others," and any government "equally divided between contrary principles . . . enters into revolution or it is dissolved." The task of statesmanship is not, per impossible, to render the influence of the few equal to the many or vice versa, but rather to identify which group dominates and to take steps to temper the tyranny that must result from its dominance.[20] "I believe liberty to be in peril," Tocqueville concludes, "when that [dominant] power finds no obstacle before it that can restrain its advance and give it time to moderate itself." When "the right and the ability to do everything [is] granted to any power whatsoever . . . there is the seed of tyranny" (241).

The fundamental inquiry practitioners of the legislative art must make can be divided into two stages: first, to identify the ruling power and to know its strengths and weaknesses; second, to know what obstacles can be placed before it that are most likely to induce it to "moderate itself," given that it will always have the last word in any political conflict. Tocqueville's conclusion that, in modern times, "a new political science is needed for a world altogether new," is premised on the occurrence of a seismic shift from ancient to modern historical periods. From ancient Athens to England in the eighteenth century, even those countries where the majority appeared to have significant influence were in fact founded on inequality. Ancient democracies were really large aristocracies, since the majority of human beings were not considered citizens (450-51). In England "large elements of democracy" were to be found, but "laws and mores" still ensured that "aristocracy had to prevail in the long term and direct public affairs at its will" (241). In such times and places, the legislative art would stress both the genuinely aristocratic virtues at which the ruling group ought to aim, but also the dangers of rule by a few and the means by which to make the ruling elite moderate its likely disdain for the needs of the majority. The entire apparatus of Aristotelian political science was based on such a reality.[21] In democratic times, by contrast, the people is for the first time the beginning and end of all things, and the question for political science is how to encourage those virtues available to a democratic populace while also slowing down its movements and moderating its excesses.

So considered, the dangers of equality and inequality appear closely analogous. Were this the whole story, political science would have to be updated in modern democratic times, yet its concern would merely shift from regulating one dominant power to another. In fact, Tocqueville believes that both the virtues and the dangers of each social state differ in content and in degree, therefore requiring what he calls a new political science. Our next section will take up the distinctive dangers posed by democratic tyranny; here we must see why Tocqueville fears that the tyranny of the majority is capable of wielding more power than any other tyranny known to man.

Liberty depends on the exercise of self-moderation on the part of a society's ruling element, which in turn requires that form of leadership expressed in the legislative art. A precondition for the practice of this art is the acquisition of reliable knowledge of the sovereign needs of the human race, or what Tocqueville calls political science. To possess such knowledge one must rise above the perspective of "this or that people" and contemplate a truth that transcends the socio-political horizons in which most citizens live (702). Thus Tocqueville remarks that a combination of "virile candor" and "manly independence of thought, . . . everywhere it is found, forms the salient feature" of those "great characters" whose influence on political affairs is so vital. Tocqueville notes with distress that the national character of the Americans is declining to the point that such great characters rarely "show themselves on the political scene." He attributes this decline to the omnipotence of the majority in America and the effect it has on thought (246-47). The influence of the social state on the great individual "who wants to speak the truth" turns out to be the most decisive problem introduced by the dogma of popular sovereignty (244).

Tocqueville's reflections on "the power that the majority in America exercises over thought" rely heavily on a contrast with prior forms of tyranny. "Thought is an invisible and almost intangible power that makes sport of all tyrannies." From the Spanish Inquisition to "the most absolute sovereigns of Europe," attempts to prevent the circulation of disfavored ideas have never succeeded. "No religious or political theory" can be suppressed in Europe, where "he who wants to speak the truth" will find support somewhere:

> If he has the misfortune to live under an absolute government, he often has the people for him; if he inhabits a free country, he can take shelter behind royal authority if need be. The aristocratic faction of the society sustains him in democratic regions, and the democracy in the others.

Here we see the tremendous advantage of mixed government, loosely defined, from the perspective of truth and justice: no segment of society is incapable of supporting the truth-seeker, and none is immune from oppressing him. Hence the coexistence of distinct sources of political authority within a society maximizes the liberty of great characters (243-45).

By providing refuge for philosophic souls, conditions of mixed authority dishonor despotism by valorizing resistance to it. In such an environment, tyranny must strike at the body to reach the soul; but "the soul, escaping from those blows, [rises] gloriously above it," whether the body also escapes or not. So fundamental is this victory that even the oppressive power often develops a sense of humor about itself: "La Brulyère lived at the palace of Louis XIV when he composed his chapter on the great, and Molière criticized the Court in plays that he had performed before courtiers" (244-45).

Modern democratic society presents a far different picture. In the United States, "one encounters only a single power, a single element of force and success, and nothing outside it." Were the democratic power to resort to violence or threats of violence—as it sometimes did in Jacksonian America[22]—there would be no escape for those who opposed it. This alone would be enough to silence many who might otherwise question settled majority opinion. Generally speaking, however, the majority does not have to resort even to the threat of force, for it "is vested with a force, at once material and moral, that acts on the will as much as on actions." This moral force of the majority stems from its position as the sole granter of power and dignity in democratic society. The writer or statesman who opposes majority opinion does not have to fear an auto-da-fé, "but he is the butt of mortifications of all kinds and of persecutions every day. A political career is closed to him," as are glory and the open alliance of others. The democratic master leaves a man free to think as he pleases without losing his civil rights, so long as he is willing to renounce his "rights of humanity." The democratic despot is usually happy to leave an opponent with his life, but it leaves him a life "worse than death." In other words, "it leaves the body and goes straight for the soul" (243-45).

The result of this new dynamic is to render tyranny immaterial, invisible, and far more effective. Majority tyranny is immaterial because it prevents not only the deed but the desire to do it, producing not only compliance with its dictates but also "remorse for having spoken the truth" (243-45). It is invisible because no segment of society visibly opposes its mandates, calling their justice into question. It is effective for two reasons. First, even those citizens who persist in seeking the truth privately will either refrain from publicizing unpopular truths or be ignored when they do so. Second, those who seek both truth and public influence will be powerfully tempted to renounce the first in favor of the second (246-47), rendering a reconciliation of the two impossible.

The final fruit of democratic despotism is therefore a decline in leadership. The people, growing used to its unlimited power, fancies that it alone possesses truth, wisdom, justice, and reason; it becomes prickly and hostile to any suggestion to the contrary (236-27, 245). At first, "the minority accepts [this majority dominance] only with difficulty," but "it habituates itself to it . . . in the long term" (236). This habituation of democracy's leaders undermines the legislative art, which ought to direct democracy from elevated grounds the existence of which democratic dogma denies. The history of this decline can be sketched from the examples of leadership, or its lack, Tocqueville draws upon in painting the American national character.

That history begins, when American national character was at its strongest, with Winthrop's speech to the Massachusetts assembly. Though the people had the right to depose him as leader, Winthrop was able to appeal to a notion of rights that legitimized his right to command and their duty to obey. Liberty, he persuaded them, is to be used only for what is just and good, concepts defined by the will of God and discerned through the wisdom of virtuous leaders such as Winthrop himself rather than being determined by the will of the people. As we have seen, religion and education firmly established limits to democracy in early New England, thus making room for the influence of leaders who might strive to constitute a natural aristocracy (35, 46, 54).

The next stage Tocqueville describes is that of the American Revolution. In this struggle against the motherland, America owed some of its "greatest men" to the semi-aristocracy of the South (46). Having opposed England in the name of the American people, however, it was impossible to prevent the dogma of popular sovereignty from leaving the township and becoming "the law of laws" throughout the land. The upper classes, perceiving that all power was now in the majority's hands, "submitted without a murmur and without combat to an evil henceforth inevitable," the unchecked reign of democracy. Retaining some of their prior influence at first, they no longer thought of banding together to resist popular opinion in any way; rather, "individual selfishness took hold in their members," and they competed with one another to gain the majority's good will by taking the most democratic measures possible (54). As a result, Tocqueville concluded that the state constitutions of his day, written during this Revolutionary period, offered virtually no resistance to the despotism of the majority, magnifying the threat of majority tyranny (235ff).

There the tale might end, if not for the occurrence of one major exception to this democratic ascendency. The Articles of Confederation by which the United States were loosely held together produced a federal government incapable of governing the democratizing states. As sometimes happens when countries are in crisis, the American people met this challenge by temporarily putting aside its "envious passions" and looking to the guidance of "superior men" (190). Reaching what Tocqueville significantly calls "the height of its glory," the people turned "its regard on itself without haste and without fear, sound[ed] the depth of the ill, contain[ed] itself for two entire years in order to discover the remedy at leisure, and when the remedy [was] pointed out, submit[ted] voluntarily to it." This triumph of reason over passion was accompanied by great modesty on the part of the people, who permitted an assembly "few in number," and including "the finest minds and noblest characters that had ever appeared in the New World," to engage in "long and mature deliberations" about the fate of the country. Only after this natural aristocracy had reached its conclusion did the people name local deputies, who were still permitted to engage in "profound discussions" before deciding whether to ratify the convention's Constitution (106-107).

Given this history, it is not surprising that the resulting Constitution was not demagogic on the model of the state governments. Rather, it contained many features designed to slow down and moderate the will of the majority: longer and varying terms of office; indirect elections; a bicameral legislature; an independent executive; and an unelected judiciary (236). The Constitution was largely the product of men whose wisdom allowed them to see that America was in grave danger from the abuses that could be made of political liberty (143-44). Realizing it was no longer possible to sustain powers completely independent of the people—as with an Aristotelian mixed regime—they nonetheless devised ways to grant certain offices enough freedom "so that, when forced to obey the permanent direction of the majority, [political leaders] could nevertheless struggle against its caprices and refuse its dangerous demands" (129).

At the time of the Constitution, "almost all" of America's natural aristocracy took this "Federalist" position, and they had enough "moral power" to establish the principles of American federal government. Tocqueville considered the Constitution "a lasting monument to their wisdom and patriotism," and the circumstances that gave them such influence "one of the most fortunate events that accompanied the birth of the great American Union." Yet he also questioned the long-term effectiveness of their measures against majority despotism. Once the crisis of the Revolution and Articles had faded, the American people reverted to its democratic passions. The Federalist party, which had never had a majority, lost its support and ceased entirely to exist by Tocqueville's day (168-69). Even had the federal government retained an aristocratic flavor, its influence in the 1830s would have been limited by the persistently superior force of state governments. Yet Tocqueville relates how, by his time, the helm of the Union itself had been given to "General Jackson," a president who "maintains himself and prospers by flattering" the passions of the majority "daily"—in short, by being "the slave of the majority" (170, 265, 377). Jackson's behavior, combined with the crude rhetoric of his enemies (174), demonstrates the difficulty of restraining demagoguery through institutions alone when the restraints are not firmly embedded in a people's national character.[23]

Again, Tocqueville does not believe that democratic despotism was often used tyrannically in Jacksonian America: "circumstances and mores" still restrained the people from doing the most serious harm possible (242). In effect, Americans were disposed to respect certain moral authorities of old, such as Christianity, while looking with increasing contempt upon the leaders in their midst (188ff). Yet this situation was precarious not only because circumstances and mores can change. It was precarious above all because the exclusive dominance of the majority oppresses, however unconsciously, those who would lead democratic society in light of truths which are sometimes hard to hear (400); and because good leaders can easily be replaced with demagogues who seek to enhance their own power by flattering democracy's every passion, including those that ought instead to be checked (377, compare 129). Without a firm idea of rights confirming the title of the natural aristocracy to lead, the talents that might have led democratic society to just goals will instead be employed to direct the omnipotent force of the majority to impious and detestable ends (240). Unlike the tyrannies of old, which could always be challenged by a rival power, and therefore always had to hear and answer their critics, democratic tyranny threatens the very existence of rival power, and risks becoming completely deaf to those who warn of the harm it can do without proper direction.

Thus far the threat posed by the unchecked ascendency of the popular element, for all its formal plausibility, may seem highly abstract. What precisely did Tocqueville fear from the demagoguery to which modern democracies were likely to succumb? We conclude this chapter by turning to the chief causes and characteristics of the greatest of all the dangers Tocqueville attributed to democratic despotism: individualism and administrative despotism.

Individualism and the Threat of Administrative Despotism

Tocqueville said that his principal goal in writing *Democracy* was to combat individualism; he also said that the two parts of *Democracy* "complete one another and form a single work" (643, 399). Though he does not define the term individualism until the second part of the second volume, the concept itself pervades his entire analysis of American democracy. In this section we shall briefly outline that concept and explain why Tocqueville considers it so fearsome. This outline will be developed and complimented in subsequent chapters as we consider Tocqueville's account of how Americans have combated and how others might combat individualism through robust civic, legal, and religious institutions.

The story of individualism begins with the dogma of the sovereignty of the people. As we have seen, Tocqueville supports popular sovereignty in democratic times to the extent that liberty tends to elevate the small to the level of the great. Yet he realizes that, as citizens of democracy, Americans themselves take a different view of liberty. In America, the "moral empire of the majority is founded in part on . . . the theory of equality applied to intellects" (236). The theory of equality applied to intellects holds that "each individual is . . . as enlightened, as virtuous, as strong as any other"—a manifest error, in Tocqueville's view, and one that explicitly undercuts his version of civic rights. Recall that rights, for Tocqueville, delineate the conditions of obedience to authority in light of the concept of virtue (227). Were all men equally virtuous, such rights would scarcely be necessary because command and obedience would be largely superfluous. When all men consider themselves equally virtuous, however falsely, it becomes difficult to say why they must obey authority at all. The answer given by Americans is that a man obeys society because (and to the extent that) "union with his fellows appears useful to him," and "this union cannot exist without a regulating power" (61). In other words, on its face the American notion of rights denies that obedience is needed for the sake of virtue, justifying it on grounds of utility as opposed to justice. Tocqueville, the avowed foe of utility without justice (11), will see the need to combat this notion that subjects all social and political relations by the standard of utility alone.

The introduction of what we might already call individualism—the belief that each man remains master "in all that regards only himself"—takes place in a discussion of the American township. In his treatment of the colonial township, Tocqueville had emphasized that rights and duties revolved around the common life of the township, so that a real political life overshadowed more individualistic notions of liberty (40ff). In this later account, Tocqueville shows how the Americans have blended township liberty with individual liberty. In all that concerns himself, they say, a man "owes an account of his actions only to God." In all that concerns the common life of the town, he is bound to obey its authority, and the town is free under God. Only in those matters manifestly concerning the state or federal governments need those authorities be obeyed. And only in those matters where society is injured by a deed or requires the cooperation of its members may it direct the actions of the individual or lower unit of government (62). In this way, the concept of individualism seems to demand a robust version of what is now called subsidiarity, or the decentralization of government. Tocqueville, who celebrates the result, might fairly be expected also to celebrate the apparent cause: individualism itself.

This expectation turns out to be true only in a very qualified sense. Later in *Democracy*, Tocqueville famously notes how the Americans have used the doctrine of self-interest well-understood to combat individualism (500ff). Since this doctrine maintains that each individual ought to cooperate with the social power on the grounds that it furthers his personal interests, it would not be amiss to say that Tocqueville sees Americans combating individualism with individualism. The paradox can be explained by noting Tocqueville's precise definition of individualism, by which he means a settled indifference to public affairs, not merely a settled attachment to one's personal affairs (482-83). With effort, the selfish citizen can be made to see the connection between the two, and can become interested in public things without necessarily abandoning the focus on his own things. As we shall see in our next chapter, the dynamic of self-interest well-understood is more complex than this by far. Here we must note that the beginning point—a dominant attachment to one's private good—has a natural tendency to result in indifference to the public good; only with tremendous effort can this seed of individualism be kept from bearing the poisoned fruit of individualism itself (compare 86, 645).

To understand why Tocqueville considers individualism itself so ominous, it is easiest to consider the face of a world utterly dominated by it. Tocqueville's account of such a world, for which he struggles to find a name, but settles on the term "administrative despotism," unfolds in the part of *Democracy* dealing with "the influence that democratic ideas and sentiments exert on political society" (639ff). In order to understand this worst-case outcome of the democratic social state, we must see the roots of individualism in the democratic intellect and heart—precisely the topics of the first two parts of volume 2 (403ff, 479ff).

The intellectual roots of individualism can be gleaned from Tocqueville's discussion of the American "philosophic method." That method is for each man to reason for himself about everything. Note that self-interest well-understood, while it requires the individual to cooperate with society for the benefits it provides, does not oblige him to defer to society for the content of his thinking. Without the intervention of contrary habits, the democratic social state undermines the notion that any man or group possesses natural authority over another. Even when citizens accept the word of another, it is on the basis of their own free judgment. They are practically forced to rely on their own intellect in all matters, and are in any case inclined to disbelieve or resent any and all claims to intellectual superiority. "Each therefore withdraws narrowly into himself and claims to judge the world from there," stubbornly denying what he is not able to comprehend through his personal efforts (403-4). Once this condition sets in, any appeal to public-spiritedness will thenceforth have to be framed in terms accessible to citizens thus self-enclosed, a requirement that would all but rule out appeals to virtue and its beauties (501).

Tocqueville's labeling of this method of thinking as "philosophic" is somewhat ironic.[24] A true philosopher understands that no man has the leisure, capacity, or energy to prove for himself every truth of which he makes use. In order to penetrate the truth on the matters he has reserved for study, the philosopher will therefore willingly "believe a million things on faith in others," embracing a "salutary servitude" in trivial matters for the sake of intellectual liberty on truly important ones. Democratic man is deeply deluded to think he can fathom the truth on all matters. In rejecting what he cannot understand, he is as apt to reject profound truths as he is to avoid shallow deceptions. In fact, he is all too likely to embrace the latter. This is because the inability to prove every truth to oneself requires every man to accept dogmatic beliefs or the opinions of others.[25] Such opinions must come either from a superior source or from one's peers. The democratic citizen, refusing to acknowledge the existence of natural (or supernatural) superiors, firmly rejects the first option; hence his beliefs on countless matters (all matters in which he does not have extensive personal experience) must be derived from his fellows (407-9).

Here Tocqueville reminds us of the tremendous power public opinion has over the mind of the individual in democratic times. The belief that no one is superior to him fills democratic man with pride, but this pride is vain in that by himself he can neither understand nor accomplish what he needs to live. He must turn to his fellows for support. Since he is uncomfortable turning to any one or a few of them as if they were his superiors, he arrives at the conclusion that truth is found in the concurrence of the greatest number. He need not be embarrassed at following the impersonal mass. The problem comes when he happens to disagree with this majority for any reason, however justified. On his own premise of equality, democratic man cannot assert his intellectual superiority over against the mass of his fellows; but he cannot resist their opinion without implying some such superiority. Hence democratic man comes to doubt his right even to hold an opinion contrary to that of the majority. The strength he thought he possessed in equality turns out to be a weakness, subjecting him to the "general will of the greatest number," a servitude so powerful that Tocqueville fears public opinion will replace thought itself in democratic times (409-10).

We can round out this account of the intellectual roots of individualism by considering the content such public opinion is likely to have. First we see that public opinion will have a definite proclivity for "very superficial and very uncertain notions." The reason is simple: most men in democratic societies are too busy to have time for sustained thinking on complicated subjects, and therefore prefer quick oversimplifications to detailed studies of difficult topics. Deference to mass opinion is therefore fatal to the "slow, detailed, conscientious work of intelligence" without which knowledge of many important things cannot be had (414). The only exceptions to this rule will be in areas where each individual has extensive personal knowledge, and especially in practical affairs, where competing truth claims can be tested by their immediate practical results (415ff, 433ff). In the place where it matters most—ideas relating to God, human nature, and the moral duties consequent to them—neither exception applies, and easy superficialities are likely to become dominant (417ff).

It follows that reliance on public opinion will have a devastating effect on religious beliefs. This is particularly important for Tocqueville, because he teaches that almost all human actions flow from the idea man forms of God, human nature, and the inter-relation of the two: in other words, of cosmic order and man's place within it. The idea of cosmic order is therefore of utmost importance to political society as well as each man individually, and yet it is of all matters the most difficult to fathom with any certainty. If society is to have any clear and precise notions on this matter, it must embrace the dogmatic account offered by religion. To the extent that each man is forced to think from scratch about these matters, most will become intellectually paralyzed under the strain, and seek to cease thinking about religion altogether. Since man requires an idea of cosmic order, this surrender represents a drastic weakening of the human will, robbing society of much of its force. With what energy they have left, citizens so affected will seek security in what is most obvious, such as material things, and will come to regard these as the only reality, denying once more what they cannot comprehend (417-19, compare 404).

In the intellectual realm, then, individualism inclines citizens to judge all matters for themselves; to refer to public opinion when necessary to fill a gap in knowledge; to give way to public opinion when they might otherwise know better; to happily accept vague and superficial treatments of complex matters; and to avoid what we might call metaphysical questions in favor of clinging to material things.

The role of sentiment in furthering individualism is easy to understand when we bear in mind Tocqueville's contention that men love what seems most permanent and powerful in the world. Since power and permanence are represented to us (accurately or not) by our intellects, the sentimental life of democratic man follows from his intellectual penchants.[26] Simply put, the democratic soul sees two things as undeniably dominant: the material world and equality itself. It is therefore inclined to adore these things or place them above all other goods. This explains why modern ideologies are usually focused on some combination of these two concepts. Since equality has two main sentimental features—the pride in having no superior and the weakness of having no foothold against mass opinion—we can identify three emotional preoccupations of modern man: a passion for material well-being; an absorption with his private affairs; and an insistence on the eradication of all privileges, real or imagined, through the subjection of human life to uniform and detailed regulations. While all of these tendencies can be combated, left unchecked each can become a blind passion in democratic hearts. Without restraint, the combination of these three passions paves the way for administrative despotism.

The passion for material well-being is often thought to reinforce political liberty. We speculate, for instance, that the growth of capitalism in China may produce a class that will demand more rights from that one-party state. Tocqueville grants that material interests can be a hook by which to interest citizens in public affairs, but he also sees a contrary tendency: for the economically productive, time is money, and time spent in the civic realm is costly to one's private business. Without the clearest of connections between one and the other, the materialist soul is likely to resent civic duties as a waste of precious time (515), or perhaps to prefer the simpler operations of a corrupt political system. When we consider that the benefits of liberty, sublime as they are, are often immaterial and enjoyed only by a few dedicated citizens after much sacrifice and effort, there is good reason to fear that commerce will supplant politics in the hearts of democratic souls, and that the prospect of a stable despotism furthering business interests will appear highly attractive to many of them (481).

This danger is accentuated by the general democratic preoccupation with oneself and one's own affairs. In keeping with the link between ideas and sentiments, the citizen whose mind is closed to studying the world will also have a closed heart (compare 404 with 484). All a despot truly requires of citizens, Tocqueville observes, is not that they support his schemes of power, but merely that they not love each other enough to come to one another's aid, and that they be content to abandon political affairs to someone else. "Thus the vices to which despotism gives birth are precisely those that equality favors," and above all the vice of individualism properly so-called, or apathy toward public affairs (485, 704).

The picture is yet grimmer when one considers the third disposition of democratic souls: the taste for uniformity in public affairs. Just as democratic man resents trusting the opinion of one or a few of his fellows, so too is he offended by the slightest sign of privilege in civil society. Since liberty always results in inequality, the only way to achieve uniformity is through the concentration of power in a central state apparatus capable of subjecting all citizens to the same rule. Taken to its extreme, the pride democratic man feels in his independence from his neighbor can induce him to prefer a common dependence on a despotic government to a mutual independence from which his neighbor seems to profit more than he does (642).

As it happens, the other intellectual and sentimental currents of individualism unite to support this perverse preference for oppressive order. The central power can easily promise that the rules it imposes will guarantee order and tranquility, allowing the materialist and individualist to forego the burdens of self-rule and enjoy the fruits of commerce and private life undisturbed. The weakness felt by each individual when left to his own resources may induce him to look for material as well as intellectual assistance; and just as he prefers to take his opinions from the mass mind, so too will he prefer to receive tangible aid from the state, rather than from "rival" individuals (643ff).

None of this means, of course, that democratic man will long for despotism in and of itself.[27] To the contrary, equality will always induce men to want to be free and to pride themselves on their independence (639ff). Tocqueville has no hesitation in embracing this tendency of democratic times, and it is in fact the side of democracy he seeks to educate toward a more genuine liberty in the pages of *Democracy* (640). The problem, however, is threefold. First, the independence democratic man prides himself on feeling is often an illusion masking dependence on a mass mind with dangerously corrosive tendencies. Next, the avoidance of these corrosive effects requires a steady and prudent effort to cultivate contrary habits and practices, and therefore depends upon the conscious influence of leaders possessing an appreciation of the dangers Tocqueville discusses. Finally, the dominance of the mass mind causes a decline in democratic leadership, rendering such a healthy influence less likely. What is instead to be feared is that the corrosive effects of popular sovereignty as expressed in the intellectual and sentimental strains of individualism will be met, not with the counter-action of wise and just statesmen, but rather with the venal or naïve encouragement of unworthy leaders.

Tocqueville is far from imputing corrupt motives to all who will contribute to the growth of despotism in democratic times. He plainly accepts that the need for centralized government will expand as a result of industrialization and other phenomena, and predicts that noble attempts to alleviate the sufferings of modern society will contribute to the future he fears (651ff). In the end, however, Tocqueville is aghast at the prospect that the democratic passions discussed above will be channeled by a newly improved administrative art capable of harnessing their power and achieving a level of governmental control over society never before known to man.

Unlike the tyranny of old, which directed a great deal of violence toward a relatively small number of citizens, Tocqueville expects the tyranny of the future to be broad and mild. The government will seek to regulate an increasing dossier of affairs for the peace and well-being of citizens, and the lives of every citizen will be ruled by these measures. The tyrant will not portray itself as an oppressor but as a tutor or guardian to those ignorant or in need—categories to which most every citizen will feel himself to belong from time to time. Lulled by the sentimental and intellectual enticements of individualism, the citizen will enjoy the petty pleasures facilitated by administrative measures and not regret the lost trouble of thinking and living for himself. Gradually, he will become used to deferring to authority on matters of even slight importance, little by little losing the use of his free will. Occasional elections will reassure him that his tutor is one he has chosen for himself, and thus he can even flatter himself with the illusion of self-government while in fact losing all ability and interest in matters of government. This decline will escape the notice of most citizens most of the time, and aspects of it will be pleasing to many when they do notice it (661ff).

Three things about this picture disturb Tocqueville. First, he considers the life facilitated by such an arrangement to be beneath human dignity. For Tocqueville, human virtue consists in the perfection of those faculties that distinguish us from animals, including the application of theoretical and practical reason to matters of cosmic and political concern. A life devoted to "small and vulgar pleasures," combining indifference to metaphysical questions with apathy toward political affairs, is worthy of "a herd of timid and industrious animals," but not of "a union of rational and intelligent beings" (665, 663, compare 227). Second, Tocqueville sees no escape in such a society for "the most original minds and the most vigorous souls" to "clear a way to surpass the crowd." If majority tyranny closes the doors to public life for those who transcend public opinion, administrative despotism, backed by the instincts of that same tyrannical majority, brings the same pressure to bear on the private lives of each citizen. Not even ignominy remains as an avenue of escape from the mass mind. Through its newfound administrative art, despotism now knows how to cover society with "a network of small, complicated, painstaking, uniform rules," thus preventing intellectual or moral virtue from even "being born" in potentially great souls (663). Finally, by sapping society of all public-spiritedness, administrative despotism prepares the way for the open tyranny of "a single master," against which no effective resistance could be offered by an apathetic people

(665). Ironically, after proclaiming themselves more than kings, democratic citizens may allow themselves to become less than men; and in this diminished condition of spurious liberty they may one day find themselves unable to prevent the loss of liberty altogether.

In this chapter, we have considered why Tocqueville fears that modern democracy may render citizens "more than kings and less than men" (665). Equality of social conditions is concomitant with the overthrow or decline of conventional aristocracies or anything approximating their influence. Yet such aristocracies, despite all their flaws and injustices, were capable of cultivating and institutionalizing the influence of that natural aristocracy without whose guidance every society is prone to injustice and error. What results is a popular power possessing more power than wisdom or justice, and experiencing fewer checks to its will than are consistent with its own good. This historically unprecedented situation of a single social power dwarfing all others has profound corrosive effects on the human soul, resulting in a combination of mass conformity and weak individualism that paves the way for administrative despotism and a life unworthy of human beings.

As noted, Tocqueville does not consider this scenario unavoidable. The question for his political science becomes how to instill virtuous habits, the opposite of individualism, in a democratic people despite the resistance of democracies to the influence of those claiming to possess superior wisdom. Tocqueville's own answers to this question, and answers we might attempt to give today, set the agenda for the second half of this book.

Notes

1. See Jefferson (1979, 75ff: letter to Adams, October 28, 1813).

2. Tocqueville's condemnation of aristocracy as unnatural, combined with his evident love for human greatness, has led interpreters to see him as fundamentally conflicted with regard to democracy. Zetterbaum (1967, 127) and Manent (1996, 22-23, 69) both see Tocqueville as placing justice and nature on the side of democracy and greatness on the side of aristocracy, with the result that justice and nature undermine virtue and happiness. This study argues instead that Tocqueville locates nature and justice in a "law" transcending democracy, aristocracy, or any other social state or set of mores, each of which contains some mixture of virtues and vices as measured by that standard.

3. See Manent (1996, 68).

4. For a detailed account of both the virtues and vices of the French aristocracy, see Tocqueville (1955).

5. Letter from Tocqueville to Silvestre de Sacy, October 1840 (Jardin 1988, 273).

6. Tocqueville recognizes that the concept of a God who created the natural realm raises the issue of the relation between the natural and supernatural, but he deals with this issue in his writings by focusing solely on those elements of God's will discernible in the natural world (6-7, 419). See chapter 5.

7. This meaning must be distinguished from the theological concept of dogma as a teaching of the Church. Theologians discuss dogmas very thoroughly, though orthodox theologians trust that dogmas are true and question them for the sake of understanding rather than doubting. See Aquinas (1947, Q1, A8, Reply Obj. 2). Tocqueville was aware of this distinction but did not give it full credence, as we shall see in chapter 5.

8. According to the classical view, a law is not a law unless it is for the good of the community, and made by the whole people or their legitimate representative. See Aquinas (1947, I-II Q90 A2-3).

9. For an example of how this plays out in actual politics, consider that Tocqueville's teacher Guizot called the loss of the liberty of French medieval communes on account of monarchical centralization "useful," while Tocqueville described the new order as "servitude" (Gannett 2003, 3-4).

10. See Koritansky (1986, 50).

11. In this sense Tocqueville's analysis would reinforce that of Harry Jaffa (1958-1999, 2000), whose detailed defense of the Declaration of Independence as capturing the essential purpose of legitimate government we shall discuss in chapter 6. Tocqueville's wariness of the Declaration is related to his fears about the abuse of the dogma of popular sovereignty detailed in this chapter.

12. Compare Strauss (1995, 4-5).

13. Mansfield and Winthrop (Tocqueville 2000a, lxxx).

14. See Aristotle (1984, III).

15. Aristotle (1984, III.9ff).

16. Plato (1968, V).

17. See Socrates' counsel that the city in speech be established by exiling all actual citizens over the age of ten and having some unknown group educate the children (Plato 1968, VII).

18. Plato (1968, VIII).

19. Aristotle (1984, IV-VI).

20. In Tocqueville's view, laws can temper but not eliminate the tyranny of the majority (Koritansky 1986, 65).

21. See Cicero (1928); Aristotle (1984, III.11ff).

22. See Tocqueville's stirring examples of mob violence and racial intimidation in footnote four (241-42).

23. Mansfield and Winthrop (Tocqueville 2000a, xxvi).

24. For a discussion of its implications for the practice of philosophy itself, see Hebert (2007).

25. See Kessler (1994, 34).

26. In a draft of *Democracy*, Tocqueville wrote that the human soul always produces ideas and sentiments in conjunction with one another. What he has separated in the parts of Volume II is united in fact; the soul is like the hub of a wheel connecting the phenomena he describes (1990b, 8nj).

27. Thus it is a stretch—though only a slight one—to say that "what the people want is soft [i.e., administrative] despotism" (Zetterbaum 1967, 72, 74).

Part II
Less than Men? Combating Individualism in Jacksonian America and Beyond

Chapter 4
Citizenship: Democracy vs. Self-Government?

According to "the natural sense of words," Tocqueville contends, citizenship stands in stark contrast to selfishness. The good citizen is one who loves his fellow citizens, aspires to take part with them in the direction of the state, and strives to unite his efforts to theirs "to create common prosperity." Despotism, whose primary condition is the absence of interference by citizens of this stripe, is naturally inclined to pervert this vocabulary of nature, commending as "good citizens" "those who confine themselves narrowly to themselves" (485).[1] If there is no one less independent than the free citizen,[2] despotism's ability to undermine liberty and citizenship is subtly but powerfully enhanced by the illusion of individual self-sufficiency, an illusion that allows despotism to advance by offering to protect the private wants of individuals while opposing their collective power, and thus to cloak itself in the rhetoric of liberty wrongly understood. Individualism as Tocqueville uses the term is precisely that tendency of democratic societies rendering them susceptible to this illusion of independence, a deception capable of disarming them against the advance of the new and "mild" but suffocating form of despotism discussed in our previous chapter.

Thus far our study has prepared us to understand two things about individualism so conceived: why it is unjust and why democracy is vulnerable to it. Individualism is unjust according to that standard of justice derived from human nature itself because it induces human beings—more or less willingly—to renounce the use of those faculties that distinguish us from animals (665). Tocqueville's knowledge of political history led him to conclude "that the power and greatness of man is wholly in his soul," that part of him that connects his daily actions to a moral order or idea about the order of all things (34, compare 417, 504-505). Without reference to such moral order, society must be stagnant: "Man is so made that he prefers standing still to marching without independence toward a goal of which he is ignorant" (87). Administrative despotism, founded

101

upon popular individualism and enforcing that individualism upon citizens who would resist it, is both the pinnacle of stagnancy and the height of injustice.

Despite the repugnance he attempts to evoke for this outcome, Tocqueville believes that individualism and even elements of the despotism erected upon it will hold a natural appeal in democratic times (645). The appeal of what is contrary to nature is possible because of the fundamental dividedness of man's soul (520). On the one hand, the soul is the seat of man's greatness because the cultivation of its cosmic orientation issues in the most sublime goods known to man: philosophic and religious contemplation (435ff, 504ff), civic virtue (89), and statesmanship (518, 702). Its potential is susceptible to neglect, however, since all of these accomplishments require extraordinary talent, effort, or both. The alternative to virtue or a life of active engagement with moral order is for man (and his society) to stand still with respect to human greatness. Men who stand still in this way will inevitably distract themselves from the reality of this moral and intellectual malaise by frenetic absorption in affairs of fleeting or superficial importance (506ff). Just as the genuine liberty of virtue is supplanted with the pseudo-liberty of individualism, so is the loss of meaningful action hidden beneath a flurry of meaningless activities.

In a democratic society, where resources tend to be divided, ambitions incline toward mediocrity, and claims to moral or intellectual superiority are typically discounted or resented, the human soul is strongly tempted by any doctrine that would justify the abandonment of the precious but costly fruits of genuine greatness. Nothing more easily justifies such laziness than the idea that life has no cosmic meaning, or—what amounts to the same thing—that it has whatever meaning each individual wants to give it (compare 425ff). This belief, which we now call relativism, relieves man of the trouble of thinking, feeling, or acting outside of the narrow confines of individual or private existence, and thereby robs him of the fruits of human greatness. This escape from one's human potential is precisely what Tocqueville calls individualism, and it is definitive of the order (or disorder) administrative despotism attempts to guarantee and impose through its network of stultifying regulations (482, 663ff).

The problem of democracy for Tocqueville is therefore the question of how individualism and its accompanying phenomena can be combated within the framework of a social state so susceptible to their influence. In a sense, this question is a mere variation of that facing all political societies in all times and places: how can the tendencies of the dominant group, which necessarily fall short of true justice, be moderated in light of that higher standard? The answer is difficult to see. If political history presents us with a clear picture of human nature and its demands, the dividedness of that nature and complexity of those demands prevent there being many examples in history of societies that have succeeded at decisively moderating injustice (39). Yet even the examples we have may not suffice, for the democratic social state is historically unprecedented, and presents peculiar difficulties that prompt Tocqueville to write *Democracy* in the attempt to formulate a "new political science for a world wholly new" (7).

The problem of moderating dominant social powers is closely linked to the concept of natural aristocracy. This aristocracy consists of those whose talents and virtue, whose enlightenment and patriotism, whose virile candor and manly independence of thought allow them to see the nature of justice, to know the limits of the existing social state, and to exert pressure upon society where it is most likely to have a moderating effect. The prospects of a given political society for genuine liberty seem tightly linked to the openness of that society to the influence of the natural aristocracy. Here we see the peculiar threat posed by the democratic social state. In aristocratic ages, no degree or type of inequality is able wholly to eliminate the power of the people or other sources of resistance to the dominant few, making assistance ever available to the wise who would moderate their rule. By contrast, Tocqueville believes that the power of the majority in modern times is capable of approaching "omnipotence" on the political, social, and even psychological planes. If this comes to pass, democracy will attain the deadly power of firmly shutting out all opposition to its own inclinations, including the moderating influence of the natural aristocracy. Individualism and administrative despotism would then be the inevitable, and not merely the "natural," result of democracy.

That Tocqueville rejects this thesis of inevitability is clear from the very existence of his book. Throughout *Democracy* Tocqueville attempts to educate a readership who will perform the above-mentioned functions of a natural aristocracy even in democratic times. Tocqueville clearly has hopes of sustaining a legislative art or political superintendence[3] capable of mitigating the dangers of democracy, or else he would not have written *Democracy*. The content of those hopes as Tocqueville articulated them is the subject of our next two chapters. Chapter 5 will consider the degree to which democracy can be induced to moderate itself on the cosmic plane, and the role that religion thus plays in securing democratic liberty. The present chapter will consider the way democracy itself—understood as a mode of government rather than a social state—can moderate the excesses of equality. In conjunction with our sixth chapter, which attempts to bring Tocqueville's reflections to bear on twentieth and twenty-first century democracy, these chapters consider the prospects that a new political science can play the role of "natural aristocracy" by discovering the most virtuous or least vicious elements of democracy and promoting them as much as is possible in particular democratic nations.

The Government of Democracy vs. Majority Tyranny

The problems of democracy for Tocqueville stem primarily from the democratic social state, because of which the principle of equality dominates the minds and hearts of citizens. As we have seen, the political consequence of this social state is to reduce the range of options when it comes to political rights: in a democratic polity, "rights must be given to each citizen or to no one." Popular sovereignty therefore appears as a happy alternative to "equality in servitude" (52-53). It quickly emerges, however, that this solution itself contains a threat: the extension of rights to all issues in the dogma of popular sovereignty, in accordance with which "the people reign over the . . . political world as does God over the universe" (55). In our previous chapter, we moved from this ominous statement to Tocqueville's account of majority omnipotence, democratic tyranny, individualism, and administrative despotism. In *Democracy* itself, Tocqueville follows his warning against democratic idolatry with a detailed account of those features of American democracy that temper the majority's power, or at least its propensity to abuse the power it inevitably has.

Tocqueville's fifth chapter calls our attention to the "necessity of studying what takes place in the particular states before speaking of the government of the Union." With it, Tocqueville introduces as fundamental to American government a dynamic roughly corresponding to what we call federalism—the division of power (expressed or implied in the U.S. Constitution) between the federal and state governments. Tocqueville puts this point very strongly indeed: the United States has "two distinct societies," "two governments completely separated and almost independent," "in a word, twenty-four little sovereign nations, the sum of which forms the great body of the Union." Thus Tocqueville follows his description of the omnipotence of the democratic sovereign with an account of that peculiar "form of government" the Americans have "founded on the principle of the sovereignty of the people." This form of government, working through "a complex constitution," divides the very sovereignty that, according to "pure" democratic dogma, resides indivisibly in one entity: the people (56).

Yet the dynamic Tocqueville hails does not end with federalism as we know it. Had the division of sovereignty stopped at the state level it would have done little to moderate democratic tyranny, in Tocqueville's view, since he found that the state governments of his day were designed to enhance rather than check the omnipotence of the majority (84, 248). "What takes place in the particular states" and is the object of Tocqueville's approbation is something else entirely: the ascendency of township government. The complexity of the U.S. constitution—and here Tocqueville is speaking of the entire network of laws and customs regulating American government and not merely the written Constitution—went far beyond power sharing between federal and state governments. In the remainder of his fifth chapter, Tocqueville actually devotes more space to outlining the powers of township government and how they limited state government than he gives to the state itself.

The complete system of power sharing Tocqueville observed in America is captured by a term of his own invention: "administrative decentralization."[4] Tocqueville found that the American states possessed a high degree of governmental centralization, inasmuch as general laws pertaining to the common interests of the state emanated from a single government, which was dominated by one of its branches (the legislative). When it came to local interests, however, power was divided among the various townships. Tellingly, such local interests included the very application or administration of the state's general laws, which the states were frequently incapable of enforcing on their own. When he first arrived in America, Tocqueville almost confused this absence of administrative power in the states with the absence of administration altogether. Under a system of administrative centralization—a *sine qua non* of government from the French perspective—the government that makes laws also enforces them, and has the power to hire and fire those who must apply them to society. Under the American system, state laws were applied on the township level, by officials appointed and removable only by the electorate. Even state taxes were levied by township officials (63).

The system Tocqueville discovered in America was so decentralized as to border on anarchy, and yet he found that it functioned amazingly well. Township officials, though they applied state laws, did not work for the state: they were elected by townspeople and normally removable only by loss of subsequent elections. For outright breach of duty these officials could be fined or imprisoned, but this process was not particularly empowering to the state. County officials—justices of the peace—were responsible for trying cases against township officers, but the states possessed no apparatus for suing the latter. In practice, the action or inaction of town representatives was subject to review only when it infringed on the interests of an individual or group thereby motivated to take the matter to court. In effect, then, each town was free to apply state laws and regulations according to its own policies, as determined by the electorate and prominent local interests. In fact, Tocqueville observes, most "prescriptions relative to public health, good order, and the morality of citizens"—those matters that come under the heading of the "police power" officially belonging to states in our system—were promulgated by townships in conjunction with justices of the peace in consideration of local needs (68).

The "complex constitution" Tocqueville found in Jacksonian America was rooted as much or more in the mores of Americans as in written law. From colonial times, liberty had been exercised most robustly on the municipal level. While time had extended significant political power to the state and national governments, the primary "nerve center" of political life remained the township (56). It was in the township that Americans expressed most fully the dogma of popular sovereignty: representative government, accepted as a necessity in state and federal government, was still eschewed in municipalities, with the people in all but the largest townships seeking to direct officials "in everything that is not pure and simple execution of the laws." In this sense, administrative decentralization comes to light not as an alternative to majority omnipotence but as an extreme form of it—as the purest form of "the government of democracy" itself. "In the township . . . the people are the source of social powers . . . a master who has to be pleased to the furthest limits of the possible" (59).

In fact, majority opinion seems to meet with dangerously fewer obstacles in the township than on any other level. Tocqueville readily admits that townships tend to be "composed of coarser elements" than larger social units, and that the resistance shown at the local level to the general laws is often a case of backwardness opposing enlightenment. At first glance, one is likely to conclude that the natural aristocracy has a much better chance of turning to good use the centralized instruments of a large polity than the parochial administration of a small town or city. In fact, the fuel it gave to intellectual ambition was an important advantage of the Union according to Tocqueville (149ff). For good reasons, Tocqueville feared, "enlightened" societies would easily fall prey to the error of equating political progress with the destruction or diminution of local liberties. Yet Tocqueville believed that experience proved that "it is . . . in the township that the force of a free people resides," and that without township liberty a country is destined for despotism (57-58).

Tocqueville's defense of local liberty must be understood in light of the distinction between majority omnipotence and majority tyranny. While localized administration is an expression of majority power, and is even compatible with frequent abuses of that power, the dynamic created by administrative decentralization actually presents an important obstacle to the growth of the particular brand of majority tyranny Tocqueville fears. In his discussion of "what tempers the tyranny of the majority in the United States," Tocqueville describes "municipal bodies and the administrations of counties" as "so many hidden shoals that delay or divide the flood of popular will" (250). In this arrangement, local popular will is brought to bear against centralized popular will. Without contradicting the idea of popular sovereignty held dogmatically by democratic citizens, administrative decentralization divides government and even divides society itself, preventing the formation of a monolithic power capable of wielding the omnipotent force that belongs in principle to the majority in democratic times. The power of the majority—never directly challenged, and even visibly enhanced in its immediate, local expression—subsists only in scattered form, with the result that the state or federal majority "does not have entire consciousness of its power" (56, 251). In effect, Tocqueville teaches that the dominance of a plurality of local majorities, with all its flaws, is less tyrannical and more favorable to liberty than the formation of a centralized power representing a larger, unified majority.

Recall that Tocqueville's critique of majority omnipotence focuses much more on its "power in opinion" than its "power in fact." Under "the moral empire of the majority," the wills of individuals who disagree with the "enlightenment and wisdom" of the masses, or who pursue an interest not felt by "the greatest number" of citizens, are confronted with a fate "worse than death" should they persist in this impudence (236-37). Tocqueville is particularly concerned that "he who wants to speak the truth" in such a setting will "not find support capable of assuring him against the consequences of his independence." Yielding to the daily assault on his "rights of humanity," such a soul will remain silent, "as if he felt remorse for having spoken the truth," or even give up his desire for the truth and turn to flattering the victorious tyrant (243-48). Such flattery will in turn enhance the majority's consciousness of its power, making it less patient with obstacles; and the inventiveness of flatterers will discover the means by which to enhance this power, especially through administrative centralization. By way of the detailed regulations multiplied by the latter regime, society will be rid gradually of any and all havens in which the oppressive will of the majority does not dominate (661ff).

The key condition of the majority's power in opinion is consensus: "once [majority opinion] has formed on a question, there are so to speak no obstacles that can, I shall not say stop, but even delay its advance, and allow it time to hear the complaints of those it crushes as it passes" (237). This complaint on Tocqueville's part makes plain his hopes for moderating (not stopping) majority power in modern times. His strategy has two distinct but related components: one, to minimize consensus or maximize diversity in political affairs; and two, to cultivate the majority's willingness to listen to the arguments of minorities. In this way Tocqueville seeks not so much to promote the interests of any particular minority class—though he is critical of the radical injustices perpetuated against blacks and Indians in Jacksonian America with the complicity of majority opinion (compare 307ff)—as to preserve the conditions for the employment of the eminently human faculties by which man strives for a free, conscious, and reasonable association with the order of things of which he is a part.

Administrative decentralization accomplishes these goals by fragmenting the majority power that might otherwise halt the quest for personal excellence, objective truth, and the common good. When a large majority seizes hold of centralized power, it comes to regard itself as the "sole organ of reason," easily crushing opponents whose objections are not heard or assumed to be unreasonable simply because they are opposed majority opinion (84). Majority power so constituted stands in opposition not only to truth-seekers and other individuals, but also to localities: when it comes into contact with "the diversity of places and of mores," a centralized majority tolerates no differences; "men are then obliged to bow to the necessities of [its] legislation, [which] does not know how to accommodate itself to the needs and mores of men" (152, compare 645). Local liberty, however, has the effect of lending the legitimacy of majority opinion to distinctly local "needs and mores," fostering a dynamic of diversity that makes it more difficult for a central-majority consensus to form on a given issue, and thereby provides more opportunities for the virtuous (among others) to find support for, or escape opposition to, their ideas.

This lack of central consensus is not a purely negative phenomenon, the mere absence of authoritative opinions. Under the "complex constitution" of the United States, nothing can prevent there existing, in the minds and hearts of all citizens, a state and federal majority, whose opinion will exert its influence over them. Here it is crucial to stress that, in praising township liberty, Tocqueville is not proposing a return to the classical polis. Although Tocqueville describes the "real political life" reigning in the New England township as being "like" that of ancient Athens, he by no means considers them identical. Even the first Puritans, who often governed themselves as if they came under God alone, thought of themselves as British subjects and Christian missionaries, with all the duties and rights corresponding to membership in an international and potentially global social-political order. The local liberty they practiced and loved existed for them within a larger framework that colored its content and affected the use to which they put it. Likewise, the beneficiary of township liberty in Jacksonian America was aware not only of the proximate majority opinion supporting local needs and mores, but also of the central majority opinion, which was undecided as to some of these needs and mores. If the latter opinion was weakened by distance, it was also enhanced by numbers (compare 151). As a result, the citizen who assumed wisdom lay with the majority would assume that wisdom on many issues was open to debate. While local majority opinion gained from the indeterminacy of central majority opinion, so too did the individual who wanted to challenge local opinion, in the name of a universal order whose content was not as immovably fixed by majority opinion.

What we might call the fortunate powerlessness[5] of local majority rule shows itself in other important ways. In a country divided among distinct social powers, "he who wants to speak the truth" can take shelter with one power when opposed by another (244). Administrative decentralization does not create a power distinct from the majority, and hence it is unlikely to provide robust shelter for truths distasteful to any majority as such. Yet it does create multiple powers with diverse perspectives on a broader range of issues than would otherwise be possible in a democratic social state, offering greater scope for that "virile candor and manly independence of thought" characteristic of great leaders to find its way into political affairs (247). Though Tocqueville clearly did not consider this scope sufficient for the promotion of the greatest political virtues, as his lamentation of the loss of leadership in America attests, its mitigating effect on the extent of such loss is worthy of note.[6]

Much more powerful than outright resistance to majority opinion is the impetus given by administrative decentralization to the active participation of citizens in majority government. The check such involvement provides against the rise of individualism is crucial and will occupy us momentarily. Yet here we may consider the profound influence this dynamic has over the character of majority rule or democratic governance itself.

Tocqueville is chiefly concerned with "the political effects of administrative decentralization." The principal effect of its opposite—centralization—is to "[habituate] men to make a complete and continual abstraction from their wills," to "[isolate] them and afterwards [fasten] them one by one onto the common mass" (83). Local liberty has the opposite effect. The tendency of local government in Tocqueville's America was to make ample use of general assemblies and, when power had to be delegated, to divide it among as many hands as possible. Many citizens performed public offices for small remuneration in addition to their regular means of livelihood. The power thereby distributed was great enough to interest citizens in government and even increase their affection for local liberty by stimulating their personal ambition, though not so great as to give any citizen the illusion of seizing disproportionate control of affairs. The net result was a citizen who saw government emanating from his personal involvement in it and who took a "paternal pride" in its operations (63-65). In truth, this opinion of the citizen's importance within public affairs was "often exaggerated," but Tocqueville found it "almost always salutary," for it preserved the habit of employing one's will and reason to act freely and constructively in matters pertaining to the common good of society (90). As a result, the majority opinion that must dominate in democratic times was more likely to flow from sincere attempts to discern justice and the common good rather than from apathy toward or blindness to them.

A further political effect of decentralization follows from this one: the spirit of association that Americans bring to everything from the regulation of childhood games, to the conduct of private enterprise, to the formation of political parties and public interest groups. Here Tocqueville's insight corresponds with, and gave rise to, what contemporary social scientists call "social capital."[7] Briefly put, it is difficult for modern citizens, who possess no extraordinary private resources or may be resented when they do, to attempt to exert an influence on matters of social concern. Individualism is a danger in times of equality in large part because the attempt to involve oneself in public affairs seems futile. Local liberty is crucial in overcoming this obstacle to public spiritedness because townships, cities, and counties are "permanent associations created by law" and operated at public expense (180, compare 496ff). Local government reveals to each citizen that it is both possible and beneficial for him to unite his efforts with those of his fellows to produce results none of them alone could achieve. The consciousness of this power—a power that stresses individual will and reason in conjunction with majority opinion—carries over into all aspects of life. Citizens learn that they are able to use the art of association to give public expression to ideas or doctrines they wish to prevail, and to engage their fellows in cooperative efforts to make those ideas or doctrines prevail (181). Tocqueville therefore calls political liberty or self-government "the most powerful means . . . of interesting men in the fate of their country [*patrie*]" (226)—and hence of giving concrete form to the vague political instinct that stirs in the hearts of all (89).

Through this art of association, the energy generated by local majority rule is dispersed throughout society and has a further moderating effect on the power of the majority itself. The energy so radiated includes intellectual as well as practical power. By mimicking the forms of majority government outside of the official organs of government, citizens are able to identify and organize nongovernmental groups that, despite representing minorities in a nation ruled by majorities, possess a certain moral authority as *potential majorities*. Political parties, for instance, become nations within nations, able to formulate political platforms from which to criticize actual laws and governmental policies.[8] Though Tocqueville is well aware of the dangers such activities can pose to an unstable government, as witnessed by periodic revolutions in his own country, he insists that this danger must be braved in democratic times, for it is the only way to give minorities a source of moral force outside the government of the majority (183-84).

When properly regulated, liberty of association weakens the empire of the majority without seeking to overturn it. Rather than hoping futilely to abolish democracy, American parties compete to diminish support for prevailing views and, ideally, to persuade a majority of citizens to adopt their views.[9] In this way, everyone agrees that the majority rules, but it is difficult to establish what the majority wishes or commands beyond question. Through collective action, citizens believe that they can influence public affairs, whether through government or through private associations with public ends. Whether or not this belief is fully justified, it fosters a civic environment in which citizens need not sacrifice their will and reason to any social entity. In such an environment, "he who wants to speak the truth" is more often able to take refuge with one association—even one of his own creation—against the pressures of another association, or of the government itself. In such a climate, the majority itself becomes habituated to considering the criticisms and suggestions of minority groups rather than simply running them over (185).

In short, administrative decentralization, while accentuating many of the more obvious flaws of democratic government—especially inefficiency and inexperience—gives a distinctively quasi-virtuous character to its operations. This character, emphasizing civic participation, public spiritedness, and reasoned debate about public affairs, mitigates the instincts that would otherwise lead a tyrannical majority to habituate citizens for despotism. We now turn to an analysis of just how far local liberty is able to wield this weapon in combat against the worst of those inclinations: individualism itself.

The Government of Democracy vs. Individualism

"The Americans," Tocqueville famously remarked, "have combated the individualism to which equality gives birth with liberty, and they have defeated it" (486). From an author whose central purpose is to combat individualism (643), this is high praise indeed. Yet as Tocqueville warns us in his Introduction, he did not write *Democracy* simply to praise the American form of government. As his account of majority omnipotence makes clear, Tocqueville believes that genuine liberty was seriously compromised in Jacksonian America: the dominance of the majority over thought was so complete that neither great writers nor great leaders were anymore to be seen (245). A kind of individualism had long since divided the only political classes capable of moderating the excesses of democracy (51, 54ff), and demagoguery had replaced statesmanship, as exemplified by the figure of Andrew Jackson himself (265, 377ff).

If Americans had succeeded in preserving public-spiritedness, it could only be in the people themselves, who were not yet as corrupted by their power as those who served them.

> I have heard the *patrie* spoken of in the United States. I have encountered genuine patriotism in the people; I have often sought it in vain in those who direct it. This is easily understood by analogy: despotism depraves the one who submits to it much more than the one who imposes it. In absolute monarchies, the king often has great virtues, but the courtiers are always base (247).

Tocqueville's admiration for the majority's character should not be exaggerated: moments later, he denounces as intellectual prostitutes those moralists and philosophers who speak as if the majority (the American "king") has nothing but virtues. Yet this distinction between the corruption of leaders and citizens is of monumental importance for understanding the "new political science" Tocqueville presents in *Democracy*. On the one hand, Tocqueville teaches that the dominant power of any society is prone to injustice and must be checked by contrary forces. This seems to imply that majority power should be balanced by the influence of the few. On the other hand, Tocqueville notes that an absence of power, combined with the ambition to gain the sovereign's favor, is even more corrupting than the possession of sovereignty itself. Hence the danger that those very "elites" whose influence might moderate majority dominance will instead use their influence to flatter the majority in hopes of gaining personal popularity and power.

The solution to this problem can lie neither in resting content with the flaws of the ruling power, nor in blindly empowering those superficially opposed to this power but in fact disposed to flatter it. Rather, the task of democratic statesmanship requires certain individuals to rise above the quest for personal power and therefore above the flattery of those who hold the keys to power.[10] Rather than seeking overt power, these true leaders of democratic society will desire to gain and maintain enough influence to educate the dominant group—the majority—in the proper use of its power. In this way they will practice the legislative art without calling attention to their own authority. Tocqueville's political science, after proving the need for such an education of democracy, seeks to become the inspiration for and guide to a group capable of delivering such instruction in the beliefs, mores, institutions, and knowledge that can bring out the best in modern democratic society (7).

How is such an education to be provided, and by whom? Without an identifiable leadership class, and with so many leaders disposed to act as courtiers (or even courtesans), who will put Tocqueville's admonitions into practice? Broadly speaking, Tocqueville seeks to replace the declining aristocracies—and whatever support they had given to the natural aristocracy—with a political science that performs the same moderating function. But who will practice this science, and how will the people learn from it? Our next section will consider the first question, that of political science's teachers. In this section we will consider the second question, that of where and how the people receive their political education.

Here all of Tocqueville's readers will respond in unison by citing one or both of his famous remarks about the locus of political education: first, that "the institutions of a township are to liberty what primary schools are to science" (57); and next, that "political associations"—including the political parties that form to influence governing majorities—are "great schools, free of charge, where all citizens come to learn the general theory of associations." As this latter phrase indicates, Tocqueville regards the habits born of local liberty—especially the habit of citizens freely associating to express and implement ideas—as a science. In fact, he calls it the "mother science" of democratic times, applied and studied by all Americans as the "universal, and so to speak unique, means of which men can make use to attain the different ends they propose for themselves" (497). Local liberty alone, with its resulting impetus to association, can prevent the stagnancy threatened by individualism and administrative despotism. Thus it is vital for us to consider this "mother science" of association and to determine as precisely as possible the extent and limits of its victory over individualism in Jacksonian America. This will help us to see why Tocqueville places such emphasis on the "holy cult of liberty" while simultaneously cautioning us not to develop exaggerated hopes for it (12-13, compare 666).

Our prior analyses of individualism and of the decentralized government of democracy have prepared us to understand what sort of liberty Tocqueville seeks to promote through the institutions of local self-government. For Tocqueville, genuine liberty is the means by which human beings approach virtue. Virtue consists in the use of the highest human faculties both to grasp and live in relation to an idea adumbrating what Tocqueville calls "the admirable order of things" (505). Philosophers seek to comprehend this order through the use of reason alone (417); believers look to the revelation of God's will to assist their understanding and direct their response to this grand order; political leaders must look to the same order if they are to grasp the idea of justice from which the art of the legislator takes its bearings (518).

Yet excellence in any of these modes is a rare and difficult thing. Despite the most legitimate desire for equality among men, the gifts of heaven constituting the greatness and happiness of the human species are distributed "haphazardly" and unequally (5, 51, 513). Genuine political liberty will always consist in ensuring that social conditions allow certain souls to rise above the crowd before turning and inspiring other souls to rise as high as they can (663, 519). True liberty is characterized by a healthy individualism that recognizes virtue as the accomplishment of extraordinary persons who, far from being self-sufficient in a way that cuts them off from their fellows, are distinguished instead by their ability to conform themselves more profoundly in mind and deed to that order which must inform the life of society itself. Virtue for Tocqueville could be defined as associating oneself freely with the admirable order of all things (compare 505), a form of association that both elevates its practitioners above society at large and fits them to become its natural leaders (compare 11, 50).

Individualism is precisely the opposite of such virtue on both the intellectual and moral planes. Rooted in an exaggerated and illegitimate love of equality, individualism asserts that each man is equally able to relate to the world without needing the special guidance of superiors. The individualist, wanting to assert his independence without justification and without effort, assumes that the opinions and interests he begins with are sufficient for himself and indeed for all the world. Closing off his mind and heart to the actual order of things, he dogmatically asserts ordering principles passively absorbed from the social state and from other individualists around him (403ff, 482ff). Thus superficiality of thought and selfishness in deed become the norm and even the requirement for social adjustment in the kingdom erected to please this errant sovereign.

Individualism so described can only exist in a democratic social state. In times of social inequality, some citizens clearly exercise a disproportionate degree of intellectual, political, and social influence. Individuals in such times may be egoistic or selfish, attempting to turn social forces to their own advantage, but they can never be individualists, for the constraints imposed and opportunities afforded by the social order are too obvious to deny (483). A great lord, when he acts, will require the support of his vassals, and thus he will act, to the best of his ability, to maintain that support; a vassal knows he will have to act under the direction of his lord, and thus he will strive as best he can to influence the thoughts and goals of his master. A hierarchical society is permeated from top to bottom by the concept of duty as well as that of right or privilege. However corrupt in other ways, no man will succumb to the delusion that his opinions or interests exist independently of his relation to his fellows, and some simulacrum at least of the common good will be part of every individual ambition.

As partisans of democracy are wont to remind us, such a situation inevitably leads to abuses. This is especially so on the plane of material well-being, for the ruling class will consciously and unconsciously favor the perpetuation of its own dominance regardless of economic opportunities or needs that call for change.[11] On the other hand, a civilized aristocracy has tremendous intellectual and moral potential on account of the same presumption of inequality. The greatness of certain figures lends itself to the notion of virtue or the perfection in certain individuals of man's sublime faculties. On the intellectual plane this effect is sufficient to facilitate the natural tendency of the mind to ascend to the highest regions of thought (436); on the moral plane, it supports the idea, also rooted in human nature, that virtue is desirable for its intrinsic beauty, which consists in doing "good without self-interest like God himself" (500). Although neither of these tendencies actually renders the men of aristocratic centuries more virtuous than others—indeed, both ideals are often honored more in speech than in deed—the social climate thus created is especially favorable to the cultivation of those virtues to which certain men are disposed. The discernment and development of human excellence is much aided by a discourse that points to its beauty and mores that support its fruition.

Individualism, by asserting that all men begin on and demanding that all men remain on the same intellectual and moral level, tends to have the opposite effect. While liberating each man from his immediate neighbors, it also abandons him before the intimidating weight of the majority of his fellows, which is in turn reinforced by the dictates of a state seeking to flatter that majority's wishes (409, 615). The dynamic thus created threatens or cajoles souls that might otherwise rise above the crowd to remain content with the lot of the masses, and abandons the leaderless masses to their worst condition, a life unsuited for any human being (663).

Tocqueville frequently likens associations of free democratic citizens to the aristocracies of old (9, 91, 300ff, 489). In doing so, he has two related but distinct dynamics in mind. The first is the obstacle such associations place before the power of the majority, both in action and in thought, just as the old aristocracies limited kingly power. As we have seen, political associations fragment the ruling power, producing multiple majorities and thereby weakening the force exerted by the state or national majority, which might otherwise be overwhelming. As great as this benefit is, however, it serves a largely negative function, reducing the harm of majority rule by reducing the majority's influence over individual souls. Though such a moderation of the ruling power will be recognized as a great boon by anyone who holds that "there is almost never any absolute good in the laws" (13), Tocqueville nonetheless refuses to abandon the positive good, or justice, as a standard for judging political society.

Tocqueville insists that the dominant power, in addition to being limited, must be habituated so far as possible to seek what is truly good. In aristocratic times, this goal was expressed in the concept of *noblesse oblige*: the belief that those in power ought to cultivate truth, beauty, and virtue, even sacrificing themselves if necessary to uphold their duty to society. However cold and unfeeling relations between the nobles and people could be in aristocratic times, each class often showed itself prepared to go to any lengths to fulfill its mutual obligations as defined by the social state and expressed in national character (535ff). Thus the perception of a common good, however flawed in its conception or execution, was a very real factor in each man's actions. In Tocqueville's view, democracy understood as participatory self-government can also contribute to the development of a spirit approaching, though never quite reaching, this salutary sort of nobility in the democratic majority. Thus the American citizen who deplores the effects of alcohol on society will form or join a temperance association in much the same way that a nobleman of old would have set others an example by not drinking (492). It is above all on account of this collective sense of *noblesse oblige* that Tocqueville proclaims that the Americans have defeated individualism with liberty.[12]

To grasp the character and limits of Tocqueville's case for the ennobling power of associational life, recall that for him ideas and sentiments are powerfully linked in a human soul that longs to associate itself with the admirable order of things grasped by the mind. Though ideas and sentiments are distinguishable, the ideas that dominate our lives alter the objects of our passions, and the objects of our passions loom large in our thinking about the world. As we saw in our last chapter, Tocqueville mirrors this reality in his treatment of political vice, showing through separate arguments and examples how the mind and the heart of democratic man may succumb to a narrow individualism. He follows the same procedure in his treatment of political virtue, demonstrating how both the heart and mind are expanded and extended to higher objects by the influence of participatory political liberty (491).

Let us begin with the mind. Tocqueville notes two chief intellectual dangers of democratic individualism: one is the tendency of each citizen to reject particular authorities, judging the world on his own knowledge and experience (403ff); the other is the proneness of each citizen, lacking knowledge and experience, to rest content with vague and superficial generalizations, drawn from public opinion, about matters outside of his purview (411ff).[13]

As we have seen, administrative decentralization combats these tendencies negatively by fragmenting the public from whom such opinions can be drawn. Yet the practice of self-government also combats over-generalization in a positive way. Tocqueville notes that general ideas can enlarge the sphere of human knowledge when they are the product of the slow and conscientious work of the intellect (414).[14] He also notes that men reject superficial ideas in matters that are the "habitual and necessary objects of their thoughts," such as their private trade. The more dangerous a blind taste for general ideas is when applied to a certain subject, Tocqueville reasons, the more important it is to make that subject a daily practical concern for democratic citizens. Thus it is especially important to avoid "general ideas relative to politics," which may issue in an utter loss of liberty and degradation of humanity. By rendering government a habitual and necessary object of the thoughts of the average citizen, local liberty tends to rectify the democratic inclination to seize upon general ideas where they do the most damage (415-16). In this sense, the local government of democracy is itself a political self-education capable of moderating the excesses of the democratic social state.[15]

Tocqueville also extols the benefits of active self-rule in two areas forming a bridge between ideas and sentiments: the spheres of rights and interests. In matters of interest, which we shall explore momentarily, democratic man is prone to the delusion that he is capable of looking after his own affairs without the guidance or cooperation of his fellows. When he does seek assistance, he wants it to appear extraordinary and to be impersonal, and thus he prefers state aid to that of his neighbors. In this way, even his own weakness does not force him to acknowledge the myriad ways in which his individuality depends on a greater political and moral order. Believing himself much more independent than he is, modern man is inclined to view himself as an isolated individual over against society as a whole. This disposes him to make overly generalized or absolute claims to individual liberty or rights, on the assumption that society must either protect his right to do as he pleases in a given matter, or impose its will upon him. The third option—that society would protect his right and that of his neighbors to govern their lives together—either strikes him as inadequate or does not occur to him at all.[16]

Tocqueville's wariness of this tendency toward individualistic rights is evident in his peculiar treatment of the concept of rights. The first time he refers in his own voice to individual liberty as a *natural* right, Tocqueville quickly insists that the liberty of association is almost as inalienable a right (184). His next reference to equal liberty as a natural right comes in the chapter on the dangers of general ideas, of which equality is clearly one (413). Tocqueville then goes on to praise the Americans for not being as enamored of general ideas as the French, illustrating the latter's excesses with reference to the Constituent Assembly (1789-91) that issued the Declaration of the Rights of Man and Citizen (415). As his antipathy toward this and toward America's Declaration demonstrates,

Tocqueville seeks to avoid acknowledging the natural rights of individuals in a context that does not sufficiently affirm the dignity that individuals can realize only through political and religious forms of association.

Though Tocqueville never mentions the Declaration of Independence in his account of American democracy,[17] he does cite the Mayflower Compact and John Winthrop's "beautiful definition of liberty." One of Tocqueville's alterations of Winthrop's speech helps us to understand his selection of texts. It pertains to the positive goal of liberty: where Winthrop declared citizens free to do "that only which is just and good," Tocqueville proclaims them free "to do without fear all that is just and good" (35, 42). Tocqueville's more liberal version—replacing the word "only" with "all"—is apt to remind readers of the French Declaration, which defines liberty as "the power to do all that does not injure another." Yet Tocqueville's turn to Winthrop distances him from the individualism underlying the French articulation of liberty. For the liberal Tocqueville, unlike for Winthrop, the burden of proof remains with those who would restrict liberty; but unlike his revolutionary compatriots, Tocqueville does not divide political society into individuals seeking their private goods and a state existing only to prevent them from harming one another. Instead, Tocqueville's preferred model of liberty and rights is the New England township, with its concern to realize a commonly held moral order in the practical details of a participatory political life, one that educates citizens in their duties as well as their rights, and judges government by its response to social and intellectual as well as individual and material needs (32ff). It is the regular and practical involvement of the average citizen in self-government aimed at a common good that renders the American notion of rights a good thing—virtue applied to the political world—rather than a dangerously general opinion, in Tocqueville's judgment.

Despite Tocqueville's description of political associations as "free schools," however, the education Americans receive through associational life in the art of being free does not come without a cost, and its cost poses an obstacle to its acceptance by democratic citizens. Democratic man is driven toward individualism not only by ideas—whether that of individualism itself, or that of individualistic rights. He is also driven by sentiment, especially by the feeling of all he stands to lose by exercising the right to participate in political affairs and all he might gain by relieving himself of this duty. Liberty, taken in the moral and associational sense Tocqueville gives to it, demands the sacrifice of time, which in a commercial society translates (at least in the short term) into lost profits, diminished status, and less material well-being. The benefits it offers, such as the expansion of the minds and hearts of citizens, and the greater flourishing of society as a whole, come only at the cost of the strenuous application of personal energies to many matters outside the private interests inevitably dominating citizens' lives. Also instrumental to liberty's educating function is the willingness of citizens to consult, consider, and accommodate themselves to the interests and insights of others, which may initially or even permanently clash with their own (485ff). What would inspire democratic individuals—who are both liberated by the opportunity and burdened by the need to make their way in the world—to set aside their private business and become absorbed in the "real political life" of the township, not to mention the state or nation? In Tocqueville's view, the answer must be an appeal to "self-interest well understood," to an idea meant to detach citizens from their immediate sentimental inclinations and encourage the rational assessment of long-term private interests more clearly connected to the public weal.

Tocqueville is justly famous for his discussion of "the doctrine of self-interest well understood," one of the most important concepts he discusses in the section of *Democracy* dealing with the sentiments of democratic citizens,[18] and one that would appear to advocate the subordination of sentiment to reason. It is not so often recognized how ironic Tocqueville's praise of this doctrine is.[19] In unpacking this irony, we shall see that what at first appears as a mechanism for overcoming sentiment in the name of rationality is actually intended to develop in the democratic soul a higher range of sentiments, whose purpose and very existence will typically remain obscure to the reason of most citizens.

The doctrine of self-interest well understood asserts that "man, in serving his fellows, serves himself" (501). Americans, Tocqueville observes, have adopted this view and applied it without reservation to all aspects of their life, even religious observances (505). When asked why they are ready "to sacrifice a part of their time and wealth to the good of the state," Americans uniformly respond that they do so out of "enlightened love of themselves" (502). Tocqueville is not unimpressed with this aspect of American national character, and he certainly agrees with his Americans that this version of selfishness is more enlightened than the alternative. A crude doctrine of self-interest, such as he sees dominating the France of his day, would have men chained to the delusion that they can look exclusively after their private affairs, with the result that no one sees to the common good and both public and private affairs languish. In America, where citizens are willing to sacrifice part of their lives to politics, the common good is attended by a plethora of political and civil associations, resulting in a real political life that tends to social needs and in a vibrant economy that enriches private citizens (231ff). From this Tocqueville draws the general lesson, well appreciated by Jacksonian Americans, that one must sometimes look beyond well-being to secure well-being (521-22).

The happiness of Americans in avoiding the narrow egoism of the French is largely the result of local liberty. As concerned as they are (and must be) with their private affairs, American citizens are forced to look after public affairs by administrative decentralization: if the township does not legislate or apply state legislation, or if the same ends are not secured through private associations, chaos will ensue. Charged with this responsibility, and encouraged by the proximity of the meetings and offices through which local government acts, citizens are more apt to take part in public affairs. At first, a given citizen might join the assembly only when it is a matter of putting a road through his property, at a certain obvious cost to his own well-being. Gradually, he will learn by experience both that his own interests are more intimately bound to the common good than he had previously imagined; and that, by combining with his fellows, he is capable of exerting much more influence on general affairs than he would otherwise have guessed. Thus, without losing his admittedly selfish orientation, he will willingly sacrifice "a part" of his private good for the sake of the public good, which now appears to him as an investment in that part of his own good he continues to enjoy privately (485ff).

Tocqueville's treatment of the doctrine of self-interest well understood is conclusively but not unqualifiedly approving. "I shall not fear to say," he boasts, that this doctrine "seems to me of all philosophic theories the most appropriate to the needs of men in our time, and that I see in it the most powerful guarantee against themselves that remains to them" (502-503). In a social state where "religions are weakening and . . . the divine notion of rights is disappearing," "personal interest . . . offers itself as the only immobile point in the human heart"—the only point to which the idea of rights may be bound (228). Tocqueville advises "the moralists of our day" to turn their minds "principally toward it . . . even should they judge it imperfect," for if not perfect it is nonetheless "necessary" in democratic times (503).

The goodness of self-interest well understood is best illustrated by considering the fate of a society unwilling to add enlightenment to egoism. Tocqueville's French contemporaries interpreted egoism to mean that each man should look after his private affairs and leave the business of government to someone else. As a result, citizens lived like colonists in their own country and regarded the government as a powerful foreigner who had to be obeyed but not loved or assisted. The apathy and resentment of citizens built to the point where citizens could not even be prevailed upon to contribute to their own security or well-being, thus defeating the intentions of the unenlightened egoists. Where American citizens would pool their private resources to repair infrastructures before local government was even aware of the need, French citizens would write to Paris and wait indefinitely for the central government to act. Where American citizens would gather spontaneously to track down criminals evading justice, French citizens would hide criminals from the law out of sympathy for the former and coolness toward the latter. Where American citizens would prefer to do things themselves rather than let government intervene, French citizens would neither take action nor assist the government in its actions. In this fashion the French took self-interest to the point of self-injury, condemning themselves to a true misery in the midst of apparent tranquility (88, compare 10).

Yet if Tocqueville is willing to embrace enlightened self-interest as a doctrine necessary for democratic citizens—and hence a key part of the legislative art and the national character it ought to shape in modern times—he is unwilling to pass over its imperfections, which are both intellectual and moral. The doctrine of self-interest well understood is intellectually and morally defective because it ignores the innate and immaterial interest all human beings have in living in relation to a meaningful order of things, an order that engages them in thought and deed, in mind and heart. In a social state that does not facilitate the use of our higher faculties, self-interest (enlightened or not) easily "offers itself" as the sole fixed point of the human heart; but in truth the human heart is always divided between self and cosmos, earth and heaven (520). The transition from narrow to enlightened egoism is only the first step in a longer path down which Tocqueville seeks to lead the democratic soul.

The irony with which Tocqueville treats self-interest well understood is best exposed by looking more closely at his treatment of Jacksonian Americans, who would seem to embody the ideal of enlightened and self-interested public-spiritedness. Tocqueville initially contrasts this new and American idea of rational patriotism with the old European notion of passionate, unreflective, or religious love of country. On closer examination, however, the sharp line separating the two fades away. True enough, modern-day patriots approach the public realm by means of rational self-interest. Grasping that the public interest affects his own, the citizen "interests himself in the prosperity of his country at first as a thing that is useful to him" as an individual. Yet almost immediately this "rational" approach to the public weal breaks down. Seeing the effect he can have on public affairs, the citizen eventually comes to love them "as his own work." Far from expecting others to attend to his prosperity, the citizen takes pride in acknowledging and fulfilling a duty to contribute to the general prosperity, expanding his concept of personal interest to include the good of the community. Without entirely losing sight of his "cupidity," he nonetheless develops a "spirit of the city," so powerful that his national pride takes on all the features of individual vanity. By this point, the premises of neither rationality nor personal self-interest continue to hold: in America, Tocqueville wryly notes, one is permitted to say nothing bad about the country. If one so much as speaks freely about "the climate and the soil . . . one finds Americans ready to defend both as if they had helped to form them" (225-27)!

Though there remains an element of egoism in the patriotism of Americans—who love the public good as their "own work" and their country "as if they had helped to form [it]"—it is an egoism that identifies the self with a greater whole rather than separating the two. Yet the "reasons" underlying this civic pride cannot be called rational: the public weal is not greatly dependent upon any individual, and the climate is not the product even of the whole people.[20] In describing the development of American public-spiritedness, then, Tocqueville shows that what begins as a matter of "enlightened self-interest," exercised in opposition to the individualistic sentiments drawing democratic citizens away from civic affairs, ends in a reality that transcends individualism altogether, and does so precisely on the plane of sentiment, or the feeling that one is responsible for the good or bad state of collective affairs.

Americans, Tocqueville observes, do themselves an injustice in attributing most of their actions to motives of enlightened self-interest. "It often happens" that this explanation falls short, in Tocqueville's judgment, "for one sometimes sees citizens in the United States as elsewhere abandoning themselves to the disinterested and unreflective sparks that are natural to man," even if they "scarcely avow that they yield to movements of this kind." Unlike aristocratic souls, who praise the beauty of self-sacrifice even while acting selfishly, "enlightened" democratic citizens proclaim their own selfishness even while *disinterestedly* seeking the common good. The latter, who "would rather do honor to their philosophy than to themselves," show themselves no less motivated by noble passions than any other generation of men, even if they are less inclined to take credit for these higher motives (502)—and hence, in an important sense, *more* public spirited than the former.

Thus the examples of the French and Americans prove, in opposite ways, the insufficiency of self-interest to explain human behavior. In truth, "man is so made that he prefers standing still" to living without reference to a goal transcending narrow self-interest (87). The laws must take account of "that vague instinct of the native country (*patrie*) that never abandons the heart of man," an instinct that finds collective expression only in "patriotism or religion" (89). Unless the presence of the *patrie*—heavenly or earthly—is felt in the daily lives of citizens, public life will halt and even private life will decline (90). Thus the French, having abandoned the *patrie* for a narrow egoism, no longer have the spirit even to care for their private affairs. The Americans, on the other hand, drawn into public life by an "enlightened" perception of their selfish interest in doing so, soon find themselves redefining "their own" to include public things, and casting themselves into public affairs in a manner that is objectively disinterested. Even their protests to the contrary demonstrate their eagerness to place public philosophy before personal praise. At no point do either people rest content with a thoroughly "rational self-interest," demonstrating that pure egoism, conflicting as it does with human nature, cannot be the crux of a truly rational theory of human behavior.

For Tocqueville, a genuinely rational account of human action must culminate in the praise of virtue, the free or conscious choice of what is good for man.[21] Since the human good transcends material and selfish interests, neither the sentimental nor the "enlightened" pursuit of these goals can by itself constitute a truly reasonable, just, or virtuous policy. Yet modern democratic man labors under the false doctrine—rooted in the political thought of Machiavelli, Hobbes, and others, and reinforced by equality of social conditions—that reason is merely a tool of the passions, and that the passions are rooted in man's material nature.[22] In this view, the "disinterested sparks" Tocqueville identifies as natural to man can only appear as symptoms of irrationality. Even those "romantics" among moderns critical of rational self-interest as a standard tend to identify reason with material self-interest, faulting the early moderns only for assuming that man is rational enough to take his bearings from his true interests.[23] This explains why the Americans of Tocqueville's day were disinclined to admit to harboring such sentiments, which they may have considered irrational; and why many Americans who later did embrace them did so with a sentimentalism of which Tocqueville would not approve.

Tocqueville, by contrast, sees that man's attachment to an order of things surpassing his individuality can be, but is not always irrational or unreflective. Recognizing his innate need to live in relation to a cosmic order, man can strive to penetrate this order with his mind. Once he grasps this order, man can wil-

lingly sacrifice his lesser interests for the sake of the more sublime good consisting in the contemplation of and association with this admirable object (504-505).
A sacrifice of this nature, though truly a sacrifice because it involves the loss of
lesser goods, is truly rational in that lesser goods are exchanged for greater ones.
Though the path be rigorous and the goal rarely achieved, Tocqueville insists
that man take his bearings from a virtue or greatness consisting not in the triumph of reason over sentiment or vice-versa, but in the perfection of both together.

Thus the highest compliment Tocqueville can pay to administrative decentralization is to say that, by making the *patrie* felt in the daily lives of citizens, it
draws them away from narrow egoism and endows them with a genuine notion
of rights, without which "there is no great people" (227). What virtue is to the
individual, rights are to a people: the source of its greatness. Yet virtue or individual greatness remains distinct from and superior to that collective greatness
based on respect for rights. Explaining this distinction and evaluation of the two
will help us to see the limits of administrative decentralization as a corrective to
individualism.

True virtue, in order to perfect both reason and sentiment, must be conscious of the goal it embraces. In aristocratic times, many selfish men falsely
believed themselves to be acting disinterestedly; but those who practiced virtue
were assisted by public morality in developing the self-understanding without
which virtuous sentiments cannot be complete. Americans, by contrast, do not
appreciate their own public-spiritedness for what it is: an expression of the natural desire of man for cosmic order. They have the sentiment of virtue without the
idea of it, and thus their virtue is incomplete. Participation in public life "brings
them near to [virtue] insensibly through habits," but "does not lead directly to
virtue through the will" (502). It brings them closer to the absolute good, but
does not prompt them to make the free choice of that good. Through involvement in political affairs, Americans develop a "lofty notion of political rights,"
one that elevates them on an objective plane of morality (228, 502); but their
elevation is not completed through incorporation into their subjective self-
evaluation. Administrative decentralization brings Americans very close to the
patrie, so that the activity and discussion of politics constitutes "half" their lives.
Yet this magnification of their lives never fully penetrates their consciousness,
stopping short of virtue or happiness properly so-called (231ff).

The praise Tocqueville heaps upon American self-government therefore
does not conflict with his general contention that the absolute good is almost
never found in the laws, and that no political society is without its serious shortcomings from the elevated perspective of natural justice. The greatest benefits of
local liberty, though defined by their proximity to virtue or human perfection,
stop short of achieving that perfection. Though the art of the legislator must be
employed in maximizing this approximation of virtue in democratic society, it
must also accept the likelihood that, in most cases, it will have to rest content
with virtue's mere approximation.

From Primary School to Higher Education in Liberty?

Tocqueville's description of local politics and associations as primary schools of liberty corresponds to his awareness that the virtues they instill do not become fully self-conscious in that context. Though the practices of liberty give Americans a lofty notion of political rights, to which they cling under the impulsion of passions that transcend narrow self-interest, the self-understanding of Americans as enlightened egoists cannot help but diminish the quality of public life. When local magistrates openly discuss their profits from hanging criminals as if they were describing the sale of cattle, the social costs of "rational self-interest" become abundantly clear (75).[24] Tocqueville's endorsement of American liberty is therefore tinged with irony, and reflects not only his admiration for those virtues instilled by participatory democracy, but also his profound patience with the inevitable flaws of political society.

For all his patience, however, Tocqueville does not believe that the system of self-government is self-regulating. For him, society as such is defined by its ability to recognize and follow the influence of the natural aristocracy in its midst. Those for whom virtue is a vague feeling or shadowy opinion must take their bearings from those who see it more distinctly. In one sense, the complex division of sovereignty Tocqueville observes in America compensates for the loss of virtuous leadership by elevating the intellectual and moral level of the people. In another sense, the very complexity of the system capable of approximating virtue increases the need for the guidance of those possessing virtue in its fullness.

Generally speaking, false but clear ideas are more influential with peoples than true but subtle notions. In democratic times especially, the simplicities of majority tyranny, individualistic rights, and uniform centralized administration will tend to have more of an inherent appeal to the masses than the intricacies of the art of liberty. The maintenance of liberty under such conditions will necessarily involve a struggle, and can only succeed when something like Tocqueville's "new political science" influences the activities of all ranks of society (155-56). We have seen part of what that political science recommends, but it remains to be seen who, if anyone, will be in a position to master it and teach it to modern democratic citizens when they are tempted to abandon it.

In considering the openness of democratic citizens to political instruction from above, the first thing to remember is that local liberty, by fragmenting the majority whose power threatens to crush civic spirit and the spirits of citizens, tends to render democratic society more open- and high-minded. In aristocratic times, the power and influence of a few individuals brought the idea of human greatness to light, and "he who want[ed] to speak the truth" could take refuge with one part of society if opposed by another (244). Under the decentralized government of democracy, any citizen whose views are or might be shared by a significant minority may set a "great example" by forming an association, and he who would speak a truth unpopular in one locality or with one association may seek refuge in another (489). In this way the "manly independence of thought" characteristic of great leaders and contemplatives is more likely to find encouragement in a democracy characterized by local liberty, at least on a "primary school" level.

Local liberty opens minds in two other crucial ways. First, it brings citizens into contact with a broader range of their fellows than they would encounter in daily life. This creates a greater likelihood of dealing with minds sharper and more enlightened than one's own. Of all the superficial and general ideas to which democratic societies are prone, that of the equality of intellects is perhaps the most corrosive, inciting resentment toward those who claim—sometimes rightly—to see justice more clearly than others. If the practice of liberty tends to diminish the thoughtless reliance on general ideas, regular relations with superior minds and characters both enhances the intellects of citizens and makes them less likely to spurn further assistance in the future (233). This is all the more likely because, as it turns out, democratic resentment is placated more by the sight of superior men willing to associate with the crowd than by any of the more material benefits by which the privileged seek to gain popularity. By giving citizens of various capacities an experience of lifelong mutual service, local liberty enables the natural aristocracy to manifest its virtues and establish an influence in society (487-88, compare 50).[25]

By virtue of the intellectual openness generated by local liberty, many leaders might hope to respond to Tocqueville's call by stimulating greater self-awareness on the part of democratic citizens concerning the genuine merits of associational life. Yet the openness of public-spirited citizens to such lessons is counterbalanced by the rarity of enlightenment and virtue, or even the aspiration to them. Though large enough to contain the elements of administration, townships small enough to be governed actively by their citizens are unlikely to be the setting for great political or intellectual ambitions or talents. In one sense this is advantageous. The Union government is large enough to facilitate the spread of ideas and enterprises, drawing talents and enlightenment into government (154); but the shoals of local government restrain the temptation to use those talents to build a centralized system destined to become an administrative despotism. The very pettiness of local politics has the virtue of undermining grand schemes that might serve as pretexts or preparations for tyranny.

In another sense the mediocrity of local politics is unfortunate, since it will stand in the way of those leaders who do aspire to greatness, and whose grand ambitions will apparently require centralization for their realization. This conflict between greatness and self-government may eventually inspire contempt for local liberty in such leaders and their would-be followers. Though local liberty may render the people great, individual virtue can often outshine collective virtue, especially of the local sort (227). In contrast to seemingly virtuous centralizers, the most vocal defenders of local liberty will often be motivated by a mediocrity and backwardness that will ultimately undermine their own cause. Certainly a key component in the loss of local liberty in America since Tocqueville's day has been the moral clout of figures such as Abraham Lincoln and Franklin Roosevelt, whose very greatness brought to light the incompetence and injustice of local and state administrations.[26]

Tocqueville's position on such figures is clear: the type of greatness they represent is not viable as a long-term platform for politics in modern democratic times. A society dominated by equality of conditions will never place itself under the regular guidance of highly virtuous figures. In times of crisis the people may be capable of looking beyond its passions and prejudices and embracing the directives of its wisest members (168), but it is neither possible nor desirable to make crises the basis of ongoing political life. The scale of national politics does attract enlightened citizens to public life, and the checks and balances of the American Constitution do provide a mechanism for such citizens to moderate and educate popular opinion before putting its dictates into effect. Yet the idea of moderating the will of the majority to which one must inevitably submit is not highly flattering to those with self-consciously great ambitions, and more apparent power will always be available to leaders who opt to demagogically advance popular causes regardless of their genuine wisdom. Tocqueville saw proof of this problem in Andrew Jackson, whom he accused of gaining a reputation at home and abroad for great strength (if not for virtue as a whole) by being "the slave of the majority," anticipating its needs and fulfilling them with a bluster calculated to make cowardice look like courage (377).

Tocqueville's political science confronts the paradox that regularized greatness in democratic times depends upon local liberty and voluntary associations, whose strength seems opposed to the fruition of the outstanding greatness of virtuous leaders. Yet without the guidance of virtuous leaders Tocqueville would not expect the general virtues of administrative decentralization to last long. This paradox can be resolved only by identifying a type of leadership tailored to the preservation of self-government. This species of leadership is necessarily a very humble one: to achieve its highest potential, democracy needs leaders willing to encourage or even force the people to solve problems on their own, rather than offering centrally administered solutions to enhance the leader's own reputation. It is in this sense that Tocqueville definitively rejects the attempt to instill "aristocratic" virtue in democratic times, while advocating the development of a type of greatness more compatible with democracy (675, 666-72). Yet this humble greatness remains aristocratic in the natural sense of the term—that is, it aims at virtue and the common good.

Due to the pressures of self-interest, most politicians cannot be expected to exhibit such selfless leadership in any zealous fashion. If they practice restraint at all, it is most likely to be a result of social pressures to do so[27]—pressures that other leaders (those practicing the deeper political art of influencing mores) will have to encourage the people to apply to their elected officials. The problem for Tocqueville is to locate those in democratic society who might be able and willing to implement his political science, in whose name one has to limit leadership to facilitating, improving, or inspiring the active self-rule of democratic citizens. Luckily the influence of the natural aristocracy, exerted through what Tocque-

ville calls "the art of the legislator," need not be confined to those in governmental office. In several key statements, Tocqueville appeals to all citizens who
exert influence within democratic society to practice this art (7, 452, 472, 519,
666). Our next chapter will consider positions outside of government that might
provide a regular platform for such leadership. In the remainder of this chapter
we will examine the one place within government where Tocqueville believes a
natural aristocracy is likely to emerge in democratic times and to wield a power
not only compatible with but enhanced by institutions of local self-government.
That place is the judicial system.

In several brief but pregnant sections of *Democracy*, Tocqueville covers the
general character of courts and citizens who practice law; the variations on that
character democracy is likely to effect; and the influence that character exerts
over the particular version of democracy practiced in America. The result of
these three considerations is evident from the fact that they culminate in two
sections of a chapter dealing with "what tempers the tyranny of the majority in
the United States," in which category Tocqueville explicitly places the "absence
of administrative centralization," "the spirit of the lawyer," and "the jury"
(250ff).

Courts are well placed to exercise a moderating influence on any regime
because of the universal nature of judgment. A court is an institution designed to
settle disputes about the law, and its function both presupposes and fosters a
sense of impartiality toward those parties who dispute the law or its application.
Regardless of who makes the law—be it the many, the few, or the one—courts
serve little purpose unless they at least appear to possess independence from that
sovereign power. Such independence cannot be absolute—e.g., rules of jurisdiction prevent local cases from being tried in foreign countries for the sake of
complete impartiality[28]—and yet the identification of judgment with the legislative power would yield not only the essence but also the appearance of tyranny.
So long as courts seem capable of interpreting the sovereign's laws without the
undue interference of the sovereign, however, their power (a power of opinion)
tends to be regarded with a kind of reverence that may even compete with that
normally accorded to the exercise of sovereignty itself (93ff).

In all democratic societies embracing the rule of law this moral force of
courts is a potential moderator of democratic tyranny. In America, this potential
is further increased by the genius of constitutional government. Tocqueville was
amazed at the frequency with which American courts intruded on political affairs, noting that the absence of administrative centralization made this intervention indispensible (elected officials could not be removed unless found guilty of
crimes). Yet how could a self-governing people tolerate this interference with
self-government on the part of the least democratic branch of its government?

The answer lay in what Tocqueville regarded as a very clever and very instructive strategic surrender to the power of the people: the power of constitutional amendment. In France, the people had ostensibly limited itself by a constitution that no one, itself included, could change. Should legislators ignore this
constitution, however, no court was permitted to stop them, for a court able to

overturn unconstitutional legislation would have free reign to define its own powers, whereas legislators were responsible to the people. In America, where the people reserved the right to amend their constitutions, courts were permitted to enforce constitutional law even against popular legislation. This power did not threaten the people, who might always correct errant courts by amending the source of judicial power. In practice, however, the people came to rely upon the courts to interpret and apply the fundamental principles defining the powers of government and the liberty of citizens. By giving way to democracy on the power of amendment courts actually gained more sway over the notion of rights that would define and limit the practice of democracy (95ff).

This same dynamic applies to the relations between those citizens who practice law and those who do not. Universally, lawyers form a distinct class within any political society, whose membership is limited to those who master the arcane precepts and precedents of the law, and whose interest always lies in maintaining the influence of their profession. Generally lawyers have an interest in continuity and order, and are therefore conservative, though they sometimes support revolutions when current structures give them too little influence, or new ones would give them more. In democratic times, lawyers stand out as an inherently elite group with a visibly disproportionate influence over affairs, and one might expect them to be resented for that reason. Yet the indispensability of lawyers to any system of law and liberty is evident enough to shield them from outright hatred and to win at least a grudging admiration on the part even of democratic man.[29] Lawyers therefore profit from democracy, in which they become the only corps with aristocratic tendencies whose influence is acceptable to the majority of citizens (251ff).

In Tocqueville's America, the aristocratic function of lawyers was not only tolerated but actually enhanced, and once again the enhancement came by way of an initial concession to democracy itself: in this case, the institution of the jury. The jury in itself is a radical example of democracy and local self-government. At first glance, it would seem that the jury leaves decisions at law not to the elite corps of lawyers but to the common man. From a purely legal standpoint this might even seem alarming, and Tocqueville scarcely seeks to defend it in legal terms. His praise for the jury is motivated by political considerations, and he believes that the political benefits of the jury are of a very high order (258ff). In fact, Tocqueville speaks of the jury as another school of politics. Though he does not explicitly refer to it as "higher" as opposed to primary education, Tocqueville makes clear that the school of the jury builds upon but decidedly surpasses the lessons learned in township government:

> One ought to consider [the jury] as a school, free of charge and always open, where each juror comes to be instructed in his rights, where he enters into daily communication with the most instructed and most enlightened members of the elevated classes, where the laws are taught to him in a practical manner and are put within reach of his intelligence by the efforts of the attorneys, the advice of the judge, and the very passion of the parties.

So important is this "school" that Tocqueville even goes so far as to claim that "the practical intelligence and good political sense of the Americans must *principally* be attributed to the long use that they have made of the jury in civil matters (262, emphasis added).

The reason for this effect is simple. Though the jury appears to enhance the power of the people by giving them the power to decide cases, cases are to be decided according to the law, and only the attorneys and judges comprehend the law well enough to understand its application to any particular case. The jury must look to the enlightened advice of the lawyer class in order to fulfill its own responsibility. The adversarial nature of the courtroom seems to ensure that the jury will not be tricked by one side or the other, further enhancing their willingness to learn. As a result, American citizens, who are profoundly attached to their political and civil rights, are deeply affected—even within their very souls—by the understanding of those rights presented by "the elevated classes" in the courtroom (262ff).

How ought judges and lawyers to use this influence? Here we must recall Tocqueville's view that there exists a higher law, one grounded in the sovereign needs of the human race as revealed to the inquiries of reason (240). Who is better positioned than the legal practitioner to study this law of justice and apply it to the interpretation of those particular laws and rights constituting American political society? Through the courts, and especially through constitutional law and jury trials, the legal class, and those like Tocqueville who might hope to shape its understanding, can have a tremendous impact on democratic politics and the self-understanding of citizens. Here, if anywhere, is an opportunity for the unconscious virtue cultivated in civic and civil associations to become self-conscious and therefore complete through the guidance of wise leaders. Tocqueville, who was himself a minor judge before traveling to America, indicates at least one powerful means of implementing his political science—with its focus on the influence of a "natural aristocracy"—in modern political societies.[30]

This chapter has shown how the institutions of democracy, which in itself naturally tends toward individualism and administrative despotism, can be structured so as to run contrary to both tendencies. What Tocqueville styles administrative decentralization or "the government of democracy" divides and weakens the overwhelming influence of the democratic majority, and also enhances the virtue of citizens by interesting them in the common good. Tocqueville has no illusions that this good use of democracy will readily produce full-fledged virtue, and he realizes that the efforts needed to maintain even the half-conscious virtue exhibited in Jacksonian America require forms of leadership that are generally without a firm basis in democratic society. In his discussion of courts and the lawyer class, we see how the strategic cession of power to democratic institutions can preserve the influence of a class of citizens potentially enlightened by Tocqueville's political science. The boundaries of this class do extend beyond explicitly governmental institutions such as courts, however. In our next chapter we shall consider the role of another institution that both stands outside of politics in its daily form yet also lies at its foundations in the mores of citizens: organized religion or Christianity, which Tocqueville calls the "first political institution" of the United States.

Notes

1. For the root of this conception in political philosophy, see Machiavelli's description of the people as "decent" because they neither want to rule nor be ruled (1985). Contrast this to Aristotle's claim that the good citizen must know how to do both (1984, 1227a-b).

2. Tocqueville (1955, 274-75).

3. Ceaser (1990).

4. That Tocqueville had to invent a term to describe one of the key features of American government is but one indication that he thought he had grasped the theory of American government better than Americans themselves. Glendon notes the price we have paid for this inability to articulate a fundamental element of our own tradition (1991, 29ff). Tocqueville's notion of administrative centralization closely corresponds to that of subsidiarity as articulated by the Catholic Church today: "a community of a higher order should not interfere in the internal life of a community of a lower order, depriving the latter of its functions, but rather should support it in case of need and help to coordinate its activity with the activities of the rest of society, always with a view to the common good" (John Paul II 1991, 48 § 4). This common good includes the benefits to personal development only possible through participation in robust civil and civic associations (Vatican 2000, # 1880-1885). The concept of subsidiarity in secular Europe—e.g., that outlined in the proposed Constitution for the European Union—is far weaker, permitting the intervention of central government whenever "the objectives of the intended action cannot be sufficiently achieved by the Member States but can rather, by reason of the scale or effects of the proposed action, be better achieved at Union level" (European Union 2004). A key component of strong subsidiarity is the recognition of the profound and unique advantages of local self-government and the willingness to sacrifice the ideal realization of centralized objectives for the sake of preserving this invaluable component of human life. Compare Tocqueville (87-88).

5. Bertrand de Jouvenel (1947) borrows this term from medieval jurists who used it tactically to limit the power of the king. Jouvenel favorably contrasts this notion to the modern one that the sovereign is, by definition, absolute.

6. Tocqueville originally hoped to find in America a diversity of ways of life, "a picture of society in all its ages," "like a vast chain descending ring by ring from the opulent patrician of the town right down to the savage in the wilds." Instead he found a country "leveled out by an egalitarian civilization" (1959b, 332-33; compare Darcy Wudel 1993, 346-48). Administrative decentralization tempered democratic uniformity without entirely preventing it.

7. See Putnam (2001), and our discussion in chapter 6.

8. One only has to consider Barack Obama's world tour *before* the 2008 elections.

9. A potentially vicious outcome of this dynamic is the favoring of those minority views that are, because of their extreme egalitarianism or libertarianism, most capable of portraying themselves as representing the democracy of the future (Bloom 1987, 249),

This reinforces the need to empower local majorities, which are less likely to dream of subjecting whole peoples to some dangerously impractical scheme. See our discussion of "general ideas" below.

10. This is how Harry Jaffa (1958-1999) reads the career of Abraham Lincoln.

11. Tocqueville considers the English aristocracy to have been unusually open to the admission of new wealth, and yet he cites it as an example of the economic tyranny of aristocracies as such (224).

12. Thus Mansfield and Winthrop describe Tocqueville's concept of political liberty as aristocratic (Tocqueville 2000a, lxxvi, lxxxii).

13. See Lively (1962, 238-39) and Ceaser (1990, 148, 154, 157, 162).

14. Thus Lawler exaggerates in holding that Tocqueville sees *all* general ideas as distortions of reality (1993, 94).

15. Ceaser (1990, 1991) describes the democratic "enlightenment" Tocqueville propounds—his science of association—as anti-intellectual in character. Tocqueville indeed opposes that sort of easy intellectualism that oversimplifies issues in order to maximize its influence on the democratic masses (450ff, 463ff, 469ff). True intellectual virtue recognizes the complexity of affairs and takes a more modest stance toward them (450ff). In democratic times, it above all resists the false allure of perfect equality (189) and the fuel that general idea gives to despotism (650).

16. See Glendon's penetrating critique of this individualistic strain in the American idea of rights (1991).

17. Perhaps the closest he comes is in describing the triumph of "the dogma of the sovereignty of the people" in America as a result of the 1776 Revolution (54). As we saw in chapter 3, Tocqueville was much less impressed with the immediate results of this triumph—including the refashioned state constitutions—than he was with the more "aristocratic" statesmanship behind the federal Constitution of 1787.

18. Volume II, Part II.

19. Mansfield and Winthrop call attention to its status as a doctrine or belief rather than a truth (Tocqueville 2000a, lxi). Brian Danoff (2007) offers an insightful account of Tocqueville's reservations on the matter.

20. The possibility of environmental degradation and need for the community to care for its natural environment presents an important but limited exception to this rule.

21. Tocqueville (1957, 117).

22. See Machiavelli (1985) and Hobbes (1994).

23. See Rousseau (1964) and Nietzsche (1980).

24. This example comes from a draft version of *Democracy* (Tocqueville 1990a, 52), where Tocqueville records a conversation he overheard between two "gentlemen" at a Boston saloon: "'You're speaking of a good piece of business' [one of them said to the other]. Now, it was a question of nothing less than two pirates to be hanged the next day. One of the interlocutors, who was the city marshal, was obliged by his station to be present at the execution and to watch that everything was done in an orderly fashion. The law allowed him for his right of assistance a hundred dollars per hanging, and he spoke of these two condemned men like a pair of cows he had to sell the next day at the market."

25. See Kessler (1994, 159).

26. See chapter 6 for more on these leaders and their effect on the American regime.

27. Some of Jackson's efforts, however demagogically executed, were made in defense of the popular principles of federalism or political decentralization. In Tocqueville's view, Jackson (and the public opinion ruling him) failed to distinguish correctly

those powers that should or should not be given to the Union or left to local government, a fact that boded ill for the future maintenance of decentralized government.

28. Of course, the political interests of other nations would cast significant doubt on the impartiality of foreign courts, not to mention the doubts one would have to entertain about their ability to judge the relevant circumstances of a foreign case.

29. Those who argue for the relative freedom of judges to interpret the Constitution by their own lights, as opposed to the original understanding of its authors or those who ratified it, tend to ground this case on the bare social necessity that disputes be resolved by an impartial authority (see Brennan 1985). In principle, this detaches judges from the concept of law, whether it be of the positive or natural variety. Tocqueville does not advocate taking the authority of judges that far, though he does prompt judges to act as statesmen (142; see Carrese 2003). See Chapter 6 for a further discussion of this point.

30. In chapter 6 we shall assess the influence courts have had on American democracy since Tocqueville's day.

Chapter 5
Religion: Separation, or Political Institution?[1]

Human action, according to Tocqueville, is almost always born "from a very general idea that men have conceived of God, of His relations with the human race, of the nature of their souls, and of their duties toward their fellows" (417).[2] For the same reason that man is a political animal, he is also a philosophic and religious animal: virtually nothing he does can be explained without reference to a self-understanding derived from his apprehension of the social, political, and cosmic order of which his life forms a part. For this reason, the human mind is inclined to know and the will is inclined to embrace an "admirable order of all things" surpassing the existence of the individual (505). Even the materialist, who believes he has proved himself a brute, is filled with a pride in his intellectual accomplishment that proves him distinctively human in this sense (519). Civic life, theoretical science, and religious faith all seek to satisfy the natural longing of the human soul to locate itself within a moral order. Though individual self-interest sometimes seems to "offer itself" as the only fixed point in human nature (228), it is in fact always accompanied by a natural instinct for patriotism, an ever-present spark of moral disinterestedness, and an ineradicable taste for the infinite and immortal, all of which can be hindered and distorted, but never destroyed (89, 502, 510).

In every time and place, the student of human nature will find the human heart divided between earth and Heaven, despite all attempts to make one interest prevail over the other (520). If this is so, any attempt by political society to ally itself with one of these spheres to the exclusion of the other is fundamentally imprudent, tantamount to laying the foundations of a building over a fault line. Yet, as his Introduction makes clear, Tocqueville fears that those who have placed themselves at the head of the modern democratic revolution are madly or scurrilously intent on separating earth from Heaven once and for all (11-12).

One of Tocqueville's main tasks in *Democracy* is to refute the contention of those early liberal philosophers who expected the acquisitions of political liberty and material progress to displace religion in the hearts of citizens.[3] He does so by repeatedly demonstrating religion's roots in human nature and its compatibility with modern liberal democracy (283ff, 417ff, 504ff). We would be mistaken to conclude, however, that Tocqueville found nothing but harmless dreams in the hopes of Enlightenment philosophers. Though he believed religion natural to man, Tocqueville realized that the natural instinct for religion, like that for the *patrie*, is "vague," requiring cultivation, formation, and direction on the part of society, ideally under the direction of wise leaders. As society changes— especially when it changes from one social state to another, as from aristocracy to democracy—the form religion is likely to take also changes. Thus the "natural state of religion" varies according to time and place (284-87). As with the social state itself, the natural state of religion imposes constraints on those who would govern society, without completely robbing them of options. Yet, like the democratic social state, the natural state of religion in democratic times threatens to leave souls exposed to a type of individualism all too similar to the vision of the modern philosophers whose leadership Tocqueville is contesting.

Prior chapters have shown us what Tocqueville means by individualism and why he considers its possible reign an injustice to be combated by legislators and virtuous citizens. Equality of social conditions tends to isolate citizens from one another, producing individuals who are proud of their independence from their fellows but timid in the face of mass opinion, against which their very equality leaves them no right to assert themselves. For such citizens, engagement in politics is painful, offering as it does the choice between recognition of the superiority of the natural aristocracy, with whom active citizens must cooperate, or blind obedience to a faceless crowd. Confronted with this choice, democratic citizens are likely to cling to private affairs and leave politics to the administration of a state promising to guarantee their private enjoyments in exchange for their tacit renunciation of the right to think and act for themselves on matters of public concern (661ff).

The effect of democratic individualism on religious belief is similar to that on politics. Just as the problems of political life expose the inequalities in talents and virtue among citizens, so do the cosmic questions to which religion attempts to provide clear and intelligible answers. The democratic soul is inclined to resent supernatural as much as political authority, and yet without such authority the democratic mind will become confused and paralyzed attempting to solve the problems of human existence on its own. Just as politics does not disappear when the democratic individual flees from it, however, neither does the need to address cosmic questions, without answers to which almost no action, individual or collective, is possible (404, 408, 418). The result of individual autonomy in religious matters is not the rule of reason in human affairs, as the Enlightenment philosophers hoped and as Tocqueville himself, in principle, would embrace. Rather, the result is powerlessness in the face of mass opinion and a desperate clinging to whatever seems certain in the world, especially to material comforts and pleasures in the physical realm, and exaggerated notions of equality in the realm of ideas (180, 407ff, 511ff).

This account would not necessarily phase the more profound minds behind the Enlightenment, for whom popular materialism, individualism, and egalitarianism are in harmony with, if not identical to, the truth about human nature.[4] As prior chapters have shown, however, Tocqueville's resistance to individualism is grounded in his view that justice consists in adherence to the demands of human nature, even when they are in tension with the inclinations of a given political society (240), and in his understanding that human greatness and happiness depend on the cultivation to perfection of those faculties that draw human beings to an active association with the moral order of which they are a part (11-12, 88, 426, 472, 435-36, 456, 504-5, 509, 518-19, 604, 617, 663ff, 670ff). It is this break with the Enlightenment view of humanity, which applies as much to religion as to the realm of political affairs, that renders Tocqueville's political science—and the kind of liberalism it supports—so distinct.

In the case of politics, Tocqueville's political science combats individualism through administrative decentralization or robust self-government. By showing each citizen the connection between self-interest and the common good, local liberty builds a platform of habits and capacities—what we now call "social capital"—that re-acquaints citizens (consciously or not) with their own political nature. Similarly, Tocqueville is intent on finding ways that traditional religious beliefs and practices—those connecting citizens to a cosmic order supportive of human dignity and virtue—can be promoted in modern democratic political society, thereby preserving the proper orientation of the human soul and warding off the inhumane extremes of materialism, mass conformity, and despotism that threaten our times. And just as the success of political liberty depends on collective adherence to the public doctrine of self-interest well-understood, so too does the maintenance of a healthy religious orientation depend upon the acceptance of common moral and theological doctrines by all or most citizens (compare 287, 406).

This chapter will consider in further detail Tocqueville's views on religion as it relates to human nature and the conditions for human liberty. To begin with we will consider how religious authority, despite being authority, contributes to the liberty of the mind, which naturally and freely seeks to contemplate the order of things. Next we will consider the relation of religious authority to political liberty, with special attention to Tocqueville's account of the role played by Christianity in the historical development of liberal democracy. Finally we will turn to the role played by religious authority in Jacksonian America, examining Tocqueville's reasons for embracing Christianity as the first political institution in America; the threats he identifies to its continued ability to serve this function; and the strategies he identifies for defending it without transgressing the boundaries of a liberal democratic political society.

Religion, Philosophy, and Intellectual Liberty

According to an American opinion Tocqueville enthusiastically endorses, "despotism can do without faith, but liberty cannot." In a move that may be downright startling to many liberals, Tocqueville contends that the relaxation of political bonds in democratic times must be met with a tightening of the moral bond, and that nothing short of religious unity can achieve this necessary function (281-82). Tocqueville's preference for religious unity and defense of religious authority is, of all the facets of his political thought, perhaps the most foreign to modern sensibilities. Though this position clearly demands explanation, a correct appraisal of Tocqueville's insights and their ability to contribute to the self-understanding of twenty-first century democracy demands that we meet such foreign elements with wonder and willingness to learn rather than indignation. What may seem like a departure from his overall liberalism is, on closer consideration, actually the fruit of Tocqueville's profound reflections on the dynamic interrelationship between the sovereign needs of the human race, the limitations of political society as such, and the peculiar threats posed by the democratic social state. We can begin to understand this dynamic by examining Tocqueville's account of how, and to what extent, the Americans of his day had succeeded at harmonizing religion and liberty.

In celebrating Christianity as the first of American political institutions, Tocqueville notes that the "innumerable multitude of sects" one finds in America is divided "in the worship one must render to the Creator," but all sects "are within the great Christian unity, and the morality of Christianity is everywhere the same." This unity, which also includes "the principal dogmas of . . . religion" from which Christian morality flows, constitutes an exception to the usual dynamic of liberty in America. Neither the individual citizen, who is used to judging all matters by his own reason, nor any party or association, which are used to advocating particular opinions over against others, dares challenge the supremacy of Christian faith and morals in American society. In sharp contrast to administrative decentralization, which places "hidden shoals" in the way of "the flood of the popular will," religious unity itself becomes a mandate enforced by "omnipotent" majority opinion (250, 245, 287, 409). "Christianity therefore reigns without obstacles" in America, dividing the world between a political realm seemingly "abandoned to the discussion and attempts of men," and a "moral world" in which "everything is certain and fixed." "The human spirit," generally free to roam at will, when it approaches religious matters "feels it ought to halt before insurmountable barriers" (278ff, 406).

This willingness of the human spirit to apply contradictory principles to the realms of politics and religion, and Tocqueville's willingness to endorse this division, pose a problem that cannot be resolved simply by appealing to the notion of "separation of church and state." Though Tocqueville admires the use the Americans make of this juridical doctrine, applied in a certain (and limited) fashion (compare 282ff with 280, 519-21), he makes clear from the outset of his

discussion of American religion that human nature precludes the absolute separation of these two realms:[5]

> Next to each religion is a political opinion that is joined to it by affinity. Allow
> the human mind to follow its tendency and it will regulate political society and
> the divine city in a uniform manner; it will seek, if I dare say it, to *harmonize*
> the earth with Heaven (emphasis in original) (275).

The barrier posed by Christianity to the "free movement" of the human spirit,
though immediately applied only to religion and morals taken apart from politics, has an indirect but profound and inevitable effect on politics as well. Since
most human action takes its bearings from religious and moral ideas, obstacles
to "free thinking" in the religious and moral realm must impose limits on the
realm of political action. To the religious mind, political phenomena flowing
from ideas contrary to faith must appear "impious" and hence intolerable (280).

So far from lamenting such indirect limits on political action, however,
Tocqueville regards them as precious contributions of Christianity to the success
of liberal democracy. It is precisely when religion "does not speak of liberty that
it best teaches the Americans the art of being free," and it is precisely by induc-
ing the people to submit to God that religion renders it capable of being master
of itself (278, 282). Tocqueville clearly believes that the "freedom" to cast off
religious morality must be set aside if modern democracies are to cultivate that
virtuous sort of liberty whose cult he promotes in *Democracy*. Why and how this
is so becomes a crucial question for understanding Tocqueville's thought.

In discussing the political effects of Christianity, Tocqueville is at pains to
emphasize the enthusiasm of Christians, both Protestant and Catholic, for the
maintenance of political liberty. Not only do American believers regard politics
as a field abandoned by God "to the free inquiries of men," but they see it as a
good to be prayed for, and its lack, despotism, as a deformation of God's creation (276-77). The equality and liberty of men created in God's image are fundamental teachings of Christianity itself, as is a certain distinction between the
things of God and the things of Caesar (11, 413, 419-20). In this sense, Christianity is a religion peculiarly if not uniquely suited to liberal democratic society, one that both affirms and reinforces that society's core tenets. For these reasons and more, Tocqueville is among those who hold that liberal democracy is
historically inexplicable without reference to the many centuries in which the
European mind was steeped in Christian faith.[6]

Despite this historical correspondence between the two phenomena, however, a liberalism rooted in Christianity must remain radically distinct from liberalism autonomously conceived. Many liberals came to regard Christianity as a
transitional stage in a development from something less to something more mature than Christianity itself.[7] To their mind, preserving Christian dogma in modern times would be akin to clinging to adolescent dreams when one ought to
have reached adulthood. For the Christian liberal, obedience to a fixed moral
code is compatible with or even demands liberty in the realm of political affairs,

but political liberty must confine itself to those options not in conflict with religious morality. For anyone who genuinely questions such boundaries, a liberalism so confined might easily seem unworthy of the name. As Tocqueville himself makes abundantly clear, the religious and a-religious visions of liberalism are therefore ultimately incompatible.

This conflict between two sorts of liberalism seems to preclude the possibility that Tocqueville's defense of religious liberalism is merely instrumental to the maintenance of liberalism conceived in a-religious terms. In other words, the starkness of the choice between two forms of liberalism implies that Tocqueville regards the constraints imposed by religion upon political society as being genuinely justified, at least in the main. This would be easiest to explain were Tocqueville himself a believing Christian. In this case he might simply hold that the teachings of Christianity are true, that only the truth can make us free, and that political freedom therefore depends on public adherence to Christian morality.

In truth, this hypothesis cannot be maintained. Biographically, we know that Tocqueville was not a man of faith. Throughout his life he attended Mass without receiving Holy Communion, on his deathbed he initially refused Last Rites, and in his correspondence he frankly declared "I am not a believer."[8] The question about whether or not Tocqueville sincerely converted before his death[9] cannot affect our reading of his stance in *Democracy* or his other writings. In fact, close attention to his words will reveal that, in *Democracy* and elsewhere, Tocqueville's defense of Christian liberalism studiously avoids any reliance on revelation or the supernatural (419). As he puts it more than once, Tocqueville considers "religions from a purely human point of view" (284, 419). Tocqueville's dispute with a-religious liberals rests not so much on a disagreement about the divine nature as on a fundamentally different view of human nature and the needs it gives to individuals and political societies.

Like many other liberals, both classical and modern, Tocqueville believed that human opinions—and hence human action—"ought to be subject only to reason" (273). What separates Tocqueville from most of his contemporaries, however, rendering him "a liberal of a different kind,"[10] is his understanding of reason itself and its place within the human psyche. For early modern thinkers, beginning at least with Machiavelli, reason is an instrument for the satisfaction of desire. The perfection of reason—whether it be called *virtù*, science, or enlightenment—consists in the marshalling of our powers, individual and collective, to master our environment and make it suit our desires. The only bad desire, in this view, is one that cannot be realized, and the only important truth, by the same token, is the one that helps satisfy a desire: "the effectual truth."[11] This applies even to the human being whose life is seemingly devoted to truth: according to Rousseau, the philosopher stranded forever on an island would discard his books, no longer concerned with the order of a world that could no longer affect him (1979, 167).

Tocqueville, by contrast, believes that human nature is constituted by a soul (*âme*) much closer to the classical ψυχή than to the modern "self" or "psyche."[12] Recall that for Tocqueville the soul is the point at which sentiments and ideas converge, and it is the cause of our human need to live in relation to a moral order: a set of enduring principles explaining the place of things in the world, ourselves included. Human reason and desire are united in this aspiration for order, and neither can be separated from it. Yet the need for meaning does not in itself guarantee the existence of or access to the true meaning of things. Though this need within us cannot be suppressed—"the soul has needs that must be satisfied"—it can be distorted: the soul will idolize the ephemeral if deprived of access to the infinite and immortal (510).[13] When reason is regarded as instrumental to desire, desire does not cease longing for the immortal, but reason is no longer capable of checking desire's tendency to immortalize the mortal objects of desire.[14] Tocqueville's political psychology exposes the dangers of the modern, "Cartesian" view of rationality, applied by Americans to every sphere save religion, and likely to appeal to all citizens who come under the unmitigated influence of the democratic social state (403ff).

If reason is to provide a salutary check on unhealthy manifestations of the soul's needs, the human intellect must be capable of ascertaining some truth, if not the whole truth, about "the admirable order of all things" of which human lives form a part.[15] The problem for political society is that, while the need for this cosmic science is pressing and constant, access to it is immensely difficult:

> Only minds very free of the ordinary preoccupations of life, very penetrating, very agile, very practiced, can, with the aid of much time and care, break through to these so necessary truths. [And] still we see that these philosophers themselves are almost always surrounded by uncertainties . . . [and unable] to seize the truth firmly (417).

The promises and limitations of the philosophic pursuit of necessary truths explain why Tocqueville, a nonbeliever, is so supportive of religious authority in democratic times.

First we must consider the promises of philosophy. Tocqueville does not despair of grasping sufficient truth to guide human affairs. Through his careful and penetrating study of political societies he believes himself to have glimpsed the first causes of political life and the fundamental needs of human nature, including the need for cosmic order (26-29, 34, 315, 510, 520).[16] These insights, which present at least a glimpse of the natural order of things, allow him to say which faculties and expressions of the human soul are high or low, great or petty, because of the sublimity or baseness of their corresponding objects (compare 456). Above all, they enable him to distinguish between virtue and its contribution to "lasting happiness" on the one hand, and individualism with its tendency to foster complacent misery on the other (504, 521ff, 661ff). They also enable him to insist that all efforts to articulate cosmic order include both the acknowledgement of the soul and its superiority to the body, and the moderating influence of reason (compare 520 with 273 and 570). These insights are solid enough to form the basis of the legislative art Tocqueville outlines and applies to democratic societies (518, 702).[17]

The limits of philosophy are nonetheless significant. To begin with, Tocqueville does not believe that philosophy can provide a view of the order of things sufficiently complete to satisfy the cosmic longings of most human beings. What philosophy uncovers are better described as "the greatest problems that human destiny presents" than as solutions to the human problems (418). To the philosopher, this limitation need not be deadly. If human nature longs for the cosmic order, and if any part of it can be glimpsed, then any amount of effort is worthwhile that results in the glimpsing of any part of that truth. Plato's Socrates, without claiming to have discovered the cosmic account of the good he sought, was nonetheless sure that the life he chose—the life devoted to the "erotic" quest for wisdom—was the only one worth living for a human being.[18] Likewise, Aristotle maintained that the least we could know of the greatest things was more precious than the most we could know of lesser affairs.[19] Tocqueville acknowledges and admires the existence of this uncompromising and "pure desire to know" the highest things. In fact, he seems to regard it as the pinnacle of human existence. Yet he recognizes that such a "disinterested passion" for truth "lights up in the hearts of [only] a few" (435-36). The content of philosophy is therefore inapplicable to human society without the admixture of elements to make it appear less uncertain and easier to live by.

This limitation of philosophy is only exacerbated by the conditions of modern democratic society, in which citizens are reluctant to acknowledge the intellectual superiority of any of their fellows. The democratic citizen seeks to philosophize for himself, without devoting the energy or time to thinking that philosophy demands (403ff, 417ff). If the greatest of minds enjoying maximum leisure are scarcely able to settle on the most necessary truths about the greatest problems facing humankind, then popular philosophizing is bound to have woeful results indeed. If the results of true philosophy require simplification before they can be applied to human society, then the results of pseudo-philosophy will consist in little but oversimplifications of the complex problems human beings face—simplifications unmediated by the leadership of those with superior insight into those problems (411ff, 582ff). As noted, Tocqueville fears that the difficulties of philosophy may become so severe in democratic times that citizens will give up *thinking* about these cosmic problems altogether, accepting "solutions" that effectively ignore the very substance of human life.[20]

These weaknesses of philosophy point to the irreducible necessity of religion in Tocqueville's view. Religion comes to light as an authoritative means of furnishing clear and precise solutions to the primordial questions that are "intelligible to the crowd and very lasting" (418). Of course, not every "solution" offered by every religion will be worth furnishing. Tocqueville denounces the "religious folly" that results from an impetuous desire to "escape . . . toward Heaven" without the intervention of reserve, experience, or common sense (510-11). Yet he also notes the ways that religion can convey to the crowd profound truths also affirmed—if less persuasively to most—by philosophy. For example, Christianity teaches that there is an "admirable order of all things" created by an intelligent God; that the human being possesses a soul drawn not only to God

Himself but also to this order of things, which is an expression of God's will; that this order requires human beings to sacrifice their lesser and individual interests for the sake of a common good; that doing so constitutes virtue, by which human beings achieve lasting happiness; and finally, that the greatest happiness derives from the pleasure of contemplating the admirable order of things, the expression of God's will (505, 517). Though Tocqueville's treatment of these teachings reveals him to be skeptical of many of the details in which they are couched,[21] he clearly regards the overall effect of these teachings to be "magnificent" in their affirmation of those human faculties and their objects that constitute the sublime goals of human nature (504).

It is fair to say that Tocqueville regards religion as a means rather than as an end. His concern is not that God be worshipped well, but that human beings live as they ought: ends that for him are not simply identical, as they are for a believer. What Tocqueville means by living well, however, is not reducible to the maintenance of material order in society, but rather requires the elevation of the human soul. Religion has a unique ability to bring the human soul back into possession of itself by leading it to contemplate itself. For Tocqueville, religion is "only [a] general, simple, and practical means of teaching" human beings that they have souls, yet as such it is indispensible for a society ordered toward the happiness of its members. Since the danger of democratic times is that the soul will be forgotten in the "honest and legitimate search for well-being," religion, like local liberty, is an especially crucial tool for the legislator who would check the harmful inclinations of democratic society (517-19).

Inasmuch as genuine liberty requires that human beings be free to realize their potential for greatness, we can see how religion promotes liberty by preventing the elements of human greatness from being drowned in a sea of contempt and skepticism. The authority of religion, which is in one sense imposed by the majority as part and parcel of democratic tyranny (245, 287, 409), constitutes in a deeper sense a check on the inclination of that majority to impose its paralysis and apathy on potentially great souls, directly or through the tendrils of administrative despotism. The authority of religion cannot succeed in conquering American materialism or rendering Americans deeply pious (278ff, 423-24), but it does prevent them from completely losing sight of or openly rejecting the notion of a higher happiness available to human beings as such and dependent on virtue understood as self-mastery and self-perfection (517). Nonetheless, in embracing Christianity Tocqueville understands himself to be embracing an authority with whose teachings he does not fully agree. It is therefore necessary to consider how such an authority in cosmic matters can be compatible with liberty in the same matters, without which correspondence the value of Tocqueville's stance would be questionable on his own terms.

For the philosopher, there are two possible solutions to this problem. The first is best articulated by Thomas Aquinas, who taught that the truths of faith and the truths of philosophy cannot conflict because they have the same source: God, who gives us some truths in the form of revelation and others by means of our rational faculty, which He created. For Aquinas, faith appropriately transcends what human reason tells us because our reason is natural, whereas the matter of faith encompasses supernatural phenomena; nonetheless, grace or the supernatural "perfects nature" and does not destroy it. Faith therefore does not demand the sacrifice of reason, though it does demand that reason refrain from denying what faith asserts and what reason can neither prove nor disprove. In this way, Aquinas and other exponents of Christianity sought to harmonize classical philosophy, including political philosophy, with religious authority. On this view, any apparent tension between liberty and religion comes from misunderstanding one or the other or both.[22]

For reasons we can only allude to here, Tocqueville refrains from adopting this classical Christian approach.[23] Though Tocqueville continues to regard Europe under the guise of "the Christian world" (6), and though he goes so far as to imply that returning to an age of faith would be beneficial for humanity (524), Tocqueville clearly regards adherence to religious dogma on the part of a potentially philosophic individual as a sacrifice of intellectual liberty (43, 275ff). For him, philosophy is the subjection of the great human problems to the analysis of human reason alone; as soon as one accepts solutions from an outside source, one places one's mind in servitude, however salutary it may sometimes be. For the philosopher, however, such servitude is acceptable only in matters of less importance. "There is no philosopher in the world so great that he does not believe a million things on faith in others or does not suppose many more truths than he establishes." On the primordial questions, however, the philosophic mind must remain free to affirm or deny all conclusions on the basis of its own testimony (408).[24] For Tocqueville, it does not matter who places the yoke around one's neck, and he regards no yoke as gentle that qualifies the rule that one must pursue truth by human reason alone (410).

Though this view places Tocqueville sharply at odds with religious believers on a point of utmost importance, it need not vitiate the sincerity of his alliance with religious souls in the project of reforming modern democracy (11). Unlike many modern liberals, Tocqueville does not regard Christianity as a significant threat to intellectual liberty. The reason is apparent from his account of majority "omnipotence" and its effect on thought. The worst abuses of religious authority—here Tocqueville cites the Spanish Inquisition—were less able to restrain the human spirit than is the influence of majority opinion in modern societies. "Thought is an invisible and almost intangible power that makes sport of all tyrannies," so long as the will to think persists. The danger of democratic times is that majority tyranny, coupled with individualism and administrative despotism, will rob human beings of the very desire to seek any form of greatness, including the philosophic (243ff, 663). So long as the majority remains subject to religious authority, however, notions of the soul and the greatness it makes possible will continue to be known and tolerated within democratic society (517). The persistence of religious authority in modern times will therefore ensure that souls are able to conceive the desire for truth even amidst a general indifference to it. Once born, this desire for truth is well able to contend with any power that tries to stop its free ascent (243, 418, 437).

Though proponents of the classical Christian view would insist that religious authority, rightly conceived, does not seek to suppress genuine intellectual liberty, even a religious skeptic like Tocqueville can see that religious authority will be in no position to do so in democratic times.[25] From the perspective of philosophic liberty—by all accounts, a central concern of liberal democratic regimes—Tocqueville contends that the real benefits of religious authority far outweigh its potential costs. It remains to be seen how such authority can be preserved alongside and balanced with the political and personal liberties that prevail in modern political society as a whole.

Christianity, Human Nature, and Liberal Democracy

For Tocqueville, liberal democracy is radically dependent on Christianity. This is true historically: "it was necessary," he claims, "that Jesus Christ come to earth to make it understood that all members of the human species are naturally alike and equal" (413). It is also true, though perhaps less categorically, for the future: whatever the merits of other religions, only Christianity "has cast deep roots within . . . democracy," and must therefore be preserved carefully "as the most precious inheritance from aristocratic centuries" (519). In order to grasp Tocqueville's analysis of Christianity as a political institution in Jacksonian America, and to be able to apply its lessons to other societies, including America today, we must attempt to get to the root of the conceptual and historical relationship between Christianity and political liberty.

Tocqueville's approach can best be clarified by turning to materials outside of *Democracy* itself, including his later work *L'Ancien Régime et la Révolution* (published in 1856). The second and third chapters of this pre-history of the French Revolution deal with circumstances nearly opposite to those Tocqueville observed in America: the viscerally anti-religious character of the Revolution and the regimes that followed it. So powerful was this anti-clerical ire in the revolutionary movement that "Napoleon, who was able to vanquish the liberal genius of the French Revolution, made useless efforts to tame its anti-Christian genius," and the heirs of democracy in Tocqueville's day still tried to "redeem their servility toward the least agents of political power by their insolence toward God," reducing "liberty—the noblest and the proudest of the doctrines of the Revolution," to a mere lack of religious devotion (101).[26] These facts seem to oppose Tocqueville's thesis in *Democracy* that no contradiction exists between the natural state of religion in democratic times and the persistence of religious authority.

As in *Democracy* before, Tocqueville's answer regarding the compatibility of religion and democracy seems reassuring at first, but less so on closer consideration. Tocqueville insists that the anti-religious spirit was incidental and not essential to the Revolution or to the eighteenth century philosophy that inspired it. The socio-political teachings reaffirmed by the spirit of the democratic age are in no way irreligious; if their proponents were, this is merely the result of the Church's unfortunate entanglement with the feudal system whose demolishment those ideas demanded. The very success of the Revolution has therefore removed the cause of complaint against religion, which is now (the 1850s) experiencing a resurgence across Europe. It would be strange, Tocqueville concludes, for institutions that empower the people to encourage impiety when the people has always been the most religious of social classes (101-102).

This argument is nearly identical to the one Tocqueville advances in *Democracy* (282ff), yet in both cases the surface optimism masks deeper misgivings about what form the natural but vague and malleable religious instinct will take in democratic times. In both works, Tocqueville pursues this problem in light of an analogy between religion and patriotism: one instinct, the desire to associate oneself with a *patrie*, earthly or heavenly, accounts for both patriotism and piety (2000a, 89; 1988, 105ff). Tocqueville's development of this theme in *L'Ancien Régime* casts much light on the nature of his political disagreement with the "usurping" leaders of democracy whose influence he seeks to counter with his new political science (2000a, 11ff).

"All civil and political revolutions have had a *patrie*"—a country or fatherland—"and have been contained within it." In every case but one, this *patrie* was bounded by earthly borders, but not so in the case of the French Revolution, which "had no proper territory."

> What's more, its effect in a way was to efface from the map all the old frontiers. One saw it bringing men together or dividing them despite laws, traditions, characters, and languages, sometimes making enemies of compatriots and brothers of strangers; or rather it formed, above all particular nationalities, a *common intellectual patrie* of which the men of all nations were able to become citizens (1988, 105ff; emphasis added).

Remarkable as it was, this feature of the French Revolution was not wholly unique. The French Revolution reminded Tocqueville of nothing so much as the Protestant Reformation, which had also cut across national boundaries to unite and divide citizens in the name of an intellectual *patrie*. Like the Reformation, the Revolution achieved this transpolitical effect by preaching, propaganda, and proselytism (106). What could explain this uncanny resemblance?

Tocqueville's answer provides valuable insight into the unique role Christianity plays in his strategy for educating modern democracy in the art of being free. The resemblance between the Revolution and Reformation is explained by a common cause present in both and more or less absent in other cases: an idea of moral order explicitly grounded in human nature. "The habitual character of religions," Tocqueville explains, "is to consider man in himself, without stopping at the particularities that the laws, customs, and traditions of a country (*pays*) have been able to join to this common base." Religion as such seeks "to regulate the general relations between man and God, [and] the general rights and duties among men, independently of the form of society." "Taking [its] foundations in human nature itself," religion "can be received equally by all men and applied everywhere," rendering its revolutions uncontainable by "the territory of a single people, or even of a single race." All of these features, which explain the civilizational impact of the Protestant Reformation, are equally attributable to the French Revolution, and equally explain its impact. In other words, the French Revolution resembles a religious revolution not for any accidental reason, but because the Revolution itself was "a sort of new religion—an imperfect religion, it is true, without God, without worship, and without another life, but one that nonetheless, like Islam, has inundated all the earth with its soldiers, its apostles, and its martyrs" (107-108).

Tocqueville's account of the French Revolution as a quasi-religion helps us to understand why its anti-Christian tendencies seemed so essential to its "apostles," and why Tocqueville is so insistent that the revolution's doctrines—equality and liberty—be recast in harmony with Europe's Christian heritage. To the revolutionaries, the abandonment of Christianity seemed possible and even necessary precisely on account of the "common cause" behind both "religions." Both Christianity and the Revolution were founded on the notion of universal human nature, the rights and duties it bears, and the type of behaviors and relationships it demands. Both exerted an influence over wide swathes of humanity by influencing the very idea (or complex of ideas) from which almost all human action is born. The difference, as we saw above, is that Christianity regards human nature as subordinate to its Creator, to whom the greatest duties are owed, and from whom the greatest benefits are to be expected. The Revolution, to the contrary, sought to go "back always to the least particular and so to speak the most *natural* facts of the social state and government" (108; emphasis in original). The Revolution, as a religion without God, based itself on a concept of human nature excluding dependence on God, and was therefore a religion of man. Tocqueville's reasons for rejecting this new religion "without God [and] without worship," illuminate by way of contrast his motives for embracing the idea of Christian liberal democracy.

Tocqueville is in agreement with the revolutionaries on one important point: the primacy of nature over convention and over the supernatural understood as convention. Though Tocqueville sees human nature as naturally longing to know "the admirable order of things," and though he repeatedly associates this order with the will of the Creator, Tocqueville deliberately limits himself to what human reason can tell us about the natural order of which we are a part (compare 6-7, 284, 419, 504-5, 519). Justice, the guiding star of the legislative art, is for him reducible to the sovereignty of the human race (240). In saying that legislators ought to arrange political affairs so as to elicit the higher potentialities of human nature through daily affairs, on analogy to the cultivation of piety through daily worship (64-65), Tocqueville advocates something that we might call a human or political religion. He himself unabashedly calls it "the holy cult of liberty," and trumpets his adoration of a liberty ultimately conceived in naturalistic and humanistic terms (12, 666).

At the same time, Tocqueville is supremely cautious, in *Democracy* and elsewhere, to avoid using the unqualified term religion for any phenomenon that does not provide clear, precise, and intelligible solutions to the primordial questions of human life based upon the subordination of humanity to its Creator. This is so despite the abundance of pseudo-religions—systematic ideas by which citizens seek to explain their world, embraced by the majority of them without question—Tocqueville discovers in democratic regimes. The love of equality (52, 189, 480, 645), self-interest well-understood (500ff), pantheism (425ff), materialism (506ff), the indefinite perfectibility of man (426ff): Tocqueville describes them all as quasi-religious, and therefore as possible substitutes for genuine religion, but is unwilling to christen them with the name of religion itself. In *L'Ancien Régime*, he refers to the Revolution as a "new sort of religion," and one that is "imperfect" at that. What is it about God, worship, and the afterlife that, "from a purely human point of view," Tocqueville finds essential to any religion capable of supporting liberal democracy?

A general answer to this question can be gleaned from Tocqueville's treatment of "honor in the United States and in democratic societies" (589ff). "Honor" as Tocqueville uses the word here refers to the sum of rules by which one obtains the esteem of one's peers. It is distinct from what we have called moral order in that it influences men through an element of their will—namely, their desire to be esteemed—rather than through their beliefs, which may or may not correspond to the demands of honor. It is also distinct from morality inasmuch as morality is derived from the permanent or general needs of the human race, whereas honor is derived from the needs felt by particular peoples, classes, or castes. Thus honor drove the nobility of old, whose ascendency was based on force, to fight duels even when decency would decline them; and honor drives the American citizen, whose people is taming a wild continent, to cast himself relentlessly into the accumulation of wealth with an avarice that would shock general reason and the universal conscience of humanity. For Tocqueville, who defines justice in terms of the sovereign needs of the human race, honor is clearly a problematic phenomenon, and one might expect him to advocate its replacement by adherence to morality grounded in nature.[27]

Two points cut against so facile a rejection of honor, however. First, honor holds sway over men with a force inversely proportionate to the size of the group adhering to it. The weakening of honor's grip may free citizens to follow a more truly moral code of behavior, but it also weakens the ties that bind them to any code of behavior, that of morality included. Thus Tocqueville notes that the nobility and peasantry of old, regarding one another as distinct species, had no pity for one another's sufferings; yet, so long as the old regime endured, they were prepared to die for one another when doing so was a matter of duty or honor. Americans, by contrast, tend to regard all men as their fellows (*sembables*, "those like them"), frequently being moved by compassion to assist their neighbors in small matters; yet it is rare to find anyone willing to make great sacrifices for another in the absence of a specific code of conduct (535ff). Though elements of honor remain in America—such as the glorification of commerce and condemnation of leisure—honor overall is weaker and less detailed, failing to provide the specific guidance or strong motivation required for most quasi-virtuous acts (589ff).[28]

A second consideration against the abandonment of honor relates to the problem of gaining access to the grounds of its alternative. It is "the vast . . . association" of the "human race . . . that [has] given birth to moral laws," and "all men have naturally attached in all places and all times the idea of blame and of shame to the nonobservance of them" (589). Yet no society consistently succeeds in representing the human race as a whole. Rather, every society is dominated by some faction, be it composed of few or many, whose particular needs and gifts, virtues and vices, color its understanding not only of justice, but of humanity itself (240ff, 675). Aristocratic souls do not perceive fellowship where it exists by nature; democratic souls are hostile to hierarchy even when it is perfectly natural (411ff). Even with the best of intentions, a society seeking to govern itself by a morality purified of honor will instead regulate itself by a sort of honor—the peculiar perspective of its ruling element—disguised as morality.

At first glance, then, Tocqueville seems to imply that honor is ineradicable and morality is a hopeless cause. Closer consideration reveals that Tocqueville is pointing to the reasons that morality must be advanced in a particular way: through the legislative art. Practically speaking, the appeal to "pure" morality in any given society will translate into a call to renew its adherence to the demands of the social state.[29] "Honor," on the other hand, roughly corresponds to what Tocqueville previously referred to as "national character": a set of habits defining a particular people or class, and rooted in their particular history and self-understanding, that may or may not correspond to the demands of the social state of that people (28ff). Like honor, national character tends to divide the human race into distinct and semi-autonomous subgroups, and in this sense is contrary to nature and natural justice. The virtue of both honor and national character, however, is their ability to cut against the claims of the social state, which are sometimes also unnatural and unjust. Thus honor and national character, though seemingly sources of parochialism and prejudice, can in the right hands—the hands of the wise legislator, statesman, or influential citizen—serve as a means of gaining the leverage to oppose the faults and reinforce the strengths of a given society (compare 13, 520).

What does this have to do with Christianity and its role in liberal democracy? Though religion, as a matter of belief, does not strictly correspond to what Tocqueville calls honor, Christianity's relationship to the democratic social state and the beliefs the latter encourages renders it a part of the American national character with several features very much resembling those of honor. To begin with, Christianity, like the honor codes of the Middle Ages—though with far less specificity—presents us with a "detailed code in which all [is] foreseen and ordered in advance" (597, compare 43, 276). In fact, Christianity as a tradition is itself an "inheritance from aristocratic centuries," and was for many generations intertwined with the thought patterns of the medieval soul (519, 420-21). For this reason alone, Christianity contains elements that counterbalance the deficiencies of the democratic spirit, such as the linkage of virtue and happiness to self-mastery and self-perfection (517).

In addition, Christianity has an air of particularity that gives it a greater purchase on the human will than a mere set of generalizations about human nature could possess. Exteriorly, Christianity divides the world between those peoples who have been evangelized and those who have not; interiorly, it divides peoples between the elect and the damned, and individuals between the spirit and the flesh. This, along with the connections it fosters to the communion of saints, the faithful departed, the Church militant, the pastors of the flock, and an incarnate God, gives Christianity the force of a particular code regulating the esteem given to the actions or inactions of its adherents (compare 406, 413).

In this respect, Christianity appears superior to the Enlightenment or the quasi-religion of the French Revolution. By seizing upon the concept of human nature too directly, these movements provide no basis for distinguishing between human nature per se and what passes for human nature in the view of the social state. Thus they provide no leverage against the excesses of the social state itself, at least on a popular level. In his correspondence, where Tocqueville was much more frank in addressing the comparative strengths and limitations of different religious beliefs than he was in his published works, Tocqueville worried about the consequences of the decline in traditional Christianity and its replacement by increasingly vague spiritual systems such as Unitarianism or even deism. Tocqueville considered these latter doctrines sufficient to guide the superior classes themselves, but incapable of checking the proclivity of the majority to embrace material self-interest.[30] In the end, Tocqueville would consider it sad but not strange for the majority, longing for religion but perplexed by doubt, to settle for the worship of well-being and what a more recent thinker has called "the road to serfdom" of a new and peculiarly democratic sort: administrative despotism.[31] Christianity, in its particularity and specificity, is capable of influencing the beliefs and wills of citizens in a contrary and counterbalancing direction; the religion of man, in its comparative vagueness, is not.[32]

If the particularity of Christianity renders it superior to substitutes for religion, in Tocqueville's view, then it is the simultaneous universality of Christianity that causes him to prefer it to other genuine religions as the basis for liberal democracy. Here it is worth reconsidering Tocqueville's startling statement that it took a supernatural event—the Incarnation—to make the natural similarity and equality of the human species understood (413). This jarring claim is accompanied by Tocqueville's strange accusation that "the most profound and vast geniuses of Rome and Greece were never able to arrive at the idea" of human nature, an accusation he later directs against Cicero in particular (539). Tocqueville, an accomplished student of Tully[33] and an advocate of the careful reading of ancient texts (450ff), could hardly have missed Cicero's coinage of the term "natural law," his account of cosmic citizenship based on the perfection of human nature, or other features of classical thought that undermine the caricature he puts forward in these passages of *Democracy*.[34] The strangeness of both of these accounts—the supernatural revelation of nature and the seemingly careless repudiation of ancient thought—can be explained by reference to Tocqueville's appreciation of the uniquely promising political possibilities introduced to the world by Christian morality.

Here Tocqueville's *L'Ancien Régime* is again helpful. In that work, Tocqueville qualifies his characterization of religion as appealing to human nature by noting that "the pagan religions of antiquity . . . were all more or less tied to the political constitution or social state of each people, and retained even in their dogmas a certain physiognomy that was national and often municipal." Thus they inspired zeal but not proselytism (107-8). This means that pagan religions, unlike Christianity, were oblivious to a universal human nature, and too steeped in particularities to oppose the injustices of honor or national character by appealing to morality as such (compare 2000a, 593). Political philosophy, though it had discovered human nature and even devised an account of ethics grounded in reason and applicable to the lives of citizens and statesmen, lacked the means to reach the hearts and minds of the masses, who remained rooted in the pure particularity of their time and place. This imperviousness of the masses in turn prevented classical political science from gaining a secure purchase for its potential reform of political society.

Tocqueville seems therefore to support the explicit and implicit claims of Christian political thinkers that Christianity, by making all citizens cognizant of their membership in a universal brotherhood, presents statesmen and moralists with a superior foundation for the reform of political society even in light of the standards elucidated by the unaided reason of pagan political philosophers.[35] This explains why Tocqueville calls for the careful study of ancient literature by the leaders of democratic society, who ought to examine the basis of virtue in human nature itself, but not for the masses, whose connection to virtue is best mediated through the institutions of the township, the jury, and worship (517). The township and jury, which embody participatory democracy "as in [ancient] Athens" (40), represent the need to preserve something of the particularity of the ancient polis. Yet Tocqueville's defense of Christianity reflects his view that the insights of political science, rooted in political philosophy, cannot be fully implemented without a religion that speaks of a universal, heavenly city (32ff).

Finally, a full grasp of Tocqueville's preference for Christianity must consider his critique of Islam. Mohammed, he claims, "had not only religious doctrines descend from Heaven and placed in the Koran, but political maxims, civil and criminal laws, and scientific theories." Christianity, by contrast, "speak[s] only of the general relations of men to God and among themselves" (419-20). This is enough to regulate not only the private actions of men, but also their political deeds, for almost no deed is not derived from one's idea of the relations Christianity defines. Yet the chain of ideas from these primordial notions to the plethora of actions taken in political society is not a short one; deliberation is required to apply even the fixed tenets of Christianity to the shifting conditions of the world. In this task, Christianity gives guidance but leaves its adherents largely free to determine their own specific path. The command to "render unto

Caesar" implies both the limits of politics, which can never usurp the rights of God, and the liberty of political actors within those limits (43, 276, 280, 419ff).

Again we return to the observation that Christianity is uniquely suited to reinforce the practice of political liberty while placing salutary limits upon it. Now its uniqueness can be described more fully as the virtue of making men aware of their universal nature, of the need to bring that nature to perfection through virtue, and of the liberty to develop that nature freely within certain salutary limits, all by way of a tradition particular enough to resist the easy generalizations of the social state. Though Tocqueville himself declined to embrace key tenets of the Christian faith, for the reasons outlined above he considered it an indispensible component of any attempt to prop up a genuine or virtuous liberty in the conditions of modern democracy.

Separation and Civil Religion

The final problem we must confront in Tocqueville's account of Christian liberal democracy is no small one: how can religious authority serve as the basis for a free political system without either obstructing liberty or itself being swept away in the torrents of freedom? Tocqueville answers this question in what might appear to be a paradoxical fashion: in America, the dominion of religion in society is secured principally by "the complete separation of church and state" (282ff). As with the legal class discussed in our last chapter, it is precisely religion's lack of apparent political power that enables it to cultivate a maximum influence over the religious opinions of citizens, an influence which is then carried into politics by the free actions of those believing (and even by many nonbelieving) citizens. Tocqueville's analysis of religion's role in modern liberal democracy culminates in a strategy for fostering faith through a legislative art operating mostly outside of the institutions and actors we usually call "political," one that fosters a civil religion shaping the language and actions of political society without the need for direct Church intervention in political affairs.

In his usual manner, Tocqueville articulates this democratic strategy in contradistinction to that employed by religious authority in aristocratic times. In *Democracy* as in *L'Ancien Régime*, he attributes the anti-religious sentiment of European democracy to the Church's accidental association with the old political regime. Nothing in Christianity, or even Catholicism, attaches it necessarily to aristocracy or repels it from democracy, and Tocqueville appears to blame Church leaders for seeking to found religion's strength on the shifting sands of law and political power rather than on the unfailing desire for immortality in the heart of man (1988, 103; 2000a, 284ff). Would not a Christianity founded purely on an appeal to man as man have succeeded in exercising religious influence with greater continuity in both aristocratic and democratic ages?

Our prior analysis of the religion of man prepares us to see the gentler subtlety of Tocqueville's critique of Church politics. An appeal to man as man is possible in any time and place, but to exert real influence over a society ideas must speak to the concrete circumstances in which human beings live and act. The Middle Ages were drastically different times, when political society was much more hierarchical, stable, and impervious to new influences. Christianity, many of whose tenets run contrary to the assumptions of aristocratic inequality (compare 11, 413),[36] had to seek social status and therefore political power for its clergy if it was to check the excesses of the reigning regime. Only by placing serf-priests in the midst of nobles—only by taking its place as *le premier état*, to use the medieval term—was Christianity able to introduce the notion of equality into the heart of the feudal world (4). Feudalism and the variants of inequality that followed it were long-enduring conditions, and Tocqueville implicitly concedes the political wisdom with which the Church adapted to them.[37]

Tocqueville criticizes European Christianity, and holds up its American daughter as a model, on the separate but vital question of how to adapt to the new but equally durable conditions of modern democracy. Here the wisdom and foresight are to be found in the new world rather than the old, and in a strategy quite the opposite of that which succeeded in the old regime. Aristocracy is characterized by a diversity of authorities, each secure in its privileges but (more or less) accepting of the co-existence of other powers; thus it was natural for the Church to become one social power among many, even if this produced a tension concerning certain aspects of feudal honor. Democracy, by contrast, is characterized by the complete dominance of the majority, which recognizes no limits to its authority save those of rights equally held by all citizens as such. In democratic times, the people reign over the political world like God over the universe: they are the source and end of all things (52-55). A Church that tried to maintain the support of laws and political institutions under such conditions would become susceptible to the flux of democratic opinion. It would then lose even the appearance of permanence and transcendence, without which it would no longer have anything to offer the hearts of citizens longing for the infinite and immortal. American priests are therefore right to remain scrupulously neutral on questions that appear purely political in nature. If religion is to maintain any hold on the democratic soul, it cannot be by means of political authority; it must confine its appeal to the religious longings of each citizen and family of citizens, and to those political beliefs fundamental to the proper ordering of liberal democracy (277ff).

This is not to say that Tocqueville advocates anything like the complete privatization of religion or the strict exclusion of religious language and symbolism from the public sphere characteristic of mid-twentieth century American Constitutional jurisprudence.[38] To the contrary, Tocqueville notes with approval (or without protest) the many ways in which Christian beliefs and morality permeate the political atmosphere in Jacksonian America.[39] It is precisely to enhance these political effects of Christianity that Tocqueville counsels Christian leaders to steer clear of direct involvement in politics. Just as Tocqueville attributes the power of the American legal system to its apparent subservience to the people, represented in the Constitution and the institution of the jury (93ff,

258ff), so too he understands the political power of the clergy as enhanced by its apparent deference to the ultimate authority of the people. In both cases the appearance of submission to democracy renders the authority trustworthy in the public eye, while the complexity of the issue—law, rights, or religion—renders the average citizen susceptible to the guidance of a learned authority. Such guidance could never succeed if it simply repudiated the premises of democratic society, and therefore it must work within the limitations of the social state. Yet the proper cultivation and application of legal or religious authority can provide the means for a "natural aristocracy" schooled in Tocqueville's "new political science" to accentuate the strengths and correct, however subtly, the flaws of democratic political society (418ff, 504ff, 517ff). Ironically, then, the separation of church and state, properly understood and implemented, becomes the platform by which clergy can take their place as practitioners of Tocqueville's "legislative art" and "art of being free." Separation is then the means of maintaining and even enhancing the political influence of religion in democratic times.

Like any political strategy in Tocqueville's view, this one is not without its potential pitfalls. The gravest danger besetting the American solution Tocqueville favors derives from the inescapability of majority opinion in democratic times. The mass mentality prevails as much in the private sphere as in the public realm, though in importantly different ways. The risk of appealing to the private consciences of citizens is that religion, or various of its proponents, will enter into a competition for souls that will tempt them to dilute the content of Christianity beyond recognition. Tocqueville notes in *Democracy* that, in order to reach their audiences, American preachers refrain from condemning the goods of earth even while they praise the goods of Heaven; in fact, they often praise both, even in terms that make one wonder which goods they consider best (423-24). In a letter he wrote shortly after arriving in America, Tocqueville is more detailed and blunt about this problem.[40] He accuses preachers in America of having all but abandoned dogma or the authoritative, but highly disputed, portion of the faith for an over-emphasis on those points of morality shared by all Christians. Though Tocqueville strongly supports this shared morality, he also holds that Christian morality derives from Christian belief (compare 29), and that the erosion of the latter must eventually undermine adherence to the former.[41] In their struggle to avoid alienating listeners divided and confused by the multiplicity of sects, Christian leaders, he thought, were in danger of abandoning the real basis of their influence altogether (422). The result, as we have seen, would be the descent of the populace into materialism, pantheism, and other noxious quasi-religions.[42]

Tocqueville's response to this problem comprises three main features, all of which place him in tension with many liberals of his day and ours. The first is an emphasis on religious orthodoxy. Though democratic souls will be uncomfortable with many of the more definite articles of faith—whether it be the emphasis on the supernatural, on virtue, or on the formalities of worship—Tocqueville advises religious leaders to be prudent in the concessions they make or do not make to such popular resistance. They should carefully identify what is essential and what is accidental to the faith, and bend only with regard to the latter (422ff). Thus Tocqueville supports the preservation of religious orthodoxy, even if it is of a less aggressive sort than before.

In the letter cited above, Tocqueville again goes into greater and less politic detail on his understanding of Christian orthodoxy.[43] Religion, he argues, is essentially premised on divine authority and its claims over the intellect of man. At the center of Christianity is therefore the Catholic Church, which unabashedly stakes its claims over all human minds, from the peasant to the philosopher. Protestantism, in Tocqueville's view, was inaugurated by the claims of reformers to subject some doctrines of the Church to critical scrutiny, while accepting others on authority; essentially defined by this precedent, Protestantism leads gradually and in practice to the acceptance by individuals of whatever appeals to them in Christianity, and the rejection of whatever they dislike (compare 275ff, 405). The combination of Protestantism and general doubt, accentuated by the democratic social state and by the growing multiplicity of sects, is for Tocqueville a recipe for deism and disbelief.[44]

In a conclusion that he also expresses in *Democracy*, though with greater tact, Tocqueville predicts that the religious sphere in democratic times will gradually become polarized. Those attracted to religion for the certainty it provides (and, in Tocqueville's view, ought to provide) on the primordial questions will increasingly gravitate toward "the truths of the Roman Church," while the majority of citizens will fall away from religion properly so-called, embracing an increasingly watered-down Christianity or the ersatz religions whose advent Tocqueville dreads (425). Clearly, Tocqueville intends his analysis to encourage a reconciliation between the Catholic Church and those pursuing his model of a virtuously liberal modern democratic society.

The second part of Tocqueville's response would have been controversial to some liberals of his day, but is more so in ours. Tocqueville locates the height of religious influence in the private rather than public sphere, and he also endorses the division of labor by which women are mainly concerned with domestic life (279, 573ff). As a result of this division, Tocqueville speaks of American women as less possessed than their male counterparts by the frenetic spirit of commerce and the tumultuous mentality of democratic politics, and consequently more open to the dominion of religion in the place where it counts most: in the soul itself. Tocqueville has doubts about the authenticity or depth of belief of many professed Christians in America, noting the sizable overlap between religious zeal and the perceived conditions of political liberty, material prosperity, and self-interest well-understood (278ff, 504ff). Where religion is merely capable of moderating the worldliness of the American male, however, Tocqueville observes that "it reigns as a sovereign over the soul of woman." This is especially significant, since "it is woman who makes mores" as the primary educator of children (279).[45]

To the extent that Christianity holds genuine sway over souls in America— and Tocqueville believes it does (278)—it does so because of the willingness of clergy and women[46] to separate themselves from the flux of commercial and political affairs and cultivate the faith in a realm whose separation helps to preserve its integrity and influence over individuals. That Tocqueville does not consider such separation degrading to either women or clergy can be seen by considering the third group he advises to remain aloof from political affairs: students of ancient literature and of the classical virtue it articulates (450ff).

The writings of ancient authors can serve as a valuable corrective to the deficiencies of democracy, but only if cultivated outside the stream of democratic affairs and applied prudentially by wise leaders to the radically different circumstances of modern times. In his discussion of the role of women in American society, Tocqueville describes American women as exemplifying the main features of classical prudence: self-control, astuteness as to the perils and promises of human affairs, and a critical perspective on the ability of dominant democratic pursuits to provide happiness (563ff, 573ff). Likewise, Tocqueville describes the effect of Sunday public worship and private Scriptural study as opening the democratic soul to an account of its own potential virtue and happiness (517ff). Though it may seem odd to associate the domesticated woman with the leisured pursuant of classical wisdom, it is well to consider the definition of leisure given by Xenophon's Socrates: the leaving off of a lesser work to take up a greater one.[47] Education in a true sense requires a turning from the ephemeral to the enduringly true, and the nexus of religion, classical wisdom, and domestic life can aim at the implementation of this insight even in the heart of a regime all but completely turned to material success—so long as this nexus is preserved by respect for the distinct sphere in which it is pursued.[48]

None of this is to suggest, however, that Tocqueville believes that religion can hold sway in total isolation from political affairs, or that political authority plays no role in bringing "men back toward spiritualist [sic] opinions or [keeping] them in the religion that evokes them." To the contrary, Tocqueville gives advice on this score that he knows will harm him "in the eyes of politicians":

> I believe that the only efficacious means governments can use to put the dogma
> of the immortality of the soul in honor is to act every day as if they themselves
> believed it; and I think it is only in conforming scrupulously to religious moral-
> ity in great affairs that they can flatter themselves they are teaching citizens to
> know it, love it, and respect it in small ones (521).

Without violating the separation of church and state, the authority of the latter can reinforce that of the former—which in turn contributes to the continued liberty of political society—through the example of leaders willingly limiting themselves by a transcendent notion of justice most clearly communicated to society through the medium of religion.

What results did Tocqueville expect his strategy for preserving the influence of Christianity in modern times to yield if properly implemented? As we have already intimated, Tocqueville does not believe that modern democracy will ever become permeated by the spirit of classical virtue or its otherworldly supporter, Christianity. Tocqueville admits outright that, in a Christian liberal democracy, many professed believers will be entirely cold to the faith, paying it public respects out of self-interest, public-spiritedness, or an unwillingness to disturb the consciences of others (278).[49] As with other elements of his political thought, however, Tocqueville insists that virtue be pursued without demanding that the law, per impossible, deliver the absolute good (13).

Even when it does not penetrate all hearts, "a public opinion in favor of religion" has many salutary effects for individuals and for political society. It checks the instability of desires and renders citizens more law-abiding while simultaneously encouraging vigilance against the "impious" claims of political authorities to possess unlimited power (278ff). It therefore fosters civil liberty, grounding it in beliefs about the universal brotherhood of humankind, while checking the excesses of liberty that might otherwise lead to liberty's self-destruction. It cannot bring the average democratic citizen or democracy as a whole to give up the relentless pursuit of material well-being and the resultant neglect of moral and intellectual goods (423). Yet it does create an environment in which souls remain aware of these higher alternatives and are less embarrassed to pursue them (517ff). It therefore contributes monumentally to liberty by checking the forces that would otherwise browbeat the soul into accepting the inevitability of a degrading confinement to petty and material pleasures, freeing a path by which the most vigorous souls can break free from the crowd and pursue those goods that constitute the greatness and happiness of the human species (663ff, 509). In this way Tocqueville sees Christianity not only as an indispensible foundation for the institutions of modern liberal democracy themselves, but also as a necessary guarantor of that genuine liberty and justice rooted in the natural needs of the human race (11, 43, 240).

Notes

1. An earlier version of this chapter was presented at the 66th Annual National Conference of the Midwest Political Science Association in April of 2008.

2. Tocqueville's language expresses an emphatically natural relationship between action (effect) and idea (cause): "*Il n'y a presque point d'action humaine . . . qui ne prenne naissance dans une idée tres generale. . . .*"

3. Tocqueville here distances himself even from his great mentor Montesquieu. Despite his "complex" view of human nature and organic approach to implementing modernity (Carrese 2003), Montesquieu regarded religious sentiments as byproducts of frustrated material desires (1989, 61, 479ff). Tocqueville twice airs his reservations about Montesquieu's materialism in *Democracy* (89, 567).

4. For an account of how René Descartes might respond to Tocqueville, see Hebert (2007).

5. Ceaser notes that Tocqueville sees "the entire structure" of liberal democracy as resting on a foundation deeper than the separation of "the political . . . the cultural, the religious, or the economic"; at this deeper level, "there is constant interaction among

these spheres," interactions that "hold the key to whether the foundation can support the edifice built upon it" (1990, 33-34).

6. See especially his letters to Gobineau of October 2 and 22, 1843 (1959a, 204ff).

7. See especially Kant (1983), whom Tocqueville describes as a post-Christian thinker (1959a, 208).

8. See Jardin (1988) and Kessler (1994).

9. See Jardin (1988, 528ff).

10. Tocqueville (1985, 29); Lively (1962, 8); Zetterbaum (1967, 145). Ceaser notes that Tocqueville "is one of the few genuine supporters of traditional religion among the great liberal democratic thinkers" (1990, 166).

11. See Machiavelli's *Prince* (1985), especially chapters III and XV.

12. The latter is most clearly articulated in Hobbes (1994, I-XI).

13. Thus Tocqueville predicts that democratic peoples will lean toward pantheism. This doctrine appeals to both sides of the human heart—its desire for material and for spiritual goods—while destroying the tension between them with its claim that material and immaterial things are part of a gargantuan undifferentiated mixture (419). Tocqueville refuses to call pantheism a religion because it destroys the hierarchy between these desires in the soul, and the cosmic order to whose contemplation the higher longings of the soul draw us, thereby rendering human greatness impossible (517ff). See Bellah (1975; 1988-2007, 231ff) and Kessler (1994).

14. As a saying inspired by G. K. Chesterton has it, when one ceases to believe in God one will believe in anything.

15. The negative view—that human life requires the "horizon" provided by cosmic order, while reason exposes the non-existence of any such order—is articulated by Friedrich Nietzsche (1980). It leads him to conclude that man must "create" what does not objectively exist, that meaning must be the product of an extraordinarily powerful human will, in defiance of "true but deadly truths." In this way, Nietzsche takes to its ultimate conclusion the premise that reason is the instrument of passion, reducing truth itself to a weapon with which one clears the way for new creations of the human will, whose ends are once again cosmic in scope.

16. See also Tocqueville's Speech to the Academy of Moral and Political Sciences (1991).

17. For a contrasting view, see Lawler (1993, 81-93). Lawler nicely traces the ways in which, in Tocqueville's account, reason and nature can guide the proper ranking of human achievements, rendering political science possible, before himself concluding that Tocqueville is too Pascalian to believe this. This study tends to support Robert Eden's characterization of Tocqueville's doubts as a "skepticism . . . inseparable from a defense of his own intellectual health and freedom" (1990, 380ff).

18. See Plato's *Phaedo* (1998), *Symposium* (1997), and *Apology* (1984).

19. See Aristotle, quoted in Aquinas (1947, Q1 A5), and Strauss (1959, 11).

20. Here it is interesting to consider the analogy drawn by Mark Kremer (2004) between the Platonic character Cleitophon, whose disappointment with philosophy misconceived as the guarantor of social harmony drives him to embrace a thoughtless legal positivism, and contemporary post-Enlightenment disillusionment with reason. Our "post-modern" world tends either to reject all systems of belief as groundless, or to embrace contrary beliefs indiscriminately in blissful indifference to their conflicting bases.

21. Not surprisingly, Tocqueville's formulations of Christianity differ subtly but significantly from orthodox expressions of the faith. Specifically, Tocqueville emphasizes the contemplation of God's will, which can be seen in the natural order of things ascer-

tainable to human reason in this life; missing from his account is any reference to the vision of God Himself attainable only through the infusion of divine grace in the next life. Compare Aquinas (1947, I-II Q3 A8: "God alone constitutes man's happiness"), and even Rousseau's Savoyard Vicar (1979, 277, 293, 283, 311), who is more orthodox on this point than is Tocqueville. Compare Kraynak (1995, 215).

22. See Aquinas (1947, especially Q1).

23. See Tocqueville (1990b, 18): "In the Middle Ages . . . philosophy, that natural antagonist of authority itself, itself . . . took the form of authority, having cloaked itself in the character of a religion."

24. Thus Mitchell goes too far when he attributes to Tocqueville the belief that all men are made for obedience (1995, 63ff).

25. Tocqueville does observe that public opinion in America prevents the publication of books attacking religion (245), and he cites a case in which testimony by a professed atheist was disallowed in court (280). He also illustrates by his own behavior, however, that one need not attack religion or openly profess one's atheism in order to maintain and even to communicate one's skepticism about religion in a prudent fashion.

26. References in this chapter to L'Ancien Régime are to Tocqueville (1988) and translations are mine.

27. Zetterbaum holds that Tocqueville endorses this goal and believes democracy can achieve it (1967, 35-39). Our reasons for disagreeing follow in the text.

28. "Simple virtue," Tocqueville maintains, "lives on itself and is satisfied with its own witness," and thus transcends honor, which seeks the esteem of one's peers (598).

29. For a critique of contemporary strands of normative theory based on this insight, see Ceaser (1991).

30. See Tocqueville's letter to Kergorlay of June 29, 1831 (1985) and his letters to Gobineau of October 2 and 22, 1843 (1959a).

31. Friedrich Hayek (1994).

32. A telling objection here would be that, on Tocqueville's own account, the quasi-religion of the French Revolution was capable of inspiring soldiers, apostles, and even martyrs. This objection is partially correct. Tocqueville explains the zeal inspired by doctrines of natural rights in terms of the particular struggle that must be waged against their foes (2000a, 10). The zeal fades in proportion to the success of such struggles. Thus the defeat of the nobility removed the cause of hostility to the Church, which had been entangled with the enemy class (1988, 103). The zeal inspired by democracy itself—often identified, rightly or wrongly, with the zeal for natural justice—will be kindled to the extent that obstacles to perfect equality remain. In this sense, the zeal inspired by democratic quasi-religion can be expected to grow as advances in equality make remaining inequalities stand out and appear all the more frustrating (2000a, 645). Tocqueville's core objection is that this zeal will impel citizens toward an increasingly unreasonable and inhumane mode of governance and way of life, rather than moderating democratic extremes as does Christianity.

33. See Jardin (1988, 59-60).

34. See Cicero (1928, De Re Publica I.13, III.22; De Legibus I.4-12, I.22-24, II.4-5).

35. See St. Augustine (1993, II, IV, VI-VII), Ernest Fortin (1996, Volume II, Chapter 1), Mary Keys (2006).

36. In the Middle Ages, "a man regarded it as an enormous injury to receive a blow on the cheek and was obliged to kill in single combat whoever had thus lightly struck him" (591). Compare Matthew 5.39.

37. In *L'Ancien Régime*, Tocqueville lauds priests' and even bishops' participation in political affairs. He has high praise for the "Catholic clergy," whose landed property once made them "one of the very great elements of liberty" in France. He concludes that "despite the brilliant vices of some of its members, there has never been in the world a clergy more remarkable than the Catholic clergy of France when it was surprised by the Revolution – none more enlightened, more national, less wrapped up in private virtues alone, better supplied with public virtues, and at the same time with more faith" (1988, 199ff).

38. For a brief discussion of this, see our next chapter.

39. He notes that, in Jacksonian America, observance of Sunday rest is frequently mandated by law (681ff); belief in God is a prerequisite for testimony in court (280); all public figures "are obliged to profess openly a certain respect for the morality and equity of Christianity," which is considered the bedrock of liberal democracy (280-81); and "the greater part of education is entrusted to the clergy" (283).

40. See his letter to Kergorlay of June 19, 1831 (1985, 46ff).

41. "This so-called tolerance," Tocqueville wrote, "in my opinion, is nothing but a huge indifference " (1985, 48-49). Unlike Locke, who defines a Church as "a voluntary Society of Men" (1983, 28), Tocqueville wrote that "a religion (the word is used here in the vulgar sense) is an association where one alienates his liberty in a permanent manner. It is necessary to have associations of this kind" (1990b, 20). "In metaphysics and in morals and in religion," he wrote, "authority appears to me more necessary and less injurious than in politics, the sciences, and the arts" (1990b, 215). "General ideas relative to God and human nature are . . . the ones it is most fitting to shield from the habitual action of individual reason and for which there is most to gain and least to lose in recognizing an authority" (2000, 418). The primacy of faith (hence voluntary obedience to authority [compare 43]) is a doctrine necessary to religion, whose "consequence is a certain amount of intolerance," but "the damage . . . to human morality thereby caused is far less than would result from moral systems that have emancipated themselves from religion altogether" (1959a, 205-6).

42. This threat is well articulated by Manent (1996, 86-103) and Kessler (1994, 97, 125, 182, 149ff), both of whom doubt that Tocqueville's strategy can overcome it. They fear that popular civil religion will fail to find leverage outside the utilitarian and self-regarding proclivities of the majority. We may briefly respond by noting that Tocqueville finds his ultimate leverage in human nature itself, and that the point of his strategy is not necessarily to usher in a new age of faith, but to stave off the most extreme forms of democratic individualism – an accomplishment both authors agree even this civil religion can accomplish. See also Kraynak (2001, 190, 220).

43. See 1990b, 15 (in a draft of *Democracy*): "The Protestant Religion (perhaps it is not necessary to touch on religions, or as little as possible, for fear of burning my fingers)."

44. By contrast, Nathaniel Morton understood Reformation without any reference to reason or doubt: it is "witnessing against Humane Inventions, and Additions in the Worship of God, but minding most the positive and practical part of Divine Instructions. . . . To walk with God, and one with another, in the enjoyment of the Ordinances of God, according to the Primitive Pattern of the Word of God" (1937, 1-2). In Tocqueville's view, however, there ultimately can be no means of fixing the true "pattern" of religion without resort to the authority of the Church on the one hand, or to individual reason and will on the other. Without Church authority, therefore, religion is ultimately defenseless against the perils of modern democratic individualism.

45. For insightful accounts of Tocqueville's discussion of women in America, see Kessler (1994, 123), Kristol (1991), Elshtain (2000), and Winthrop (1986).

46. Delba Winthrop brilliantly analyzes this parallel (1986).

47. See *Memorabilia* (1994).

48. See Tocqueville's end-note on "the trials to which the women of America who consent to accompany their spouses [to the frontier] are often subjected." Tocqueville emphasizes the concern of women to preserve the religion, intellectual life, and hospitality of Christian culture. In their hands, the frontier cabin becomes "the ark of civilization lost in the middle of an ocean of foliage" (699-701).

49. As Kessler notes (1994, 156), Tocqueville makes much of religion's role throughout *Democracy*, but silently drops references to it in his closing chapters, including his final list of methods to "make liberty issue from the bosom of democratic society" (666-73). Koritansky (1986, 17, 61, 99ff, 119-20, 140-45) notes that Tocqueville employs numerous means of elevating democratic souls, including poetry, history, commercial honor, and even warfare, all of which are intended to preserve the use of our highest faculties against the stultifying effects of individualism (Tocqueville 2000a, 426-33, 458-63, 465-72, 589-99). Religion and political decentralization remain Tocqueville's primary weapons against individualism, but they are put forth for the consideration of statesmen who must respond to varying actual circumstances in a prudential, and not in a doctrinaire, spirit.

Videte quoniam non soli mihi laboravi,
sed omnibus exquirentibus veritatem.

Chapter 6
Democratic Statesmanship Then and Now

"A fine book that, though special to America, ought to be familiar to statesmen of every country" (108). Thus did Tocqueville describe the *Federalist*, a work whose defense of the American Constitution undergirds Tocqueville's account of the genius of federal government in America. The same words might apply with at least equal force to *Democracy in America* itself. While the *Federalist* by its very nature had to deal primarily with the limited, though vital, concerns originally entrusted to the national government, *Democracy* explores the life of a great republic from bottom to top, in its external and internal operations, in light of its past and future as well as its present, and in relation to the perennial questions of moral and political philosophy. While the *Federalist* was itself a work of statesmanship, meant to secure the ratification of a particular plan of government, *Democracy* is a work written for the instruction and guidance of statesmen and other citizens whose influence (individual or collective) may run deeper than that of any government leader or legislator. It transcends disputes over specific forms of government and instead seeks to penetrate the natures of democracy and of man, so that, with the assistance of a new political science, the two may be harmonized, or their tension reduced, so far as possible. Since the means of effecting this harmony must vary according to time and place—due to geography, economy, and especially mores—the book must look beyond the particular promises and perils facing a given people at a given time.

Though *Democracy*'s purpose is eminently practical, it is practical in the broadest sense of the term. As with the political science of Aristotle and Montesquieu, to which commentators old and new have compared it,[1] Tocqueville's practicality demands the most rigorous use of our theoretical faculties, without which we cannot grasp the most fundamental problems of our political situation, much less evaluate the potential solutions to those problems. True practicality must begin by understanding the ultimate goal of human action, which for Tocqueville is nothing less than justice or the "absolute good" of man understood as the fulfillment of his nature through association with the order of the cosmos of which he is a part. Only in light of this standard can one study the

159

socio-political terrain of one's time and place with an eye for what is truly significant within it: the obstacles it poses and aids it proffers to the achievement (or approximation) of this absolute good. What's more, Tocqueville holds that this political terrain is itself divisible into proximate variations (the most significant being the national character of a people) and semi-universal, semi-permanent features, such as "democracy" or "aristocracy," equality or inequality of social conditions. Any actual political environment will be defined by a wide panoply of influences ranging from the natural to the semi-natural to the unique and accidental; any actual statesman (or citizen) will have to factor in all of these variables as much as humanly possible in order to decide on any particular course of action.

The above considerations point to two conclusions. First, Tocqueville's *Democracy in America* aims at providing the framework for a new liberal-democratic politics that can and ought to be practiced not just in the United States or France of Tocqueville's day, but in any society defined by conditions of social equality. In other words, his thought should be as relevant to the America of today as to that of the mid-nineteenth century. Second, the evaluation of Tocqueville's thought and its application to contemporary issues is no simple task. Tocqueville's relevance cannot be confined to a host of observations about Americans that still ring true, or to a handful of predictions that have come uncannily close to the mark, though both elements contribute to the charm and credibility of his writing.

In fact, it is especially where Tocqueville's precise descriptions no longer apply and where his anticipations grow obscure that we encounter the gravest threats to and greatest hopes for the health of modern democratic life, and thus stand in greatest need of Tocqueville's political science. For instance, one can no longer say that Americans have definitively defeated individualism as Tocqueville defines it through the mediation of local civic institutions that form half the existence of citizens (486, 233), or that Christianity is avowedly the first political institution of the United States (280). Nor can one maintain that the globe is or will be divided between the influence of Russia and Anglo-America, each representing distinct and opposing manifestations of social equality (395). Though the Cold War and American exceptionalism still loom large in our consciousness, our self-understanding as a free people has been increasingly challenged by revolutions in practice and in theory, culminating in ever-more fundamental moral and political disagreements, just as foreign policy has been complicated by multipolarity and global uncertainty about the meaning of justice, democracy, and civilization.

The true test of Tocqueville's political science is its applicability to these ambiguous features of modern political life. Can Tocqueville help to explain why we face the challenges we do and how we might overcome them? To answer this question requires, at minimum, a thorough understanding of his political science, as well as a broad and profound familiarity with the history and current state of democracy in the world. This study has attempted to provide, however inadequately, a brief but cogent account of the first prerequisite; the second is decidedly beyond the scope of the present chapter or its author. Yet on the basis of broad and evident trends in politics, economics, morality, religion, and public discourse, it is both possible and necessary to test the extent to which Tocqueville's thought illuminates the present and future of liberal democratic society. With this in mind, the following pages will relate the influence of equality in its various forms, especially under the aegis of the doctrines of natural and human rights, to the growth of individualism in the past century and a half; compare Tocqueville's analysis of individualism to the observations of the growing ranks of commentators and scholars who have noted the decline of public-spiritedness and loss of animating purpose in contemporary American democracy; and consider the viability of attempts to mitigate individualism and promote moral, intellectual, and civic virtue in modern times.

Tocqueville: Prophet or Guide?

Tocqueville's reputation as a prophet, whatever its supports in the annals of commentary, originates in his own rhetorical devices. Tocqueville begins and ends *Democracy* by stressing the inevitable and even providential character of equality (6ff, 674ff). For Tocqueville, the democratic social state is both an "accomplished fact" and the basis for all accounts of the present and future; though other causes will continue to play a role in political affairs, Tocqueville chooses to speak of these other causes only insofar as they are affected by equality (13, 399). All of the phenomena Tocqueville anticipates in democratic times—individualism and administrative despotism included—are rooted in the exigencies of a world in which equality is the "generative fact" and "mother idea" (3, 480). Yet it would not be right to suppose that equality itself is the "mother thought" Tocqueville bids the reader to uncover in his book (14). For though equality is the basis of Tocqueville's power of prediction, Tocqueville deplores the kind of historiography—or social science, as we call it—that stakes its claims purely on predictive power, reducing human affairs to a conflux of irresistible forces and thereby robbing human actors of their dignity and freedom (469ff).[2]

Left to itself, Tocqueville predicts, equality will have devastating effects on the human soul and political society. The natural tendency of human beings mesmerized by the spirit of democracy is one of atomization, mass conformity, and bureaucratic banality. Equality will make despotism easy and even "natural," relative to the social state, while rendering genuine liberty difficult and, in the same sense, "artificial" (643ff). Yet the goal of Tocqueville's book is to combat individualism, not to surrender to it; had he believed the battle lost, he would have confined himself to groaning in secret about the fate of his fellows (643, 672). If liberty in modern times must be the product of art, modern man at least retains his artistic capacity; moreover, the attempt to secure liberty will always find support not only in human nature proper, but even in certain dispositions inculcated by equality itself (89-90, 639-40). So long as citizens retain the use of their free will, civic science and civil rhetoric can marshal reason, habit, and passion to strive against the new form of despotism Tocqueville fears. Though Providence "has not created the human race . . . entirely independent," neither has it deprived us of all freedom and power. We cannot escape the challenges of democracy, but we can choose how to respond to them. It therefore depends on us whether equality leads to servitude, barbarism, and misery, on the one hand, or liberty, enlightenment, and prosperity, on the other (676).

Tocqueville's "mother thought" in *Democracy*, therefore, is not equality alone, but rather equality seen in light of "the just and the good," and therefore in light of the choice it offers us between a certain species of happiness and a certain species of misery. The test of Tocqueville's relevance, then, is not whether he accurately predicts the minute details of our current situation—which he neither claimed to do nor would have desired the ability to do. The test is instead whether Tocqueville's account of equality itself, the dangers it entails, and the means of combating those dangers, meaningfully corresponds to the struggles and changes, the hopes and fears that have, for better or worse, marked the progress of liberal democracy to this day. In the following sections, reflection on the increasing prominence of equality and democracy in the self-understanding of Americans, coupled with significant changes in civic life, law, morality, and religious belief, will suggest that Tocqueville's fears regarding the susceptibility of democratic citizens to extreme individualism and administrative despotism were well grounded and relevant to our current political condition. It will also suggest that his hopes can still be ours, if we so choose.

Equality and the Radicalization of Rights

Tocqueville's evidence for the providential character of equality was not that equality had gone or would go unopposed in modern society. When he wrote the original Introduction to *Democracy*, France was ruled by a king backed by the middle classes, who had temporarily grown tired of the turmoil to which revolutionary egalitarianism had given birth. Tocqueville warned the apparent victors of that moment that they were vastly underestimating the power of equality. He sought to persuade them and all the reactionaries of his day to instruct democracy rather than combat it, pointing out that hitherto democracy had advanced by the efforts not only of "those who fought for it," but even of "those who declared themselves its enemies" (6). Given that conditions were becoming more and more equal in Europe, the opposition of a few to its advance only inflamed the partisanship of those who hoped to hasten its reign (10).

This paradoxical dynamic should be at least as familiar to the twenty-first century reader as it would have been to Tocqueville's immediate audience. In the past century and a half, the limitations and dangers of exaggerated or simplified versions of equality and liberty have not escaped the opprobrium of intellectuals and revolutionaries. Though Tocqueville anticipated these shortcomings of modern democracy, and though we will highlight some of them in what follows, it must be acknowledged from the outset that the greatest violations of justice in recent times have originated with those who have most vigorously opposed the equal liberty of men: slaveholders and segregationists, social Darwinists and social engineers, fascists, communists, and their sympathizers.[3] In all of these cases, the challenge to equal liberty has provoked Americans and others to rise to its defense, strengthening and even radicalizing the role this concept plays in forming the American national character. At bottom, this response is salutary, harmonizing with Tocqueville's demonstration that equal liberty is the only legitimate basis of modern political society. Yet Tocqueville also warns that a radicalized notion of equality, and a corrupted sense of liberty, can and may lead to injustices of a less violent but ultimately grave sort: those of individualism and the administrative despotism to which it gives rise. If, as this chapter argues, we face these very dangers in our time, it is now more crucial than ever that responsible citizens follow Tocqueville's advice to embrace liberal democracy, while simultaneously striving to direct it in light of a moral order rooted in the natural needs and virtuous potential of humankind.

What does it mean to say that opposition to equal liberty has provoked the radicalization of that idea? Before elaborating this critique it is necessary to stress that, in many respects, the persistent devotion to equal liberty Americans and others have displayed in the past century and a half constitutes an edifying spectacle of courage and wisdom and has been the source of many advances in human dignity. In the events leading to and including the Civil War, Americans were tempted to endorse or turn a blind eye to the systematic exploitation of their fellows, but instead fought a bloody war against it to the end. The legacy of Lincolnian America includes not only the abolition of slavery, but also the constitutional redefinition of citizenship guaranteeing federal protection of the equal rights of all citizens[4]—a guarantee that, while often honored in the breach, has served as the basis for continual and genuine progress in civil rights ever since. Similarly, confronted with the erection of an industrial oligarchy apparently indifferent to or unable to help the plight of millions of laborers, Americans embraced the creation of new institutions designed to maintain the minimal conditions of human dignity for all.[5] Finally, faced with the horrors to which racism, propaganda, and totalitarian socialism can lead, Americans joined the fight against fascism and led the struggle—material and moral—against Soviet communism through the second half of the twentieth century.

In none of these areas has America been alone. While sometimes ahead and sometimes behind on particular points of political progress, America continues to be, as it was for Tocqueville, a symbol of the freedom and equality to which all the world feels itself drawn, whether by longer or shorter paths. In many or most cases, the complaints about America that one often hears in foreign lands are reducible to disagreements over political means rather than ends, or even to mere jealousy over the possession of agreed means to agreed ends. Thus the fall of the Berlin Wall and collapse of the Soviet Union gave swift credibility to the theory that the liberal democracy for which America stands is the inevitable and desirable end-product of a progressive historical process—an argument that can still be made, though with greater effort, in the face of the challenge posed to democracy by Islamist extremism.[6]

Without belittling these achievements, the "hard friend" of democracy—to use a Nietzschean term for an equally Tocquevillian virtue[7]—is compelled to ask tough questions about the costs incurred in these advances for equal liberty, and even about the depth and nobility of the self-understanding frequently associated with the triumphs of equal liberty. Though "human liberty"—that is, the liberty possessed equally by all human beings from birth—is indeed "the source of all moral greatness," the love of equality is susceptible to a perversion, sometimes invisible to the lover, that sets it at odds with human greatness (11, 413, 52), while liberty is easily misinterpreted as a freedom from responsibility and for petty pleasures rather than the freedom to pursue true happiness by sacrificing for higher goods (42, 482ff). To what extent has modern liberal democracy made a distinction between the legitimate and illegitimate forms of equal liberty and sought to preserve and promote the conditions of genuine liberty and human greatness? Or to what extent has it abandoned (consciously or not) such conditions in the name of its "eternal love," equality? The more closely we consider this question from a Tocquevillian point of view, the greater cause we have for concern about the health of contemporary democratic civilization.

Signs of radicalization begin to emerge when we consider the leading idea by which America and, with certain reservations, most other liberal democracies, have come to define democracy: the protection of equal individual rights. Though its roots are in older British documents and its American form goes back to the Declaration of Independence, the practical and psychological weight of "rights talk" grew exponentially in the early to mid twentieth century. As Tocqueville predicted (228), the decline of religious and traditional authority left rights as protected by law the strongest if not the unique standard by which democratic liberty can be structured in modern times.[8] Against slavery, economic exploitation, totalitarianism, racial discrimination, communism, and other evils, the language of rights has served as a touchstone for the advancement of liberty and justice in the modern era. It constitutes both the core of American national character and, to a lesser but growing extent, the focus of a growing global consensus around a regime of "human rights." It is here that we must begin our evaluation of the manner in which modern democracies, and especially the United States, have understood the concept of equal liberty and applied it to the myriad problems of modern life.

At first glance, the contemporary notion of rights would seem right in line with Tocqueville's recommendations for modern societies. Tocqueville opens his book by declaring the necessity of giving rights "to each citizen or to no one" (52); he closes it with a call to limit social power in the name of individual rights (669-70). As we have seen, however, Tocqueville never discusses the idea of equal or individual rights without explicitly referring such rights and the liberty they protect to moral order and the conditions for human greatness. Indeed, he goes so far as to define the notion of rights as the idea of virtue applied to the political world, and to limit liberty to doing "all that is just and good" (272, 42). The rights of the individual cannot be understood apart from the nature of the individual, and it is precisely on this point—human nature and the proper ends of human action—that Tocqueville stands opposed to prevailing modern rights theories.

As our study has shown, Tocqueville sharply distinguishes two types of individualism. The first, which he refers to as virtue or greatness, perfects the individual by drawing him out of his petty affairs and engaging him through political, spiritual, or intellectual association with the order of things around him: political society, human nature, and cosmic or divine order. Such virtue may be perceived as a threat or a promise, a boon or an injury, by any given society, but it scarcely permits its possessor to live unnoticed by or indifferent to the fate of his fellows. The second individualism, which Tocqueville calls by that name, seeks precisely to confine the life of each citizen to his own private realm, dissuading him from cultivating any meaningful engagement with the larger world, and reducing most human interactions to the instrumentality of private interests. It is against such individualism that Tocqueville developed and promulgated his political science, but it is toward such individualism that a great many developments of the modern concept of rights have, wittingly or unwittingly, taken us.

Under what conditions do rights promote human greatness or its opposite? In speaking of rights as virtue introduced into politics, Tocqueville is thinking primarily of political rights: those rights by which "each [citizen], in his sphere, takes an active part in the government of society," developing a sense of duty toward and pride in the political order resulting from his cooperation with his fellows, and hence achieving what Tocqueville poetically styles "the spirit of the city" (226-27). Such public-spiritedness does not preclude personal egoism; indeed, Tocqueville famously observes how Americans derive a "lofty idea of political rights" from the moral starting-point of self-interest well-understood (228, 500ff). Yet the spirit of the city cannot be reduced to any utilitarian calculus. Though it is useful to show the skeptical citizen the intersection between the public interest and his own—the proposal that a road be put through his property, for instance (487)—such instances, however numerous, can never add up to a genuine concern for the public good as such. There is a world of difference between the citizen who takes pride in contributing to the common good of his fellows, seeing it as his own, and one who cares for public business only when and to the extent that it promotes his private advantage; and it is the transition from the latter to the former condition that stirs Tocqueville's admiration for the victory nineteenth century Americans had won versus individualism (488, 502).

In part, the difference between these two citizens is practical: citizens who are selfish in the latter sense can contribute neither to reasoned discourse about the public interest—discourse that aims at what is truly good rather than at a mere compromise among selfish desires—nor the personal sacrifices upon which public prosperity ultimately depends. On the deepest level, however, the impracticality of narrow egoism stems from its qualitative deficiencies. Tocqueville admits that the replacement of citizenship by the centralized administration of political affairs is capable of achieving manifest gains in short-term efficiency. This renders it attractive both to citizens fixated on immediate material gain, and to administrators who believe their regulations can bring true and lasting benefits to society. What this semi-enlightened perspective misses, according to Tocqueville, is the fundamental human need to live in association with an order greater than oneself. By eliminating the sphere of politics properly so-called—deliberation about the means to the public good—and by severing citizens from what is left of politics, the regime of efficiency dries up the well of civic and even natural virtue, weakening the bond among citizens and between citizens and government. It changes the very experience of being human, reducing man from a citizen to a mere "administrated thing" (82ff, 64). This spiritual hollowing prepares the way for social decline, external conquest, domestic tyranny, and the seduction of religions and ideologies inconsistent with liberal democracy, but appearing to offer richer experiences of meaning and purpose than those found in "bourgeois" life. Thus do the unmitigated effects of equal liberty threaten to abolish equal liberty itself.

Tocqueville's appreciation of the value of association does not end at the political level, however. The soul's longing for meaning is ultimately nothing but the desire of each individual to associate himself with the admirable order of all things, an order to which all his actions will be directed, whatever his conception of it may be (504-5, 417). The thoughtless identification of this cosmic order with the particular features of one's social or political environment is the essence of barbarism for Tocqueville.[9] The human capacity to look beyond this immediate environment toward a cosmic order that transcends it is expressed in both philosophy and religion, but the serious pursuit of philosophy is by its very nature a rare thing. Only genuine religion is capable of turning the souls of an entire nation toward an order capable of moderating the excesses of the national character and even of the social state (417-18). For example, Tocqueville notes that American Christianity is both supportive of political liberty and critical of abuses of that liberty (275ff); both accommodating of the desire for wealth and insistent that true happiness only comes through the self-sacrificial practice of virtue (423, 517). Only religion can hope to depict, on the plane of public consciousness, the natural goodness of a truth that transcends, and the natural bounds of a justice that limits the political realm. From Tocqueville's perspective, then, it is essential to the cause of human liberty that the notion of rights never be divorced from the context of religious belief and worship.

Despite the necessity for and even the virtue of the defenses of equal liberty previously mentioned, their combined effect has been the shaping of a modern notion of rights increasingly disconnected from both forms of association mentioned above: the political and cosmic. The idea of rights entertained by leaders and public alike in modern democracies has come steadily closer to the radical individualism Tocqueville feared than to the healthy piety and civic-spiritedness he found in 1830s America. This shift, along with its civic and philosophical roots, has not escaped the attention of pundits and scholars, who have deplored and probed the causes of our contemporary loss of community, public-spiritedness, and common purpose. Several prominent scholars have traced these symptoms in part to a hypertrophy of "rights talk" and the shift toward a language of rights that regards them as unrealistically and unhelpfully absolute, individualistic, irresponsible, unsociable, and insular.[10] Before evaluating the soundness of such critiques, it is necessary to review briefly the development of this new American perspective on rights and its connection to the chief dangers Tocqueville associated with the unchecked influence of equality: political centralization and administrative control coupled with a radical individualism consisting in practical materialism, philosophic conformism, and moral relativism.

Administrative Centralization and the Decline of Citizenship

When Tocqueville wrote *Democracy*, America's political center of gravity was local. The Union, he wrote, was little more than an abstract notion in the minds of citizens, whose hearts were drawn to the idea of liberty as lived in states, counties, and townships (352). This attitude can be seen in the actions of men like Robert E. Lee, who fought for the South not so much for the ideas it advocated as from a sense of duty to his country: Virginia.[11] The Civil War, and the struggles for civil rights that followed it both immediately and at great length, were tests of the fundamental character and ends of the American people and their government. Unfortunately for us, these conflicts saw the principle of local self-government line up consistently against the principle of equal justice for all citizens. Over and over again, it was or appeared to be necessary to suppress liberty understood as self-rule in order to protect liberty understood as the equal protection of the law. What appeared to many to be a mere means (local government) to a higher end (equal liberty) seemed repeatedly incapable of achieving that end, until they concluded it would have to be laid aside for the sake of that higher end. To this day, the appeal to federalism or states' rights remains tainted by association with the perpetuation of local prejudice and injustice in the face of national standards of enlightenment and equity.

This association of political centralization with fundamental justice was reinforced by the economic challenges of the postbellum era and the character of the nation's response to them. As Tocqueville predicted, industrialization produced vast conglomerations of business interests against which individual citizens and groups of citizens seemed powerless (658). Since these corporations were national in scope, it was apparently only a matter of time before the powers of national government had to be enhanced in order to regulate an increasingly ubiquitous "interstate commerce." The failure of states and localities in this regard was literally dramatic. Films such as John Ford's *The Grapes of Wrath* portray the apparatuses of state and local police as archaic and venal, imposing a senseless multiplicity of rules obstructing the free flow of labor, and readily sell-ing out to the purchasing power of big business. Only the federal government seemed capable of amassing enough power and wisdom to restructure the eco-nomic and political life of the nation so as to restore and even recreate, on a new basis, the enjoyment of freedom and equality. The New Deal established a new set of rights that, though still not enshrined in our Constitution, have never since been repudiated by any major politician or political party—rights that are guar-anteed to the individual by the federal government with minimal influence from intermediate bodies of government or society.

A further contributor to the centralization of American politics, de facto and de jure, has been the involvement of the United States in global conflict, both military and ideological. As Tocqueville noted, war is the greatest administrative centralizer of all (378, 621). Though the distant nature of the wars in question has no doubt moderated the effects of military mobilization on American socie-ty,[12] maintenance of "superpower" status depends on a national government in possession of vast and unobstructed power over a broad scope of economic and civic affairs. Were it necessary to repeat the extraordinary efforts of Washing-ton, Madison, or Lincoln to raise and keep an army fit for victory, the U.S. could not play the role that it does today in world politics.

In the realm of ideas a similar dynamic has applied. Our struggles against fascists, communists, and radical Islamists have heightened the importance of articulating a national creed based on human rights with which to distinguish ourselves from our foes. Though the idea of self-government has admittedly played a dominant role in this creed—witness the exportation of "self-determination" by Woodrow Wilson and the encouragement of "democracy" abroad by George W. Bush—this concept has had to be suited to its purpose. Asserted by certain "advanced" nations in their relations with others, it has not drawn attention to local civic or civil associations, at home or abroad. Though foreign policy is highly distinguishable from domestic policy, the change in em-phasis regarding America's self-presentation on the world stage—from demon-strating the success of democracy domestically to projecting democratic power worldwide—has exerted a further centralizing effect on the meaning of citizen-ship and rights for modern-day Americans.

Habits of liberty, once formed, do not die with a whimper. Discomfort with the loss of traditional freedoms is reflected in the noble efforts that have been made to uphold customary principles of self-rule and personal dignity even while erecting the mechanisms of centralized administration. America's "fourth branch of government," the bureaucracy, is neither a communist dictatorship, nor even as socialist an enterprise as many European democracies have adopted. Yet the concern to preserve the benefits of personal and local autonomy amidst the national regulation of affairs is as likely to create as to solve conundrums. Theodore Lowi has found, for instance, that, soon after their expansion under Franklin Roosevelt, federal agencies came to adopt a decentralized approach to the regulation of those spheres of life under their control. In doing so, they have tended to consult local groups composed of those specially interested in each sphere. Though it aims at the worthy goals of decentralization and checks and balances, this arrangement offends against the government of democracy in two important ways. First, it grants unspecified powers to agencies who are then able to rule with relatively little public accountability. Second, it grants special influence to various interest groups rather than to the entire community or its representatives. In other words, it cuts directly against the virtues of public-spiritedness and concern for the common good that constitute the chief advantages of local administration in Tocqueville's view.[13]

Another compromise with mixed blessings at best is seen in the practice of indirect regulation through federal grants. Local associations, from states to townships to contractors and universities, are technically free to govern themselves in a number of ways; but many or most have become wholly dependent on federal funding, which comes with strings attached.[14] For example, the legal age for consuming alcohol has effectively been nationalized through the carrot-cum-stick of federal highway grants, which induce states to sacrifice local control over health and morals for the sake of their economic infrastructure.

In itself the implementation on the local level of rules made at a higher level is consistent with administrative decentralization as Tocqueville defines it. Yet the erosion of original decision-making power at levels of government accessible to citizens tends to have a degrading effect. This is so not only because local citizens may have a better sense of local needs than distant bureaucrats. Even when the reverse is true, governmental centralization robs citizens of the fundamental goods of self-government: serious deliberation and the intellectual and moral benefits it brings. In light of the goodness of democracy as self-government, succumbing to federal control retains something of the character of being bought off, even when one is being bought off by a higher level of government over which citizens have some (if miniscule) control. Inevitably, the non-use of those intellectual and moral faculties necessary to make important decisions tends to have a stultifying effect on the human soul (665). The widespread apathy regarding politics frequently deplored today is no doubt connected to the removal of vital issues from the local level and the reduction of local government to an effectual subservience to federal agencies.

Much more could be said about the corrosive effects of bureaucracy on political life. In Tocqueville's day, central government, whether federal or state, handled a few general matters; it submitted these matters to the deliberation of legislators selected by the people for this purpose; and it often counted on the cooperation of separately elected local officials for their enforcement (63). It thus blended democracy both of a participative and of a representative sort, weaving a web of checks and balances that, for all its complexity, clearly rested on the will of the community as expressed in an ever broadening suffrage (165ff, 691n8). Today, by contrast, central governments (both federal and state) handle an endless array of issues; submit them to legislators who must delegate most details to various aides and advisors; and entrust their further development as well as enforcement to a massive bureaucracy over which neither the people nor their representatives proper exercise much control. It may be an exaggeration to say that the people's liberties have been reduced to selecting its schoolmasters (664), but it is hard to deny that modern democracies have taken a decisive step in the direction of the benevolent despotism Tocqueville warns against in the final pages of *Democracy*.

Judicial Power and the Rise of Individualism

Of all the institutions Tocqueville thought capable of opposing individualism and sustaining civic virtue, there is one whose record in recent years has been particularly disappointing: the courts, whom we have entrusted with the power to regulate any and all governmental actions according to the provisions of our federal Constitution. When we think of rights today we are far more likely to credit their defense to courts than to any other institution of government. To a considerable degree, Americans have accepted the growth of bureaucracy and entrusted their central governments with greater administrative authority because of the confidence inspired by the judicial guarantee of individual rights.[15] Tocqueville foresaw this connection between courts and the protection of rights. As we have seen, he noted the tremendous power of courts in the American system, and the influence of the legal class in educating the citizenry in the existence and nature of their liberties. He hoped that this power would be used to mitigate the extremes of equality and individualism, and called upon lawyers and judges to practice true statesmanship in this regard (93ff, 142, 251ff, 668ff). As it happens, the power of courts and legal practitioners has proved every bit as influential as Tocqueville predicted. Yet, as we shall now see, the individualistic brand of liberty often promoted by our courts has on the whole contributed to the disdain for local autonomy, the decline in public-spiritedness, and the obfuscation of moral purpose plaguing our civic life today.

The centrality of courts to our self-understanding as modern democratic citizens is witnessed by the obedience and even veneration given to certain of their pronouncements by virtually all of us. Consider the popular awareness and acceptance of "Miranda rights," whose meticulous imposition on local law enforcement has little to no constitutional or historical basis outside of a 1966 Supreme Court opinion.[16] Or consider the constitutional "separation of church and state" and the "right to privacy," both of which have radically altered and rigidly constrained the understanding and practice of American democracy with even less legal precedent or justification.[17] It is no jest to say that the rule of law has come very close to signifying the rule of lawyers—or of the elite among them, at any rate, whose opinions have produced an ever broader and more detailed set of rules constraining the choices of private and public actors. These rules have time and again effected drastic changes in the behavior of executives, legislatures, communities, associations, and individuals, and have even prevailed in the face of explosive or enduring opposition.

Given the degree and character of judicial influence, it is no surprise that both the substance of many rulings and the general principles underlying the exercise of judicial review have been subject to increasingly acrimonious dispute in recent decades. The stakes have risen for proponents of all interests and ideologies to obtain rulings furthering their favored policies.[18] As a matter of principle, however, theories of judicial review tend to fall on either side of a certain divide between those who insist upon the "strict" construction of legal texts and those who favor a freer adaptation of prior concepts to suit the interests of the moment. Broadly speaking, those taking the former line seek to constrain judges to follow the will of the majority or supermajority in whose name the law or other directive was made, while the latter group valorizes the role played by judges as transcendently wise figures who must regularly frustrate majoritarian injustices or douse the flames of tumultuous partisan quarreling.[19]

What light can Tocqueville shed on these disputes? Tocqueville's perspective on the matter can best be gleaned by noting the difficulty of determining what is fundamental about judicial decisions: their policy or precedent. That we have difficulty with this question is evident from the shifting position of parties over time: in Franklin Roosevelt's day, progressives decried the usurpation of authority by courts ready to twist the constitution to their counter-majoritarian ends;[20] today the same language is used by conservatives aghast at the way progressives have used judicial review to advance aspects of their agenda in the absence of or even against public consensus. For his part, Tocqueville seems to share this ambivalence. He mocks the tendency of common law judges to adhere slavishly to precedent, while lauding the stabilizing influence their tradition-bound behavior will exert over an otherwise careening democracy (255ff). Tocqueville declares the right of courts to decide cases to be inferior to that of society to make the law, but he also bids judges to follow in each case the law that is most binding upon them, while emphasizing that the "law" of natural justice is higher and more binding than that of "this or that society" (96, 240). He asks courts to resist majority tyranny and protect individual rights against state action, but also deplores the erosion of self-government under the influence of extreme individualism (668ff). One might conclude that Tocqueville presents no clear criteria for the exercise of judicial power in modern democratic times.

Though it would be futile to expect from Tocqueville a precise agenda for the courts of our day, he does have important advice on this subject, and working through the ambiguities in his presentation can be a helpful prelude to working out the complexities of our judicial politics. Those ambiguities can be resolved by reference to his fundamental principles. The goal of politics, according to Tocqueville, is the absolute good of man, but no set of laws can produce this good or even flawlessly facilitate it. The art of politics—which properly understood is the art of being free in a virtuous sense—consists in adapting imperfect means to the variable conditions of the day in order to approximate as closely as possible the unmoving goal of humankind. While it is generally advisable and even necessary that courts defer to the authority of the people as expressed in its Constitution and by its elected representatives, nothing can justify slavish adherence to any of these expressions when they flatly contradict natural justice. This means, among other things, that the equal rights of man ought, whenever possible, to be upheld by judges even when positive law would suggest otherwise.[21] Even in unexceptional cases, judges need not simply defer to the popular understanding of a given right when that understanding can be improved with reference to natural right.

Lest we confuse Tocqueville's position with that of the "living constitution" camp, however, we must observe that Tocqueville's advice is not for judges to rule in favor of equal justice, whatever they (or society as they read it) happen to believe that means. From the point of view of the philosopher or statesman, justice, and equality insofar as it is just, can only be understood on the basis of a profound comprehension of human nature and its needs (240). For this reason, interpretive methodology cannot be the ultimate question when justice is concerned. Naturally, Tocqueville would consider judges who are fundamentally mistaken about human nature to be, at bottom, bad judges, and so much the worse judges the more they show themselves independent of the guidance of others, including legislators whose text they are interpreting. In other words, it is naturally desirable that a wise judge have more latitude and an unwise one less in matters of jurisprudence. Yet it is precisely the unwise who are more likely to stake a claim to wisdom and therefore to employ this wider latitude. In light of this conundrum, Tocqueville's choice to hint at the propriety of such latitude for the benefit of those who will follow his arguments most closely, while leaving the overall impression that such judicial intervention is generally inappropriate (96), is perhaps the wisest course.

The most fundamental question, though, is not whether judges ought to interpret positive law in light of higher law, but what the higher law is in light of which they cannot help but interpret it, even if unconsciously. To be more precise, the Constitution (and other laws) contain words and expressions that range from perfectly evident to highly ambiguous. Very few schools of interpretation argue for decisions that contradict an explicit legal text; most disputes concern the identification and handling of ambiguity. The existence of such disputes makes it impossible to read the law without reference to higher principles, which place limits on the range of possibly legitimate meanings. Since the law ought to effect justice, those principles ought to correspond to what reason tells us about the just and the good. Only a legal culture informed by genuine political science can provide such judgments on a regular basis. This Aristotelian insight (1984 III.15-17) captures the spirit of Tocqueville's treatment of law.

When one considers Tocqueville's work as a whole, it is clear that the "individual rights" whose cause he places before judges consist in those rights that tend to elevate the souls and stimulate the virtue of citizens, and not those rights that tend to encourage the political and spiritual dissociation of individuals. One can usefully refer to this as a distinction between participatory and passive rights.[22] Since local self-government and traditional religious worship are generally necessary to promote virtuous rights in the modern age, justice cannot be served by privileging the individual vis-à-vis social authorities as such.[23] Rather, the rights of the individual must be defended in such a way that the mediating institutions of democratic life—from the family and township government through private associations and religious bodies—retain their vitality. Certain individuals or groups may be offended in various ways by the operations of such institutions, and they may even claim plausibly to suffer unfair treatment. Yet the Tocquevillian statesman cannot ignore the great good that accrues to individuals whose individual liberty is exercised in an environment that requires them to pursue happiness in association with others. Such citizens, though free to do all that the community recognizes as just and good, and even right to challenge the community when it misconstrues the nature of justice and goodness, cannot claim an exemption from public debate about the objective nature of these standards, or from public deliberation about the necessary means of securing them. Such citizens must strive to associate their thought and will with those of others, sometimes succeeding at changing the hearts and minds of others, sometimes learning to accommodate theirs to their fellows (497). This give and take is of the essence of citizenship,[24] and a Tocquevillian jurisprudence would seek to promote it by reminding citizens that individual dignity and rights are rooted in a moral order linking human beings together, and must be pursued whenever possible within the imperfect but virtue-building institutions of free democratic government and civil society.

There are doubtlessly countless court decisions in our history that follow this Tocquevillian approach. Yet when we review the most influential cases in American jurisprudence, and particularly those of the Supreme Court, it is difficult not to conclude that the dominant notion inspiring our highest courts has been one of radical individualism rather than virtue. This trend was not visible in Tocqueville's day, when the primary task of the federal judiciary had been to save the Union from debility by prudently establishing judicial review itself and shoring up those powers expressly or implicitly ceded to the federal government by the Constitution. The first manifestation of extreme individualism came later, with a series of decisions (given between 1890 and 1937) that elevated the economic rights of individuals—most notably the rights to "property" and "freedom of contract"—above the regulatory interests of the political community.

Three things must be stressed about the *Lochner*-era Court.[25] First, it seems to have accorded personal economic rights a primacy vis-à-vis community interests that was grounded neither in sound constitutional interpretation nor in sober political theory.[26] Second, its rulings were aimed at all levels and types of political community. Though the court invoked Tenth Amendment federalism to block national economic regulation, it used federal (Fourteenth Amendment) rights to prevent states, townships, and civil society (unions) from regulating local business according to local community needs. Third, the long-term effect of this jurisprudence was not to maintain a perfectly laissez-faire economy, but rather to ensure that future economic regulations would flow from a centralized administration rather than from local efforts. The stoppage of regulation at all levels nationwide, combined with the widespread sufferings of the Great Depression, created a national consensus that enabled Franklin Roosevelt to face down a stubborn Supreme Court, breaking its will and ushering in a new era of federal economic regulation virtually unlimited by any application of judicial review. Though the American people were no doubt engaged by Roosevelt's fireside chats, and shaped profoundly by the tremendous collective sacrifices of World War II, the nation as a whole lost its opportunity to address social ills through grass roots action. Instead, it turned perforce to what could only become a vast impersonal bureaucracy to regulate the details of the commercial realm, even as this realm came to absorb ever more of the time, energy, and spirit of the average citizen (658). A wiser jurisprudence might have permitted effective regulation of a wider set of economic concerns on a local level all along, reducing the need for federal legislation and regulation and preserving the strength and appeal of participatory rights to a far greater extent.

After provoking and then conceding to the New Deal, the Court entered into its present era, one defined by a distinct and perhaps even more radical brand of individualism. On economic matters the motto "laissez-faire" was now applied to the interventions of federal power. Excepting a few anemic defenses that prove the rule, federalism has been dismissed as a formalistic anachronism, such that the rights of communities have little to no constitutional protection. A telling example of this is the fate of the Detroit district known as Poletown. Faced with destruction under a municipal redevelopment plan, inhabitants of this vibrant community had to resort to the doctrine of individual property rights to protect their common interests in court. Sadly for them, property rights are no longer the beneficiary of judicial favor, and their suit failed.[27] This failure is not a sign that municipal interests now trump individual rights, but rather a symptom of the shift to a new individualism focused less on property and more on the amorphous but seductive and immensely consequential notion of "privacy."

No one who follows judicial politics will miss the importance of privacy in the universe of constitutional rights today. A prospective judge or justice will invariably be evaluated by the litmus test of his position on this matter. The controversy surrounding privacy stems from the impact of certain precedents identifying privacy as a distinct right dubiously inferred from various clauses of the Bill of Rights, none of which mention it as such; these precedents were later used to assert the practically unlimited right of women to procure and doctors to perform abortions.[28] While significant in its own right, this dispute over "privacy" is part of a larger and more fundamental shift in mentality taken by our courts, one whose outlines must be explored in further depth if one is to understand the true import of the surface quarrels we now see raging around courts.

Had the judiciary simply dropped its concern with halting economic regulation, our high courts might play a very small role in national politics today. Instead, around the time it abandoned this priority, the Court took on another cause, which has come to define its *raison d'être* in its own estimation, in elite opinion, and in the public mind. That cause is the prioritization of individual rights understood as fundamental rights and therefore as trumping the rights or interests of society—government, civil, and religious bodies included—in all or most instances. In a series of cases too numerous to review here, the court gradually "incorporated" the Bill of Rights, transforming it from a set of limitations on the actions of federal government alone—which it had been for all of American history to that point—to a source of basic individual rights, express or implied, against which no unit of society may legitimately act without extraordinary justification.[29]

To be fair, the Supreme Court has frequently sought to formulate judicial rules for "balancing" the interests of society, as expressed in various acts of legislation and governance, against the interests of individuals in exercising fundamental rights.[30] Such balancing tends to classify various rights as more or less fundamental, and therefore raises higher or lower hurdles for society to clear before it may licitly abridge a particular right in a particular way. Yet it remains the case that, on the basis of an ever-expanding set of claims, individuals (who invariably represent or become adopted by groups advancing particular agendas) may invoke the awesome authority of the Supreme Court, speaking on behalf of inalienable human rights, to undermine the efforts of society to secure various components of the common good. All the while, the burden of proof is cast upon the community to justify its incursion on "individual rights," in an atmosphere that deems certain features of individuality as such to be of more fundamental importance than increasingly suspect claims to promote the public interest.[31]

Lest the above be taken as a wholesale condemnation of this new rights movement, it bears repeating that it has achieved many priceless goods, such as the long overdue advances in civil rights mentioned above. Yet the damage done to civic life and moral and intellectual virtue by the excesses of this movement cannot be ignored if we are to heed Tocqueville's warnings against the perils of individualism. This damage results from two features of the rights revolution that must be addressed before the notion of rights can be redeemed in modern times: its tendencies toward governmental centralization and passive citizenship on the one hand, and moral relativism on the other.

The institutional difference between a centralized and decentralized political system is subtle but clear according to Tocqueville. All governments must delegate some decisions to local officials, but centralized administrations tend to delegate minimally and exercise maximum control over local actors, whereas decentralized administrations delegate maximally and exercise minimal control over the same. The test of a system's identity is therefore resolved in part by considering the treatment of issues that might be left either to local or central authorities. One such issue, according to Tocqueville, is civil rights. Though civil rights are of interest to an entire nation, they are primarily exercised in particular communities, and a political system respectful of local autonomy and the public spirit it fosters will, like Jacksonian America, leave their regulation as much as possible to those localities (350ff).

A decentralized approach to civil rights is reflected in the original Constitution by its leaving to states the task of determining electoral qualifications, as well as by its limitation of federal authority to the exercise of enumerated powers while leaving to states the limited but open-ended "police power" of regulating the safety, welfare, and morals of their citizens.[32] This arrangement was partly and necessarily altered by amendments thirteen through fifteen of the Constitution. In order to abolish slavery and eradicate, so far as possible, the lingering effects of prejudice, citizenship had to be federalized and the right of states to regulate its exercise significantly curtailed. In fact, the chief problem in this connection was too little timely intervention on the part of the federal government to rectify the gross injustices of legal segregation.[33]

As it happens, the same Court that provoked a federal backlash of economic regulation with its radicalization of economic rights also declined to enforce these constitutional protections of the civil rights of blacks.[34] When such enforcement finally came in the mid-twentieth century,[35] it was accompanied by a seemingly endless torrent of new or reconceived individual rights, all of which had to be enforced by federal courts, legislation, or regulations, at the expense of local authority. Though states officially retain their "police power," and though many social functions are still under their primary care, there is virtually no important realm in which their activities do not come under the scrutiny of a new regime seeking to impose one set of detailed rules on all Americans rather than allowing the people to adapt a broader set of common rules to fit their diverse characters and needs. Though many of the new federal rights are laudable in principle, the manner of their imposition by federal courts has deadened or dulled any distinction between truly essential principles of justice such as racial equality and a host of policies best left to individual or local specification. This failure to balance federal and local determination of rights has contributed to the erosion of self-government in America by burdening its institutions with endless regulations and legal challenges and by labeling all local variation in civic matters as ipso facto benighted and atavistic.

Examples of this new rights regime abound in law enforcement, education, and censorship, among other traditionally local realms now hemmed in with numerous and drastically limiting federal rules. Needless to say, all of these areas exercise a profound influence on the character of citizens, and therefore over their civic spiritedness and other virtues. Yet the courts seem oblivious to the effect of their rulings on "the spirit of the city," encouraging citizens to think of citizenship primarily in terms of the nation, in whose institutions the vast majority can have practically no meaningful representation. Rights so conceived foster a spirit of passive reliance on distant authorities that fails to provide for the formation of virtuous habits valuable in themselves and necessary for the long-term preservation of liberty. Meanwhile, Americans raised on the new "rights talk" are encouraged to look with a skeptical if not hostile eye at those mediating associations that foster liberty of a more meaningful and durable sort.

Nor is this all that can be said against the Court's attempt at statesmanship in recent decades. As other sources of moral authority have withered in modern times, courts have been increasingly called upon to expound the essence of ordered liberty and the philosophic basis of the rights and duties structuring a liberal democratic society. Without some such vision of the whole, Tocqueville contends, no coherent set of actions—or rulings—is possible. Yet lurking behind the new rights regime is a fundamental conviction that the world we live in is defined by moral chaos rather than moral order. Beginning with Brandeis's seminal dictum that the most fundamental liberty is the right to be let alone,[36] this conviction has expressed itself in the elevation of "privacy" over the most basic duties of the individual toward society: responsible procreative behavior and the protection of innocent life.[37] More recently, it has developed into a theory of liberty that posits in each individual the right to define the meaning and purpose of the cosmos for himself.[38] According to the court, human dignity can have no meaning if it does not have this impious and impossible one.

These dicta, which form the backbone of some of the most influential court decisions in recent history, give superlative expression to the willful self-enclosure of the Tocquevillian individualist, who claims to judge all things from his own impoverished perspective while lazily and brazenly shrugging off any effort to engage, mentally or morally, the objective order of things (404, 426). These words, emanating from our highest tribunals, have not failed to have their effect on the public mind. As Glendon relates, and the reader may verify, even those who seek to defend public goods such as patriotism all too easily slip into the language of rights as the freedom to do as one pleases.[39] Our courts, which Tocqueville hoped would assist in the vital task of interpreting rights so as to encourage a sense of duty, public-spiritedness, self-sacrifice, piety, and objectivity among citizens, have clearly chosen, at least in their most prominent rulings, to do precisely the opposite. Rather than aiming at the moderation of individualism through an interpretation of rights centered on virtue and its social conditions, they have opted to exacerbate individualism, prodding the American people farther down the path of moral decline than they would otherwise be prepared to go at any given moment. The extent to which Americans have accepted this misdirection will be our next subject.

Individualism and the Loss of Moral Order

Thus far our analysis of governmental institutions has shown Tocqueville to be sadly correct in his fears that the enthusiasm for equality would tilt modern democracies in the direction of centralization and extreme individualism, rendering active civic life and serious moral and intellectual engagement much more laborious and far less attractive to citizens. Before considering what we might do about this, it remains to be seen how these developments have affected the souls of modern citizens. Here, too, Tocqueville was all too prescient in his fears that individualism would sap the desire for excellence and consign its victims to a life of pragmatic relativism and joyless conformism.

An assessment of the moral state of a people is difficult to conduct with perfect objectivity. The best, or at least the most practicable, method at present will be, in imitation of Tocqueville (659), to ask the reader to compare what follows to his own experiences and observations. For his part, the author has found no better analysis of the state of morality today—along with a helpful treatment of its theoretical roots in religion and philosophy—than that given by Allan Bloom in his *The Closing of the American Mind* (1987). Bloom's focus on the mores prevailing in our leading institutions of higher education allows us to examine the intellectual and moral condition of our present and future leaders: our would-be natural aristocracy, in Tocqueville's language. If Tocqueville's strategy for combating individualism through political science is to achieve major success, it would almost certainly have to begin in the universities, where the sciences available to our citizenry are cultivated.

Bloom's account of the contemporary student (and, by implication, the teachers who have shaped him) can be read as an updating of Tocqueville's description of the individualist, who closes upon himself and claims to judge the world on the basis of his impoverished knowledge and experience.[40] The modern soul, according to Bloom, is shaped by one powerful and stultifying conviction: that all moral judgment is relative. This misjudgment is not only self-contradictory in its assertion of the truth that moral truth does not exist. (That the "truth" relativism asserts is indeed a moral one can be seen from the indignation heaped upon those who dare to question it, including Bloom.) It is also wholly unreflective, typically offering and seeking no proof of its claim. The modern soul, according to Bloom, is mindlessly "open" to all beliefs and ways of life. Yet insofar as all beliefs and ways of life other than that of modern relativism claim to be based on truths concerning the nature of things, the modern mind is in fact closed to all beliefs and ways of life other than its own.

The apparent sophistication and "openness" of this relativism renders it exceedingly dangerous. As Bloom rightly notes, students today are almost all trained to be relativists. This applies as much to the conservative and religious students as to their more progressive and secular peers.[41] Regardless of the content of his personal beliefs, the student has been taught to regard them as his "values" or "ideology" rather than as what appears to him to be objectively true. When confronted with the arguments of others, including that of the non-relativist professor or author, students will often go so far as to translate the language of truth, virtue, and duty into that of values, feelings, and desires, praising the great figures of history for the subjective force of their convictions rather than for their grasp of or service to objective truths and goods. Though students of course have reasons for believing what they do, their formation makes it difficult for them to enter into liberal education by examining systematically the objective evidence and arguments backing competing claims to moral truth. As Tocqueville observed, souls overburdened by an excessive sense of autonomy would frequently rather cling to their opinions because they are theirs than bear the burden of having to justify or alter them after a difficult search for the truth (179, 418). As a result, students experience a barrier to understanding, much less appreciating, testing, or prudently applying the fundamental principles of politics and morality that have shaped modern civilization.

As Tocqueville predicted and as Bloom confirms, the moral chaos of relativism does not issue in total anarchy in personal or civic life—at least not all at once. For one important exception to the general relativism of modern souls is the material realm. While moral truths must be believed on authority or discovered through careful observation combined with sustained reasoning, the fundamental reality of material things is too obvious for most to deny (180, 434ff, 508ff). When it comes to learning, then, those sciences that can be applied to the manipulation of material things are considered "hard" or capable of finding objective truth. In the matter of morals, however, what is taken to matter is not truth per se but rather what Machiavelli called "the effectual truth": the ability of a certain intellectual or moral habit to "win friends and influence people." Virtually no student is indifferent to his future earning potential, and so a certain degree of order and even superficial virtue are achieved in education on purely pragmatic grounds, for the sake of future professional success. Attempts to direct such pragmatism to higher ends through the doctrine of self-interest well understood, however, presuppose a knowledge of and interest in higher ends that are all too rarely given forceful articulation even in institutions of higher education. Often, the impression is given that the only alternative to narrow selfishness is a normativism whose basis is mysterious, and whose content often seems dictated by a blind love of equality. In this environment, students must struggle to find precious assistance in harmonizing the practical demands of democratic life with the regular practice of civic, moral, and religious virtues, settle instead for an individualistic mixture of pragmatic and idealistic activity, or heroically strive to reinvent the wheel of virtue and happiness on their own.

It is not difficult to see how these reflections on morality in higher education apply to the status of philosophy and religion in society at large. In the realm of politics and religion alike, claims to truth are frequently reviled as dangerous, indicating a desire to divest people of rights, which are assumed or asserted to rest on relativism rather than any type of truth, whether self-evident or revealed. Although large numbers of Americans call themselves religious, just as most claim to be happy and to be dutiful citizens,[42] the religious beliefs one most frequently encounters today tend towards a formless and individualized religion demanding little or no sacrifice, just as Tocqueville feared they would (see Orwin 2004). And though we often buy the insight in busyness, in moments of lucidity citizens today frequently perceive that in much of their lives they enjoy only a bland happiness consisting in grudging work coupled with a multiplication of petty pleasures, while exercising a passive citizenship consisting in a superficial knowledge of current events and the ineffectual expression of opinions about them. No one can deny that, despite these obstacles, many in our society somehow succeed at cultivating the virtues of religion, philosophy, and civic life. Nor can it be said that we have lost all collective consciousness of the need to pursue these virtues. Nonetheless, no honest examination of contemporary popular culture and discourse can ignore the marginalization, trivialization, and even vilification of these virtues it ceaselessly exhibits.

How should we respond to this individualization of our society, reaching from the halls of higher learning down to the conduct of daily life? We should respond to these actual problems as Tocqueville urged us to respond to the problems he anticipated: these trends ought not to induce despair, but should rather inspire us with a "salutary fear" (673). This fear ought to be real for several reasons. First, individualism is inherently degrading to humanity, which longs to associate itself with the truth and beauty of "the admirable order of all things." The widespread reduction of life—almost always in theory and all too often in practice—to animal urges, personal vanity, moral whims, and clever ways to satisfy all three, would demand rectification even were it to advance no further than it has. Yet it is foolhardy to think that without rectification it will go no further. The diminishment and even denigration of genuine curiosity, civic spirit, and moral purpose so prevalent today renders the fabric of political society incredibly fragile. Without virtue, citizens become vulnerable to a host of threats including the intimidation, blandishment, and deceptions of potential oppressors both foreign and domestic. There is no sense in attempting to predict a particular form of demise when history reveals such a variety of fates to which societies in decline succumb. The only sensible response to these fears, rendering them salutary rather than paralyzing, is to seek reform with all sobriety and confidence, in the knowledge that whether or not we succeed in achieving specific results, at least we can act in a spirit worthy of success (compare 400).

Political Science and the Recovery of Moral Order

The reform of our overly individualistic tendencies, if it at all possible, must begin with a discourse, scholarly and public, capable of presenting a reasoned and constructive critique of our bad choices and bad habits, as well as an identification and encouragement of our good ones, all presented in terms that will reach and possibly persuade citizens today. This is no small order. Fortunately for this study, such a discourse is well underway, even if its influence is not yet strong enough to affect the lives of most citizens. This discourse by no means dominates either the academy or our public institutions, not to mention popular consciousness, and its practitioners remain divided on a host of fundamental issues. Yet there is a growing awareness in political science and related disciplines of the dangers posed by the modern day atomization of society and the need to cultivate civic virtue within the framework of liberal democracy. Much of this discourse is directly inspired by Tocqueville, and most of it is at least cognizant of and sympathetic to him. Before turning in conclusion to the question of what general measures might revitalize civic virtue today, we shall briefly review the insights into individualism contributed by several key contemporary authors and schools.

Perhaps the most famous of recent treatments of individualism have been Robert Putnam's *Bowling Alone* (2001) and Robert Bellah and others' *Habits of the Heart* (1988-2007). Employing different methods and distinct though related conceptual frameworks, these studies have reached a wide audience and conveyed important messages about the decline of political society in recent decades and what might be done to reverse it. Putnam's focus is on empirical data proving that Americans' involvement in the institutions of civil society has sharply declined since the 1960s. Putnam also attempts to show that the "social capital" citizens build through such participation has tangible benefits in fostering both personal happiness and the success of public policies, and that Americans would therefore be well advised to embrace once more the vibrant associational life they once enjoyed. Bellah and others cover similar ground through a series of case studies of American citizens grappling with the tension between individualism and public spiritedness. Readers benefit from hearing the accounts these citizens give of their own lives combined with the authors' analysis of the issues, with particular attention to the internal and external forces moving individuals toward and away from civic engagement. Looming large in this study is the importance of a public philosophy capable of inspiring citizens to find meaning and purpose in civic partnership. This last theme has also been persuasively advanced in the field of political theory by Michael Sandel (1996), William Galston (1991), and Alasdair McIntyre (1981).

What benefit might students of Tocqueville seek to gain from this literature? Brian Danoff (2007) provides a useful Tocquevillian analysis centered on Tocqueville's ambivalent endorsement, for modern times, of the doctrine of self-interest well understood. On Tocqueville's view, the democratic social state obscures the longings inherent in human nature for a moral and intellectual association with the order of things. Moralists therefore face a peculiar dilemma in democratic times. They cannot speak of the intrinsic beauty of virtue without losing an audience incorrigibly preoccupied with private gain. Yet they cannot reduce virtue to self-interest without doing injustice to the human heart, including the hearts of the citizens they influence. A rhetoric of virtue without reference to self-interest will never get off the ground, but a rhetoric of self-interest without reference to the higher order inspiring virtue will not stay aloft. If civic virtue is to be maintained in modern times, leaders must seek to draw citizens into civic participation through appeals to self-interest, keep them there long enough for habits of association to develop, and crown their civic lives with a discourse pointing to the higher meaning of it all. Danoff, following Harry Jaffa, credits Abraham Lincoln with having mastered this Tocquevillian art and applied it to the problems of his day. In ours, this art would require a blend of the approaches demonstrated by both Putnam and Bellah and others.[43]

At this point we are compelled to ask two broad questions of civil society literature. The first (compound) question is: who can revive civil society, and how can it be done? Here the work of Robert Gannett (2003) is especially important for reminding us of the primacy of governmental associations over private associations in Tocqueville's analysis. Although the habits built by both forms of association are mutually reinforcing, Tocqueville is clear that the dynamics of the democratic social state will tend to dissociate citizens unless *political* means are used to build up contrary penchants. In the mid-nineteenth century, political life was sufficiently decentralized in America that citizens were practically forced to engage in local associations (governmental and civil) if social problems were to be dealt with at all. Thus Tocqueville might have counseled statesmen to resist pressures toward centralization whenever justice and necessity did not absolutely demand it. In our day governmental and administrative centralization seem all but irreversible, so the advice must differ. From the legislative point of view, it is imperative that we seek models for the use or abstention of federal power to encourage or permit the free, dignified, and meaningful participation of citizens in whatever initiatives address social functions such as education, welfare, law enforcement, and public morality.

Given Tocqueville's well confirmed insight into the powerful influence of courts over democratic life and thought, a reform of individualism today must consider the judicial as well as legislative branch of government. Here the work of Mary Ann Glendon (1991) comes to the fore. In her thorough and penetrating study of the development of contemporary "rights talk," Glendon exposes the degree to which court decisions have furthered a radicalized understanding of individual rights inconsistent with the conditions of meaningful civic participation and sober civic deliberation on the ends and means of political society. She calls for renewed attention on the part of judges and others to the social conditions that promote the virtues that sustain liberty, including a public discourse that balances the rights of individuals with their duties toward society, and a practical implementation that leaves far greater space for participatory democratic institutions to work out the details of this balancing whenever feasible. Such a revolution in the way the courts treat citizenship might have a profound effect on the future of individualism in America.

Glendon's work is particularly useful to us because its critique is aimed primarily at American jurisprudence, which she places in perspective by contrasting it to the more theoretically balanced legal traditions of Europe. Glendon admits, however, that the virtues of European legal theory are not necessarily reflected in policies that are ultimately better at promoting civic health. Glendon also abstracts from the question of what public philosophy might ground a more balanced view of rights, appealing at times to the influence of Plato, Aristotle, the Bible, Rousseau, Kant, and others over the contemporary European mindset, in contrast to the sway of Locke and Blackstone over ours. While her discussion of these various philosophic roots is extremely valuable, it raises fundamental questions worthy of further study about the theoretical and practical alternatives to individualism available to us today.

Paul Carrese (2003) contributes to such a study of the public philosophy of rights by tracing the influence of modern (Machiavellian) political thought on contemporary American jurisprudence through the writings of Montesquieu and the influence of Oliver Holmes, Jr. Carrese reminds us that the seed of nihilism whose fruit is so visible in the dicta of our present-day Court was also transmitted to Europe, whose Rousseauian notions of social justice likewise have Machiavellian roots worth exploring. After all, Rousseau penned some of the most stark portraits of philosophic individualism imaginable, and conceived of civic virtue as the radical denaturing of man (1978; 1979). If it is not nature that draws us to society—whatever artifice may have to be employed in its aid—then what prevents society from embracing that "impious maxim" that it has the right to do whatever it pleases to and with its members?

This brings us to the second, and perhaps the most important question that a contemporary science of individualism must explore: what, precisely, is the basis of our critique of individualism, and our articulation of an alternative to it, in nature itself? This is a question that very much occupies Tocqueville in *Democracy*, though he treats it with exceeding delicacy. Modern man, he believes, labors under a false notion of his own nature that blinds him to the profound need he has as man for moral beauty and cosmic truth. This obscurity of nature is partly the result of the modern social state, and partly the fault of moral and civic figures who have usurped the leadership of democracy, encouraging it to believe it can function without notions of justice transcending utility, beliefs informing science, and virtue surpassing material well-being. Tocqueville explicitly calls for the adoption of a new political science not grounded in these modern errors. In his development of this science, however, Tocqueville frequently relies on modern authors to understand the workings of modern society, while more or less quietly distancing himself from their materialistic or individualistic errors. He refutes these errors without calling much attention to that fact, and in doing so relies upon a highly classical notion of contemplative and ethical virtue, usually without explicitly invoking the authority of ancient authors. Why is Tocqueville so cautious about disclosing his relation to classical and modern approaches to political thought, and what might we learn from his approach about the practice of political theory today?

Tocqueville's caution can be explained with reference to the distinction between political means and ends. The coherence of political society, Tocqueville maintains, depends upon the strength of certain common beliefs held dogmatically or without radical examination by the majority of citizens (407). Politics is capable of contributing to a just, peaceful, well-ordered, and meaningful life when it draws citizens into active participation in the deciding and implementing of means to achieve such commonly held ends. To the extent that politics involves disputes about the ends that ought to be pursued, it renders common action increasingly difficult, and may even result in civil war or anarchy.[44] Though philosophically stimulating, such questioning of ends is not politically responsible unless undertaken with supreme prudence. The existence of morally serious ends in political society is itself sufficient to stimulate the ascent of philosophic minds to the highest regions of thought; once there these geniuses need not disturb society by openly exposing flaws that may not admit of safe correction. This is why Tocqueville promotes a simultaneously transcendent and timely statesmanship, one rooted in a radical philosophical understanding of the true potentialities of humankind in contrast to the errors and limits of any given day and age, but one also content to employ this knowledge for the gentle improvement rather than the forceful transformation of political society.

This view of statesmanship leaves Tocqueville in a peculiar position as he pens *Democracy*, a position we would do well to reflect upon. On account of his classical view of nature and politics, Tocqueville believes it necessary to oppose the hegemony of modern political thought whose unchecked influence might usher in an unprecedented state of political and spiritual misery. On account of that same classical view, however, he must restrain himself from imprudently attacking modern political notions that have been adopted, for better or worse, by society at large. Tocqueville's formula for the reform of modern politics begins with the cultivation of a perfect mastery of the classics by a small band of potential leaders of democracy, followed by the exercise by these leaders of a salutary influence over the souls of their fellows, who will seldom seek or achieve such theoretical knowledge. The attempt to bring the virtues of the ancient world directly to bear on modern life could only lead to the destabilization of that life and the loss of whatever virtue it can achieve (450ff). Instead, Tocqueville seeks to identify traditions, institutions, beliefs, and arguments that have been or could be employed within the limitations of modern democracy to elevate its life in a manner consistent with classical theories that need not be referenced by those promoting these reforms (675-76).

However sound its premises, this complex formula is by no means easy to apply, especially to the changed conditions of twenty-first century democracy. Fortunately for us, the questions and concerns Tocqueville raises about political philosophy and statesmanship have been taken up by several profound and prolific minds of recent times. In the field of political philosophy an influential movement has developed among those who examine the distinctions between ancient, medieval, modern, late-modern, and post-modern political thought not with the intention of satisfying historical curiosity, or of recounting stages in the development of modern methods and views, but in the hope of better understanding the human condition and the truest needs of our time. Figures such as Leo Strauss, Eric Vogelin, Hannah Arendt, and Alasdair McIntyre have inspired a new generation of political scientists intent on discovering the possible truth and wisdom in neglected or wrongly discredited ways of thinking. Although differences abound within this rather loose "movement," its significance in carrying forward the kind of reform Tocqueville called for cannot be overstated. The immense resources provided by these teachers and their students can aid us in understanding Tocqueville himself and his place within the tradition of political thought, as well as the ideas Tocqueville brings to bear on contemporary problems and their possible solutions.

Not even a cursory review of this literature is possible here. Instead it must suffice to consider three issues at play in contemporary political philosophy on which Tocqueville's thought can be usefully brought to bear. The first concerns the recovery of classical political thought about which Tocqueville was so cautious. That caution, and the reasons for it, have been carefully explored in the context of classical political philosophy by Leo Strauss and his students. As Allan Bloom (1987) and Thomas Pangle (1992a, 2004) explain, however, Strauss was compelled by the powerful influence of what we now call postmodern thought—rooted especially in the teaching of Martin Heidegger—to launch an elaborate and explicit defense of reason, philosophy, and natural right, all of which are denigrated or distorted by historicism and moral relativism. Since

Strauss, like Tocqueville, detected the roots of contemporary nihilism in the Machiavellian replacement of contemplative and ethical virtue with "the effectual truth," his defense of the former had to make explicit the differences between classical and modern philosophers, and therefore had to expose the flaws in the foundations of modern political society. Though Strauss was careful to note the similarities as well as dissimilarities between ancients and moderns and to point out important virtues of the latter, especially as regards the decency of modern liberal democracy, his influence has made it necessary to revisit in the light of day certain problems at which Tocqueville only dared to hint.

One such problem consists in defining the concept of natural right and determining its place in civic education today. In his book *The Ennobling of Democracy* (1992), Thomas Pangle calls for a recovery of the classical understanding of natural right rooted in Socratic philosophy. Recognizing the impossibility or undesirability of forcing foreign elements into political life, Pangle treats Socratic dialectics as the proper provenance of a liberal education ideally offered by universities. Noting the ways in which the United States has blended modern liberalism with elements of classical republicanism, especially in education, Pangle seeks to recover a civic education rooted in this (for us) traditional blend of Locke, Cicero, and the Bible, with the chief difference being a greater emphasis than before on the classical elements. Thus would the tension between classical and modern natural right be dampened in relation to a much enriched civic life, while the intellectual energy produced by this tension could still be harnessed to explore "the greatest problems that human destiny presents" in the philosophic realm.

Beginning from a similar understanding of the problem, Harry Jaffa and his students have taken a somewhat different approach. In his early masterpiece, *Crisis of the House Divided* (1958-1999), Jaffa maintained that Abraham Lincoln, in his critique of slavery and defense of the Union, had in principle refounded America, correcting its modernistic flaws with a deeper and more classical understanding of natural right. Though Jaffa has since shifted his take on the American founding and on early modern political thought—treating them as essentially consistent with Aristotelian political science—the unbroken core of his thinking remains the centrality of the Declaration of Independence to the correct understanding of justice. Jaffa argues for the supreme wisdom of Lincoln in seizing upon the Declaration as the founding document of the United States and the guide to the proper understanding of both liberty and virtue. If Jaffa keeps Tocqueville at arm's length, the reason is clear: as his student Thomas West points out (1991), Tocqueville never once mentions the Declaration in all the pages of *Democracy*. As we have seen, this omission is a deliberate one on the part of Tocqueville, who seeks to found America on the politico-theological declaration of duties made by John Winthrop rather than the political declaration of rights made by Thomas Jefferson. This choice reflects Tocqueville's ambivalence toward modern natural right and his desire to counterbalance it with older but still living traditions of reverence and duty.

Who is right, Jaffa or Tocqueville? While a resolution of this dispute is beyond our present scope, a few reflections are possible. To begin with it must be noted that Tocqueville is not the only commentator to find the American Declaration dangerously modern in tone. Others have faulted it for emphasizing rights over duties, for making duties derivative from rights, for presupposing a deistic view of God, and for blithely eschewing venerable traditions of political society.[45] In all fairness, however, it must be said that the Declaration preserves a careful ambiguity of language, no doubt deliberately employed by Jefferson, which allows it to be read in either a modern or classical light. It is hardly dishonest, then, and potentially quite salutary, to emphasize the latter features of this seminal document, especially in civic education, which ought generally to blend the modern with the classical. Furthermore, even if Tocqueville's reasons for avoiding the Declaration in a book written for Frenchmen in 1835 were sound, Tocqueville's appreciation of the value of tradition makes the utilization of the American Revolution, as well as Lincoln's refounding, and the tremendous moral capital both accrued, very attractive for twenty-first century American statesmen. Tocqueville himself stresses the need to embrace a version of equality that is friendly toward liberty and greatness, and where better to find such a notion than in the arguments and actions of Washington, Lincoln, and other virtuous leaders from our past?

While these and other reasons may provide excellent grounds for emphasizing the Declaration, however, Tocqueville's fundamental reason for shying away from it ought not be forgotten. In democratic times, the idea of equality will threaten to eclipse that of greatness, and the concept of equal liberty therefore needs to be embraced with supreme caution by those practicing the legislative art. As Glendon notes, Lincoln succeeded at ennobling his countrymen by appealing to both Blackstone and the Bible,[46] whereas today our rhetoric is dominated by the spirit of Blackmun and Brandeis. In defining the roots of our national character, civic education needs to recover the traditions of religious, moral, and civic duty as much or more as those of rights-assertion.[47] It can be assisted in this task by a liberal education that takes seriously the dangers posed by modern thought to the cultivation of virtue in civic and civil life.

Our final issue relates to another problem raised by Strauss's work: that of the relation of natural right to divine right. Here Tocqueville also exercises supreme caution, noting the various ways religion benefits not only political society as a whole, but also the individual soul in search of cosmic truth and meaning. While Tocqueville appreciates the inner beauty of religion as well as its public utility, however, it is clear that he eschews religious belief for minds of his own caliber, expressing his indifference to the possibility that divine grace can actually assist humanity in its search for justice, and implying pointedly that the acceptance of religious dogma on matters of utmost importance is a mental yoke intrinsically repugnant to the philosophic soul. Given that so many of our most acrimonious political disagreements today correlate so closely to the presence, absence, intensity, or content of our religious convictions, the application of Tocqueville's thought on this subject would seem to demand a frank appraisal of questions likely to provoke deep controversy and aggravate the fault lines dividing many citizens today.

Be this as it may, the risk cannot be avoided, and the question must be posed: how is it possible to apply Tocqueville's insights into the relationship between religion and liberal democracy, and therefore to determine the proper role of religion in politics today? Considering for the moment only the theoretical component of this question, two approaches are worthy of note. Strauss himself, and many of his students, make increasingly explicit the stance taken implicitly by Tocqueville himself. While highlighting many of the benefits of religion, and while promoting a great respect for the achievements of religious minds, these scholars insist upon the radical divide that separates philosophy— seen as essentially rationalistic—and faith. While this stance may seem offputting to believers,[48] it is important to note that its major premises have been adopted by men of faith,[49] and it need not imply that religion is essentially irrational. Theology can be conceived as the application of reason within the framework of faith in such a way as to distinguish it from philosophy, which operates of necessity with no such framework.

The insistence that philosophy per se must reject faith, however, does seem to imply that faith involves the sacrifice of human reason's rightful place in the cosmos. This is why certain scholars—even those very much influenced by Strauss—have taken a more sympathetic approach to the idea that reason and faith can be shown to be in a sufficiently high degree of harmony as to render philosophy and theology distinct but not mutually exclusive enterprises. Here the work of twentieth century Thomists such as Jacques Maritain (1951), Etienne Gilson (1956), and Josef Pieper (1962), and of contemporary scholars such as James Schall (1991, 2006), Peter Lawler (1993), and Mary Keys (2006) is of special note. Convinced that grace may perfect nature without destroying it, these scholars explore the possibility that faith may provide both philosophy and political society with resources complementary to their intrinsic goals but beyond the reach of their unaided inherent faculties.

Was Tocqueville wrong to hold divine revelation at arm's length? If so, both the love of truth and the need to shore up democracy's moral foundations would demand a political science more open to divine grace than Tocqueville's. At the same time, this debate, and the others mentioned above, should not cause us to forget Tocqueville's prudence in calling upon a coalition of related but hardly univocal minds—including those more or less religious, and more or less classical in their philosophy—to embrace his political science. Philosophic and theological questions have always divided humanity, and will likely continue to do so for the foreseeable future, but Tocqueville hopes to persuade all but the most "base and servile souls" to comprehend the threat of individualism, and to add their intellectual and moral energies to its containment and defeat (11-12). For anyone persuaded to join and encourage such a coalition, the intellectual trends outlined above, and many others like them, should be regarded as a cause for hope. Without sacrificing the desire for a full and accurate account of the truth concerning the fundamental problems of humanity, a friendly alliance of thinkers concerned to preserve human greatness in modern times can and ought to become an increasingly powerful presence in the sphere of higher education and higher culture in general. How such hopes can be extended into the practical realm will occupy us in our concluding section.

Notes

1. Royer-Collard (cited by Mansfield and Winthrop in Tocqueville 2000a, xxxiii) and Ceaser (1991).
2. Ironically, Tocqueville predicted that such scholarship would become common in modern times as a result of the influence of equality. A key factor in Tocqueville's ability to transcend such influences is his willingness to apply the forces studied by social science to the social scientist himself, without positing their inescapability. This allows Tocqueville to recognize and address assumptions that might vitiate his analyses.
3. Here is it instructive to consider Tocqueville's correspondence with Gobineau, an early proponent of racial inequality whose "scientific" theories Tocqueville denounced as undermining not only the moral equality of human beings, but also the very possibility of morality and virtue itself (1959a).
4. The Fourteenth Amendment.
5. See the speeches of Franklin Roosevelt on this subject (1932-1941).
6. Fukuyama (1992).
7. Compare Tocqueville (400) to Nietzsche (1954, 169).
8. See Glendon (1991).
9. See our discussion in chapter 2.
10. See especially Glendon (1991) and Pangle (1992a). The adjectives are taken from Glendon's account.
11. See Paul Johnson (1997, 471).
12. Tocqueville notes the challenge modern democracies will face in maintaining a military capable of defending the country without desiring the overthrow of civilian government (617ff). Despite the reference in our Second Amendment to the role of citizen militias, Tocqueville sees that the general spirit of democracies will be commercial and hence peaceful, and that military discipline will tend to constitute a distinct culture. The difficulty will consist in training soldiers for war without displacing their fundamental self-identity as civilians, a task made much easier by the exceptional, occasional, and distant character of conflict. Our struggles tend to be over the need for military engagement in the first place, and with the need to re-integrate veterans of combat into a society largely oblivious to the character of their military experience.
13. Lowi (1979).
14. By 2002 almost 34 percent of state and local outlays were financed by federal grants (Wilson 2008, 85).
15. Wilson (2008, 273, 319-20).
16. *Miranda v. Arizona*, 384 U.S. 436 (1966).
17. *Everson v. Board of Education*, 330 U.S. 1 (1947) and *Griswold v. Connecticut*, 381 U.S. 479 (1965).
18. At the time of this writing, the Supreme Court has recently expanded the access of foreign terrorists to civilian courts (*Boumediene v. Bush*, 553 U.S., 2008); ruled that the death penalty may not be applied to child rapists (*Kennedy v. Louisiana*, 554 U.S.,

2008); and overturned a District of Columbia ban on handguns (*District of Columbia v. Heller*, 554 U.S., 2008). At any given moment, similar decisions affecting the daily governance of our society will be pending or emerging.

19. Compare Scalia (1997) and Brennan (1985).

20. Franklin Roosevelt, *Radio Broadcast, March 9, 1937*.

21. This does not preclude the prudential judgment as to whether a decision contravening strong public prejudices might precipitate disorder and thereby do more harm than good to the cause of justice.

22. Bearing in mind that, for Tocqueville, participation or association includes *contemplation* of the order of things. Compare Aristotle (1984, VII).

23. On the harmony between moral authority and genuine individual liberty, see Hebert (2007).

24. This is one of Glendon's chief arguments (1991).

25. So named for one of its most infamous decisions, *Lochner v. New York*, 198 U.S. 45 (1905).

26. See Sue Davis (2008, 424ff) and Robert Bork (1990). James Stoner (2003, 125ff) and Hadley Arkes (2000) argue that this perception of conservative courts stifling local police power in the name of abstract economic rights is vastly overstated; nonetheless, the perception that it was so constitutes the precedent for the near-universal modern consensus that courts must supplant local powers in the name of individualistic rights.

27. See Glendon (1991, 29-30).

28. References are to *Griswold* and *Roe v. Wade*, 410 U.S. 113 (1973).

29. See Davis (249ff, *et passim*).

30. For a discussion and defense of such balancing as it applies to the First Amendment, see Kent Greenawalt (2006).

31. Consider, for instance, *Edwards v. Aguillard*, 482 U.S. 578 (1987), finding that a nondenominational prayer at a high school graduation violates the establishment clause of the First Amendment by applying undue "peer pressure" on a graduate who does not believe in God. Here, the community is forced to adopt an effective atheism lest it offend, however innocuously, the sentiments of a lone dissenter. Among the ironies of this case and its ilk is that the individual seeks concessions from the community in the name of rights whose existence and force presuppose a given moral order, while using those rights to deny the very basis of this moral order in the public mind.

32. U.S. Constitution: Article 1, Sections 2 and 4; Amendment 10.

33. Private discrimination is necessarily much harder to rectify swiftly in a free society, but this did not preclude immediate legal reform at least.

34. *Plessy v. Ferguson*, 163 U.S. 537 (1896).

35. See *Brown v. Board of Education of Topeka*, 347 U.S. 483 (1954).

36. In his dissenting opinion in *Olmstead v. United States*, 277 U.S. 438 (1928).

37. Referring to *Griswold*, *Eisenstadt v. Baird*, 405 U.S. 438 (1972), and *Roe*.

38. *Planned Parenthood v. Casey*, 505 U.S. 833 (1992).

39. Glendon (1991, 8). This is, of course, precisely the error Tocqueville seeks to avoid by placing emphasis on the religious foundations of American democracy (see our chapters 2 and 4).

40. Tocqueville's account is in turn remarkably similar to Socrates' account of the democratic soul and its "law of equality" (Plato 1968, VIII, 555b-562a).

41. When one considers the Machiavellian roots of modern political thought, the association of progressive politics with relativism is perhaps less shocking than the latter's infiltration of conservatism. Yet one does not have to look far to find expressions of

progressivism suffused with the idea of robust moral order. No political movement can be consistently relativistic. The chief damage done by relativism is to impede the application of reason to the evaluation of political goals, which must nonetheless at some level have their reasons.

42. See Lugo (2008), Taylor (2006).

43. See, however, Frohnen's salutary warning against aspects of Bellah's thought (1993b).

44. See Harry Jaffa's discussion of this political dynamic as it applies to liberal democratic society (2000).

45. See, for example, Pangle (1992, 131ff), Glendon (1991, 11), and Kraynak (2001, 127).

46. Glendon (1991, 3).

47. As the late journalist Tony Snow put it, "If you think Independence Day is America's defining holiday, think again. Thanksgiving deserves that title, hands-down" (Kristol, 2008).

48. See Clark Merrill (2000).

49. Ernest Fortin (1996), for instance.

Conclusion
Liberty and the Recovery of Human Greatness

In doing literary combat against individualism, Tocqueville offers us a profound warning against a dangerous misunderstanding of liberty, a concept that, rightly understood, ought to be the guiding light of modern liberal democratic theory and practice. How, then, should Tocqueville's warnings and counsels affect the practical regulation of democratic life today? Despite his somber warnings about a dystopian future all too likely to seduce modern citizens and leaders, Tocqueville maintained an optimistic spirit, and was quick to celebrate the real if limited successes of actual and imperfect political societies such as Jacksonian America. Though much has changed since his day, and though few if any of his specific formulas could be maintained or adopted without modification, Tocqueville claims to offer us a political science adapted for modern democracy in general, and adaptable to the specific needs of various modern democratic societies. If the promise of Tocqueville's thought is to be realized, we must be able to demonstrate its applicability to the perils facing liberal democracy today.

What, then, are the lessons of Tocqueville's political science for contemporary practice? The first lesson we must ponder is the need to balance nature and art. For Tocqueville, human nature sets the goal—a justice directed toward the achievement of human virtue—at which all action, including the organized and regulated action of political society, must aim. At the same time, the collective pursuit of natural goals is always mediated by habits and prejudices, deriving from national character and the social state, which often divert political society from the absolute good. Tocqueville assures us that human nature causes us to long for liberty understood as virtue or the perfection of our sublime faculties. This means that the statesman or leader who seeks to pursue his own greatness and that of political society will always have at his disposal a power that transcends the limitations, insurmountable as they may seem, of a given social state and national character (89, 510, 517ff). Yet Tocqueville also helps us to see that the means of harnessing this natural power must always be artful. Appeals to

nature itself cannot substitute for knowing and working with the more particula-
ristic penchants of a given populace, and genuine progress in meeting the natural
goals of political life requires the free assent of citizens rather than the tyrannical and stultifying imposition of uniformity (703, note xxiv).

True statesmanship therefore comes to light as neither the revolutionary
replacement of the old with the new, nor the reactionary defense of what is or
was against any who question it. Instead, true statesmanship is both patient and
persistent. It is conservative in the sense that it works mostly within the parameters of a given society and progressive in that it seeks the approximation of an
ideal standing outside the easy grasp of any given society. Such statesmanship is
at bottom inseparable from the ongoing enterprise of educating one's political
society, be it aristocratic or democratic, in the art of being free or the pursuit of
genuine, virtuous liberty.

The second lesson of Tocqueville political science is the need to cultivate a
moral order capable of orienting citizens toward a virtuous conception of liberty.
This project can be challenged from two different directions. Supporters of virtue, considering the excesses often associated with the notion of liberty, might
be tempted to deemphasize the latter term. Robert Kraynak (2001), for example,
though he does not go so far as to reject liberty itself, does call for the abandonment of rights-based liberalism and its replacement by the notion of constitutional democracy whose powers are limited by piety and prudence as conceived
by classical Christianity (205, 225). While he appreciates and adopts many of
Tocqueville's insights and suggestions for modern times—e.g. local liberty
(200, 222) and civil religion (190, 220)—Kraynak criticizes prominent attempts
to harmonize the notion of liberty with that of virtue. He holds that rights subordinated to the common good are not rights at all in the proper sense, which "are
essentially ungrateful" and individualistic "claims against authority" (170ff).
Though Kraynak's critique of virtue-based liberalism raises many valid questions about the hopes of reforming present-day liberal democracy, he does not
adequately consider Tocqueville's case pointing to the truly intimate link between virtue and liberty properly understood, and therefore underestimates the
practical possibility of using the idea of rights well-understood to apply virtue to
the political world.

Tocqueville's analysis of democracy clearly supports the conclusion that
concepts other than liberty and equality, especially those of duty and virtue,
must circumscribe liberty if the latter is to be well understood. Yet we would do
well to heed Tocqueville's deliberate choice to cling to democracy precisely
where it loves liberty and to consider his reasons for making that choice. The
danger of Tocqueville's stance is that, in celebrating the idea of liberty, we will
unintentionally seem to approve of various false conceptions of liberty prevailing today. The premise of Tocqueville's strategy, however, is the ineluctable
place of liberty in the true definition of human happiness: virtue or greatness as
the free choice of the good. All other moral categories—duty, honor, courage,
patriotism, and religion included—are premised on the essential freedom of human beings to associate with or dissociate from the admirable order of all things.

By our very nature, we must either learn to exercise our freedom for the sake of the good or suffer the consequences of choosing what is bad. In this sense, liberty ought to be the guiding light of all regimes, aristocratic or democratic (666).

From Tocqueville's perspective, our passion for liberty today is not excessive, since liberty is essential to virtue and virtue can never be too much loved. Rather, our passion for liberty is defective insofar as we tend to love as liberty things that actually lead to moral and political servitude. The remedy is not to deemphasize liberty but to refine our understanding of it. Pierre Manent (1996) rightly argues that Tocqueville asks us to love democracy better. What this means, for Tocqueville, is to love liberty as much or more than democracy and to love genuine rather than spurious liberty.

From the other side, Tocqueville's call for a virtuous understanding of liberty can be challenged by those who regard the application of virtue to the political realm as impossible, illiberal, or both. Tocqueville's entire work, and our analysis of it, aim at refuting this contention. Yet we have to admit that Tocqueville's stance toward such objectors—to persuade them or exclude them from his coalition of new political scientists—is more difficult to adopt today. Even if we posit the hypothetical benefits of the moral and religious consensus Tocqueville observed in 1830s America, contemporary American society appears to be fragmented among an irreconcilable plethora of religious, semi-religious, and atheistic doctrines. To the extent that the memory of the former consensus has not died, attempts to preserve it seem doomed to fuel the apparently futile "culture war" between those who would retain public commitment to aspects of traditional morality and those who would decisively abandon it. Are we not forced, as John Rawls (2001) and others have counseled, to adopt a non-foundational approach to modern politics, seeking to ground liberal democracy in the notion of equal liberty itself, without reference to any shared overarching or "comprehensive" vision of what is good for human beings?[1]

The Tocquevillian response to this objection is to emphasize not only the theoretical, but also the practical impossibility of avoiding the question of the objective moral order. Though political art can reconcile contradictory opinions and sustain theoretically untenable policies to a point, it is neither possible nor desirable for art to supplant nature entirely. If Tocqueville is correct, human beings are so constituted that they cannot ignore the question of life's purpose, and its expression in their communal life, without becoming confused, apathetic, and ultimately inferior to themselves: more than kings, according to the dogma of equal liberty, but less than men according to the reality of their daily existence. Moreover, Tocqueville makes a case that is still convincing today for the necessity of grounding public morality in religious doctrine and worship of a traditional, rather than pantheistic, character. The attempt to exclude comprehensive doctrines, ostensibly including that of modern rationalism, from public discourse, has the practical effect of rendering materialistic philosophy—philosophy, that is, which denies the existence of the human soul and its longings for moral order—the de facto arbiter of moral-political order. As a consequence, views grounded in competing—and, quite possibly, truer—visions of nature and grace are excluded without the benefit of an honest discussion of their merits or resonance with a society's national character. Such an outcome is neither liberal nor reasonable.

Though it is well to heed the warnings against overheated arguments about fundamental moral issues, Tocqueville convincingly shows us that genuine if moderated engagement with such issues is vital to the health of modern democratic society. Intellectual and political leaders who see their task as deflecting attention from these matters or imposing artificial resolutions of them in order to shield the public from its own incapacities are in fact fostering the very weaknesses they deplore and robbing citizens of the right and responsibility to grow in civic virtue through addressing such concerns. This is not to deny that leadership is needed above all when it comes to "God and human nature," or to advocate slavish adherence to public opinion in such matters. Nor can one pretend that the achievement of consensus will be as easy today as it was in the nineteenth century. It is to say, however, that the "culture wars" are worth fighting, and indeed must be fought, though the spirit in which they are "fought" should avoid all malice and employ all charity and reason. It is also important to suggest that many leaders in our society ought to reconsider their misguided antagonism to those who would preserve much that is viable and beneficial in the religious and moral traditions Tocqueville celebrates.

The third and final lesson of Tocqueville's political science is that engagement with moral order must take place within the context of a vibrant civic culture and civil society. In this sphere one is confronted today with the accomplished fact of centralization on a scale approaching that of Tocqueville's gravest fears. It ought to be very sobering to consider Tocqueville's depiction of an order characterized by the exercise of empty liberties, from the pursuit of private and vulgar pleasures to the occasional choice of administrative tutors, all ending in the atrophying of our distinct faculties and the obfuscation of human nature. Though few would claim we have come that far, it is hard to deny that many features of our mass society mirror this nightmarish vision. Thankfully the human spirit has rebelled against such degradation to the extent that there exists a distinct, if yet inchoate, language of protest against it. From George Orwell's *1984* and its numerous epigones to the contemporary interest in community, civil society, and leadership, evidence abounds that not all of us have been lulled to sleep by the blandishments of "pop culture" and the utopian promises of administrative science. On all sides of the political spectrum complaints can be heard about the loss of purpose, participation, and political virtue in our times. In principle, then, there may be a constituency for practical responses aimed at renewing these diminishing features of political life.

A key word to consider here is sacrifice. As Tocqueville makes clear, the attractiveness of administrative centralization and civic apathy lies in the promise of an easy satisfaction of the narrow interests of each member of society. True citizenship demands that the average person give not only of his time and material resources, but also that he be willing to sacrifice for the sake of public discourse the pride by which he clings to his unreasoned private opinions. In an age when individualism has taken its toll on the theory and practice of the traditional family, the religion to which it was devoted, and the community of which it was a part, the need for individuals to make a conscious sacrifice of personal convenience and preferences for the sake of the common good is more pressing than ever. For their part, legislators, judges, and administrators can only encourage such sacrifices on the part of citizens if they too are willing to sacrifice personal and corporate power for the sake of political liberty, providing for a more robust system of subsidiarity or local rule. Though it would be irresponsible to contemplate the complete withdrawal of federal government from domestic affairs, or the noninvolvement of federal courts in civil liberties, there is ample room in both departments for measures granting greater freedom to and imposing greater responsibilities upon individuals and communities. A reemphasis on the role of civic partnership would threaten countless special interests and alarm many observers with the sight of diminishing national (and global) uniformity, but such costs can be justified by reference to the conditions of genuine liberty. Evaluation of policy and juridical choices in this light is a task to which citizens of all stripes may and must contribute.[2]

In order to succeed, the practical reform of political society will have to address a conceptual error at the heart of individualism: the self-perception of citizens as fundamentally autonomous beings only accidentally concerned with one another or with the moral and political structures uniting them. All too often today, we are led to believe that we must choose between the complete liberation of individuals from moral authority on the one hand, or their totalitarian subjection to state control on the other. In truth, neither the individual nor the state exists separately by nature. By nature, every human being belongs to a community in relation to which he has certain rights and duties, and which also has the duty to promote his well being in common with others. Virtue is the natural goal of a being so constituted, and selfishness is an inborn temptation to stray from virtue and the happiness it makes possible. Individualism, on the other hand, is an artificial and unnecessary doctrine falsifying the human condition (57, 482-83, 500ff). With his analysis, Tocqueville helps us to see the futility of operating by the false dichotomy of individual versus society: individualism, by isolating and weakening citizens, renders them helpless in the face of majority tyranny and administrative despotism, while the growing force of this soft despotism contributes to the individualistic retreat from public and cosmic issues as men seek refuge in the haven of private and unsatisfactory pleasures.

Tocqueville teaches us instead to regard all social bodies as composed of persons, unique beings possessed of rational and erotic souls, whose natures demand association of various kinds and in various ways. Embracing this concept of personhood[3] as opposed to that of the radically autonomous individual enables us to explore the legitimacy and limits of various bodies, including families, churches, communities, and voluntary organizations, as well as governments, in light of the ways they enhance and inhibit personal and public virtues. This reconceptualization of the self allows us to seek in a much more sober fashion the scope that ought to be given to individual liberty of a genuine sort, and the role that must be preserved for legitimate authorities.

Paradoxically, it is by recapturing the true basis of individual dignity—with all of its communal implications—that we can decisively reject the false but easy claims of an extreme individualism that would liberate individuals from their own humanity while subjecting them to an inhumane political disorder. The examples of Martin Luther King, Jr. (2007) and John Paul II (1993), among others who have demonstrated the connection between liberty and virtue and applied this insight to the social and political problems of our day, prove that virtue-based personalism can exert a powerful influence in contemporary times. Leaders and citizens persuaded to join Tocqueville's coalition of new political scientists ought therefore to take courage. Building upon the concept of person-hood and the many other notions of noble liberty, rights, and justice still present, if neglected, in our society, they can and ought to discover practical opportuni-ties to revive in contemporary times the peculiar approach to modern liberal democracy capable of directing souls toward human greatness, thereby avoiding the perils and fulfilling the great promise of democracy.

Notes

1. I am grateful to John Tomasi and Paul Griffiths for the powerful and memorable way they separately posed this question to me.

2. For an outline of policies that would contribute to this revival of civic virtue, see Pangle (1992a, 155ff), Glendon (1991, 130ff, 171ff), Kraynak (2001, 221ff).

3. Kraynak is rightly wary of the Kantian overtones of this term, but he also admits that it has roots in the classical Christian tradition, and can be evoked in that sense (2001, 148-64; compare Maritain 1946).

References

Allen, Barbara. 2005. *Tocqueville, Covenant, and the Democratic Revolution: Harmonizing Earth with Heaven*. Lanham, MD: Lexington Books.

Aquinas, St. Thomas. 1947. *Summa Theologica, Volume I*. Trans. Fathers of the English Dominican Province. New York: Benziger Brothers, Inc.

Arendt, Hannah. 1956. "Authority in the Twentieth Century." *The Review of Politics*, 18, no. 4.

Aristotle, 2002. *Nicomachean Ethics*. Translation, Glossary, and Introductory Essay by Joe Sachs. Newburyport: Focus Publishing.

———. 1984. *The Politics*. Trans. Carnes Lord. Chicago: University of Chicago Press.

Arkes, Hadley. 2000. "*Lochner v. New York* and the Cast of our Laws." In *Great Cases in Constitutional Law*, edited by Robert George, 94-130. Princeton: Princeton University Press.

Aron, Raymond. 1965. *Main Currents in Sociological Thought*. Trans. by Richard Howard and Helen Weaver. New York: Basic Books, Inc.

Augustine, St. 1993. *The City of God*. Trans. Marcus Dods, D.D. New York: The Modern Library.

Banfield, Edward C. 1991. "The Illiberal Tocqueville." In *Here the People Rule*: *Selected Essays*, Second Edition. Washington, DC: The AEI Press, 38-53.

Bellah, Robert et al. 1988-2007. *Habits of the Heart*. Berkeley: University of California Press.

Bellah, Robert. 1975. *The Broken Covenant: American Civil Religion in a Time of Trial*. New York: Seabury Press.

Bloom, Allan. 1990. "The Study of Texts." In *Giants and Dwarfs: Essays 1960-1990*. New York: Simon and Schuster.

———. 1987. *The Closing of the American Mind*. New York: Simon and Schuster.

Brennan, William J. 1985. "Address to the Text and Teaching Symposium." In *Readings in American Government,* Seventh Edition, edited by Mary P. and David K. Nichols. Dubuque, Iowa: Kendall/Hunt Publishing, 2004.

Bork, Robert. 1990. *Tempting of America: The Political Seduction of the Law*. New York: Free Press.

Carrese, Paul O. 2003. *The Cloaking of Power: Montesquieu, Blackstone, and the Rise of Judicial Activism*. Chicago: The University of Chicago Press.

Ceaser, James W. 1991. "Political Science, Political Culture, and the Role of the Intellectual." In *Interpreting Tocqueville's* Democracy in America, edited by Ken Masugi. Savage, MD: Rowman and Littlefield.

———. 1990. *Liberal Democracy and Political Science*. Baltimore: Johns Hopkins University Press.

Cicero, Marcus Tullius. 1948. *De Oratore, Volume I.* Translated by E. W. Sutton. Completed, with an Introduction, by H. Rackham. Harvard: Loeb Classical Library.

―――. 1928. *De Re Publica, De Legibus.* Translated by Clinton W. Keyes. Harvard: Loeb Classical Library.

Constant, Benjamin. 1988. *Political Writings.* Edited by Biancamaria Fontana. Cambridge: University of Cambridge Press.

Danoff, Brian. 2007. "Asking of Freedom Something Other than Itself: Tocqueville, Putnam, and the Vocation of the Democratic Moralist." *Politics & Policy* 35, no. 2.

Davis, Sue. 2007. *Corwin and Peltason's Understanding the Constitution, 17h Edition.* Florence, KY: Wadsworth Publishing.

Diamond, Martin. 1975. "The Revolution of Sober Expectations." In *America's Continuing Revolution: An Act of Conservation.* Washington, DC: The AEI Press.

Drescher, Seymour. 2003. "Who Needs Ancienneté? Tocqueville on Aristocracy and Modernity." *History of Political Thought* 34, no. 4.

Eden, Robert. 1990. "Tocqueville and the Problem of Natural Right." *Interpretation* 17, no. 3, 379-87.

―――. 1986. "Tocqueville on Political Realignment and Constitutional Forms." *The Review of Politics* 48. No. 3: 349-73.

Elshtain, Jean Bethke. 2000. "Women, Equality, and the Family." *Journal of Democracy* 11, no. 1 (January).

European Union. 2004. *A Draft Constitution for the European Union July 2003.* Luxembourg: Office for Official Publications of the European Communities.

Fortin, Ernest. 1996. *Collected Essays*, Vols. 1-3. Ed. J. Brian Benestad. Lanham, MD: Rowman and Littlefield.

Fradkin, Hillel. 2000. "Does Democracy Need Religion?" *Journal of Democracy* 11, no. 1 (January).

Frohnen, Bruce. 1993a. *Virtue and the Promise of Conservatism: The Legacy of Burke and Tocqueville.* Lawrence, KS: University Press of Kansas.

―――. 1993b. "Materialism and Self-Deification: Bellah's Misuse of Tocqueville." In *Tocqueville's Defense of Human Liberty: Current Essays*, edited by Peter Augustine Lawler and Joseph Alulis. New York: Garland Publishing, Inc.

Fukuyama, Francis. 1992. *The End of History and the Last Man.* New York: Free Press.

Galston, William. 1991. *Liberal Purposes: Goods, Virtues, and Diversity in the Liberal State.* Cambridge: Cambridge University Press.

Gannett, Robert T., Jr. 2003. "Bowling Ninepins in Tocqueville's Township." *American Political Science Review* 97, no. 1: 1-16.

Gilson, Etienne. 1956. *The Christian Philosophy of St. Thomas Aquinas.* Notre Dame: University of Notre Dame Press.

Glendon, Mary Ann. 1991. *Rights Talk: The Impoverishment of Political Discourse.* New York: The Free Press.

Goldstein, Doris S. 1960. "The Religious Beliefs of Alexis de Tocqueville." *French Historical Studies* I (December).

Greenawalt, Kent. 2006. *Religion and the Constitution: Volume I: Free Exercise and Fairness.* Princeton, NJ: Princeton University Press.

Gurwitsch, Aron. 1945. "On Contemporary Nihilism." *The Review of Politics* 7, no. 2.

Hancock, Ralph C. 2002. "Practical Wisdom Before and After Christianity: Aristotle and Tocqueville." Paper prepared for delivery at the 2002 Annual Meeting of the American Political Science Association, Boston, August 29-September 1.

Hayek, F. A. 1994. *The Road to Serfdom*. Chicago: The University of Chicago Press.

Hebert, L. Joseph, Jr. 2007. "Individualism and Intellectual Liberty in Tocqueville and Descartes." *The Journal of Politics* 69, no. 2: 525-37.

Hobbes, Thomas. 1994. *Leviathan*. Edited, with Introduction and Notes by Edwin Curley. Indianapolis, IN: Hackett Publishing Company, Inc.

Jaffa, Harry. 2000. *A New Birth of Freedom: Abraham Lincoln and the Coming of the Civil War*. Lanham, MD: Rowman and Littlefield Publishers, Inc.

———. 1958-1999. *Crisis of the House Divided: An Interpretation of the Issues in the Lincoln-Douglas Debates*. Chicago: University of Chicago Press.

Jardin, André. 1988 [1984]. *Tocqueville: A Biography*. Translated by Lydia Davis with Robert Hemenway. Baltimore: The Johns Hopkins University Press.

Jefferson, Thomas. 2004. "Letter to James Madison, September 1789." In *Readings in American Government*, edited by Mary P. Nichols and David K. Nichols, 387-390. Dubuque, IA: Kendall/Hunt Publishing Company.

———. 1979. *Selected Writings*. Edited by Harvey C. Mansfield, Jr. Wheeling, MD: Harlan Davidson, Inc.

John Paul II. 1993. *Veritatis Splendor*. Vatican Translation. Boston: Pauline Books and Media.

———. 1991. *Centesimus Annus*. http://www.vatican.va/

Johnson, Paul. 1997. *A History of the American People*. New York: HarperCollins Publishers.

Jouvenel, Bertrand de. 1947. *Sovereignty: An Inquiry into the Political Good*. Indianapolis, IN: Liberty Fund.

Kant, Immanuel. 1983. *Perpetual Peace and Other Essays on Politics, History, and Morals*. Indianapolis, IN: Hackett Publishing Company.

Kessler, Sanford. 1994. *Tocqueville's Civil Religion: American Christianity and the Prospects for Freedom*. Albany, NY: State University of New York Press.

Keys, Mary. 2006. *Aquinas, Aristotle, and the Promise of the Common Good*. Cambridge: Cambridge University Press.

King, Martin Luther, Jr. 2007. "Letter from a Birmingham Jail." In *Classics of American Political and Constitutional Thought, Volume 2: Reconstruction to the Present*, edited by Scott J. Hammond, Kevin R. Hardwick, and Howard L. Lubert, 653-662. Indianapolis, IN: Hackett Publishing Company, Inc.

Kojève, Alexandre. 1980. *Introduction to the Reading of Hegel: Lectures on the Phenomenology of Spirit*. Assembled by Raymond Queneau. Edited by Allan Bloom. Translated by James H. Nichols, Jr. Ithaca, NY: Cornell University Press.

Koritansky, John C. 1986. *Alexis de Tocqueville and the New Science of Politics*. Durham, MD: Carolina Academic Press.

Kraynak, Robert P. 2001. *Christian Faith and Modern Politics: God and Politics in the Fallen World*. South Bend, IN: University of Notre Dame Press.

———. 1995. "Alexis de Tocqueville on Divine Providence and Historical Progress." In *Political Philosophy and the Human Soul: Essays in Memory of Allan Bloom*, edited by Michael Palmer and Thomas L. Pangle. Lanham, MD: Rowman and Littlefield.

———. 1987. "Tocqueville's Constitutionalism." *The American Political Science Review* 81, no. 4 (Dec.): 1175-1195.

Kremer, Mark. 2004. *Plato's* Cleitophon: *On Socrates and the Modern Mind*. Lanham, MD: Lexington Books.

Kristol, William. 2008. "The Character of Optimism." *New York Times*, July 14.

————. 1991. "Women's Liberation: The Relevance of Tocqueville." In *Interpreting Tocqueville's* Democracy in America, edited by Ken Masugi. Savage, MD: Rowman and Littlefield.

Lawler, Peter Augustine. 1993. *The Restless Mind: Alexis de Tocqueville on the Origin and Perpetuation of Human Liberty.* Lanham, MD: Rowman and Littlefield.

Lincoln, Abraham. 2001. *Lincoln: His Speeches and Writings.* Ed. Roy Basler. Jackson, TN: De Capo Press.

Lively, Jack. 1962. *The Social and Political Thought of Alexis de Tocqueville.* Oxford, Clarendon Press.

Locke, John. 1983. *A Letter Concerning Toleration.* Ed. James H. Tully. Indianapolis, IN: Hackett.

————. 1982. *Second Treatise of Government.* Ed. Richard Cox. Wheeling, MD: Harlan Davidson.

Lowi, Theodore. 1979. *The End of Liberalism: The Second Republic of the United States.* New York: W. W. Norton & Company.

Lugo, Luis *et alia.* 2008. *U.S. Religious Landscape Survey.* The Pew Forum on Religion and Public Life.

Machiavelli, Niccolò. 1985. *The Prince.* Trans. Harvey C. Mansfield. Chicago: The University of Chicago Press.

Maistre, Joseph de. 1994. *Considerations on France.* Ed. and Trans. by Richard A. Lebrun. Cambridge: Cambridge University Press.

Manent, Pierre. 2006. *A World Beyond Politics? A Defense of the Nation/State.* Princeton: University of Princeton Press.

————. 1996. *Tocqueville and the Nature of Democracy.* Translated by John Waggoner. Lanham, MD: Rowman and Littlefield Publishers, Inc.

Maritain, Jacques. 1951. *Man and the State.* Chicago: The University of Chicago Press.

————. 1946. "The Person and the Common Good." *The Review of Politics* 8, no. 4.

Mather, Cotton. 1979. *Magnalia Christi Americana: or, The Ecclesiastical History of New England.* Volume I. Edinburgh: The Banner of Truth Trust.

Mayer, J. P. 1966. *Alexis de Tocqueville.* Gloucester: Peter Smith.

McIntyre, Alasdair. 1981. *After Virtue: A Study in Moral Theory.* South Bend: University of Notre Dame Press.

Merrill, Clark. 2000. "Leo Strauss's Indictment of Christian Philosophy." *The Review of Politics* 62, no. 1.

Mitchell, Joshua. 1995. *The Fragility of Freedom: Tocqueville on Religion, Democracy, and the American Future.* Chicago: The University of Chicago Press.

Montesquieu, Charles de Secondat, baron de. 1989. *The Spirit of the Laws.* Ed. and Trans. by Anne M. Cohler, Basia Carolyn Miller, and Harold Samuel Stone. Cambridge: Cambridge University Press.

Morton, Nathaniel. 1937. *New Englands Memorial.* Ed. Howard J. Hall. New York: Scholar's Facsimiles and Reprints.

Muller, James W. 1975. "Politics and Philosophy in Tocqueville's *Souvenirs.*" *The Intercollegiate Review* (Winter): 33-44.

Mussolini, Benito. 1951-63. "Relativismo e Fascismo." In *Opera Omnia,* edited by Edoardo Susmel and Duilio Susmel, 17:267-69. Florence: La Fireze.

Nietzsche, Friedrich. 1980. *On the Advantage and Disadvantage of History for Life.* Translated by Peter Preuss. Indianapolis, IN: Hackett Publishing Company.

————. 1954. *The Portable Nietzsche.* Edited and Translated by Walter Kaufmann. New York: Penguin Books.

Nozick, Robert. 1974. *Anarchy, State, and Utopia.* New York: Basic Books.

Orwin, Clifford. 2004. "The Unraveling of Christianity in America." *Public Interest* 155 (Spring): 20-36.

Pangle, Thomas. 2004. "Straussian Approaches to the Study of Politics." In *Handbook of Political Theory*, edited by Gerald F. Gaus and Chandran Kukathas. London: Sage Publications.

———. 1992a. *The Ennobling of Democracy: The Challenge of the Postmodern Age*. Baltimore, MD: The Johns Hopkins University Press.

———. 1992b. "The Liberal Paradox: Might Religion Have an Answer?" *Crisis* 10 (May): 18-25.

Pascal, Blaise. 1910. *Thoughts*. Translated by W. F. Trotter. New York: P. F. Collier & Son.

Pieper, Josef. 1962. *Guide to St. Thomas Aquinas*. Translated by Richard and Clara Winston. New York: Pantheon Books.

———. 1949. "On the Christian Idea of Man." *The Review of Politics* 11, no. 1.

Pierson, George Wilson. 1959. *Tocqueville in America*. Abridged by Dudley C. Lunt from *Tocqueville and Beaumont in America*. New York: Anchor Books.

Plato. 2007. *Gorgias*. Translated by James A. Arieti and Roger M. Barrus. Newburyport, MA: Focus Publishing.

———. 2004. *Protagoras and Meno*. Translated by Robert Bartlett. Ithaca: Cornell University Press.

———. 2003. *Phaedrus*. Translated by Stephen Scully. Newburyport, MA: Focus Classical Library.

———. 1998. *Phaedo*. Translation, Introduction, and Glossary by Eva Brann, Peter Kalkavage, and Eric Salem. Newburyport, MA: Focus Classical Library.

———. 1997. *Symposium*. Translated by Avi Sharon. Newburyport, MA: Focus Publishing.

———. 1988. *Laws*. Trans., with Notes and an Interpretive Essay, by Thomas Pangle. Chicago: The University of Chicago Press.

———. 1984. *Apology*. Translated by Thomas G. and Grace Starry West. In *Four Texts on Socrates*. Ithaca, NY: Cornell University Press.

———. 1968. *The Republic*. Trans. Allan Bloom. New York: Basic Books.

———. 1942. "Epistle VII." In *Plato, Volume VII*. Cambridge: Harvard University Press.

Plutarch. 1932. *The Lives of the Noble Grecians and Romans*. Translated by John Dryden and Revised by Arthur High Clough. New York: The Modern Library.

Publius. 1996. *The Federalist*. Indianapolis, IN: Liberty Fund, Inc.

Putnam, Robert. 2001. *Bowling Alone: The Collapse and Revival of American Community*. New York: Simon and Schuster.

Rawls, John. 2001. *Justice as Fairness: A Restatement*. Cambridge: The Belknap Press of Harvard University Press.

———. 1999. *A Theory of Justice*. Cambridge: Harvard University Press.

Roosevelt, Franklin. 1932-1941. "The New Goals of Politics." In *Readings in American Government*. Seventh Edition, edited by Mary P. and David K. Nichols. Dubuque, Iowa: Kendall/Hunt Publishing, 2004.

———. 1937. "Radio Broadcast, March 9, 1937." In *Constitutional Law and Politics*, Volume One, Sixth Edition, Edited by David M. O'Brien, 62-67. New York: W. W. Norton and Company, 2005.

Rougemont, Denis de. 1941. "Passion and the Origin of Hitlerism." *The Review of Politics* 3, no. 1.

Rousseau, Jean-Jacques. 1995. *The Confessions and Correspondence, Including the Letters to Malesherbes*. Edited by Roger D. Masters and Peter G. Stillman. Translated by Christopher Kelley. Dartmouth: University of Dartmouth Press.

———. 1979. *Emile: or On Education*. New York: Basic Books, Inc.

———. 1978. *On the Social Contract. With Geneva Manuscript and Political Economy.* Ed. Roger D. Masters. Trans. Judith R. Masters. New York: St. Martin's Press.

———. 1964. *The First and Second Discourses*. Trans. Roger D. Masters and Judith R. Masters. New York: St. Martin's Press.

———. 1960. *Politics and the Arts. Letter to D'Alembert on the Theatre.* Translated with notes and an introduction by Allan Bloom. Ithaca, NY: Cornell University Press.

Salkever, Stephen G. 1990. *Finding the Mean: Theory and Practice in Aristotelian Political Philosophy*. Princeton: Princeton University Press.

Salomon, Albert. 1935. "Tocqueville, Moralist and Sociologist." *Social Research* 2: 405-27.

Sandel, Michael J. 1996. *Democracy's Discontent: America in Search of a Public Philosophy*. Cambridge: Harvard University Press.

Scalia, Antonin. 1997. *A Matter of Interpretation: Federal Courts and the Law*. Princeton: Princeton University Press.

Schall, James. 2006. *Roman Catholic Political Philosophy*. Lanham, MD: Lexington Books.

———. 1991. "A Latitude for Statesmanship? Strauss on St. Thomas." *The Review of Politics* 53, no. 1.

Shakespeare, William. 1961. *Histories and Poems*. New York: E. P. Dutton & Co. Inc.

Smith, Rogers M. 1993. "Beyond Tocqueville, Myrdal, and Hartz: The Multiple Traditions in America." *The American Political Science Review* 87, no. 3 (Sep.): 549-66.

Stoner, James R. 2003. *Common Law Liberty: Rethinking American Constitutionalism*. Lawrence, KS: University Press of Kansas.

Strauss, Leo. 1995. *Liberalism Ancient and Modern*. Chicago: The University of Chicago Press.

———. 1983. *Studies in Platonic Political Philosophy*. With an Introduction by Thomas L. Pangle. Chicago: The University of Chicago Press.

———. 1959. *What is Political Philosophy? And Other Studies*. Chicago: The University of Chicago Press.

———. 1953. *Natural Right and History*. Chicago: University of Chicago Press.

———. 1952. *Persecution and the Art of Writing*. New York: Free Press.

Taylor, Paul, et al. 2006. *Are We Happy Yet?* Washington, D.C.: Pew Research Center.

Tocqueville, Alexis de. 2000a. *Democracy in America*. Trans. Harvey C. Mansfield and Delba Winthrop. Chicago: The University of Chicago Press.

———. 2000b. *Democracy in America*. Abridged, With Introduction, by Sanford Kessler. Translated and Annotated by Stephen D. Grant. Indianapolis, IN: Hackett Publishing Company.

———. 1991. *Oeuvres. Tome I.* Edited by A. Jardin. Paris: Gallimard, Edition Pléade.

———. 1990a. *De la Démocratie en Amérique. Première edition historico-critique revue et augmentée par Eduardo Nolla. Tome I.* Paris: Libraire Philosophique J. Vrin.

———. 1990b. *De la Démocratie en Amérique. Première edition historico-critique revue et augmentée par Eduardo Nolla. Tome II.* Paris: Libraire Philosophique J. Vrin.

———. 1988. *L'ancien Régime et la Révolution*. Paris: GF Flammarion.

———. 1985. *Selected Letters on Politics and Society*. Edited by Roger Boesche. Translated by James Toupin and Roger Boesche. Berkeley: University of California Press.

———. 1981. *De la Démocratie en Amérique, II.* Paris: Garnier-Flammarion.

———. 1977. *Correspondance d'Alexis de Tocqueville et de Louis de Kergorlay*. Paris: Éditions Gallimard.

———. 1970. *Recollections*. Translated by George Lawrence New York: Doubleday & Company.

———. 1961. *De la Démocratie en Amérique, I*. Paris: Gallimard.

———. 1959a. *"The European Revolution" & Correspondence with Gobineau*. Westport, CT: Greenwood Press.

———. 1959b. *Journey to America*. Translated by George Lawrence. Edited by J. P. Mayer. London: Faber and Faber Ltd.

———. 1957. *Journey to England and Ireland*. Translated by George Lawrence. Edited by J. P. Mayer. London: Faber and Faber Ltd.

———. 1955. *The Old Regime and the French Revolution*. Trans. Stuart Gilbert. New York: Doubleday.

Vatican, The. 2000. *Catechism of the Catholic Church*. London: Geoffrey Chapman.

Washington, George. 1988. *George Washington: A Collection*. Edited by W. B. Allen. Indianapolis, IN: Liberty Classics.

West, Thomas. 1991. "Misunderstanding the American Founding." In *Interpreting Tocqueville's* Democracy in America, edited by Ken Masugi. Lanham, MD: Rowman and Littlefield.

Wilson, James Q. 2008. *American Government: Brief Version*. New York: Houghton Mifflin Company.

Winthrop, Delba. 1993. "Rights, Interest, and Honor." In *Tocqueville's Defense of Human Liberty: Current Essays*, edited by Peter Augustine Lawler and Joseph Alulis. New York: Garland Publishing, Inc.

———. 1986. "Tocqueville's American Woman and 'The true Conception of Democratic Progress.'" *Political Theory* 14, no. 2 (May).

Wolin, Sheldon. 2001. *Tocqueville between Two Worlds: The Making of a Political and Theoretical Life*. Princeton: Princeton University Press.

Wudel, Darcy. 1993. "Tocqueville on Associations and Association." In *Tocqueville's Defense of Human Liberty: Current Essays*, edited by Peter Augustine Lawler and Joseph Alulis. New York: Garland Publishing, Inc.

Xenophon. 1994. *Memorabilia*. Trans. Amy L. Bonnette. Ithaca, NY: Cornell University Press.

Zetterbaum, Marvin. 1967. *Tocqueville and the Problem of Democracy*. Stanford, CA: Stanford University Press.

Index

absolute good, 4; difficulty of, 121;
character of, 8, 48; definition of, 7;
and social state, 31
action, human, 131
Acton, Lord, 83
Allen, Barbara, 71n39
America. *See* United States of America
American Revolution, 88, 186
L'Ancien Régime et la Révolution, 141-
48, 156n37
apathy, 23, 95-96, 118, 169
Aquinas, St. Thomas, 98n7, 98n8, 139,
155n21
Arendt, Hannah, 184
aristocracy: conventional, 22, 77-80;
natural, 22, 33, 36n21, 50, 64, 76-77,
80, 89, 103, 122-25, 150, 178; as
social state, 31, 103, 114, 121-22
Aristotle, 3; on citizenship, 128n1; on
law, 172, 182; on philosophy, 138;
on art of politics, 71n48, 84-89; on
primitive man, 69n23
Arkes, Hadley, 189n26
Aron, Raymond, 11n24
Articles of Confederation, 89
association: American use of, 109-17,
181; and human nature, 173, 195;
and intellectual virtue, 129n15; with
order of things, 8, 20, 49, 121, 166
authority: and democracy, 92, 132; its
legitimacy, 196; and moral order, 28,
67; and philosophy, 155n23; and
religion, 76, 132-41, 150-51,
156n41, 156n44, 164; and rights, 192

Banfield, Edward, 11n26
Beaumont, Gustave de, 68n6
beliefs, religious: contemporary, 179;
and democracy, 55-58, 93, 118, 132,
142, 164, 186; and mores, 34, 58;
and social state, 27
Bellah, Robert, 180-81
Bible: in civic education, 185; on idola-
try, 28; influence on law, 182, 186
Bill of Rights, 5, 175
Blackmun, Harold, 186
Blackstone, 182, 186
Bloom, Allen, 10n24, 68n8, 69n10,
69n15, 129n9, 178, 184
Brandeis, Louis, 177
Brennan, William J., 130n29
Brulyère, Jean de la, 87
bureaucracy, 168, 170, 174
Bush, George W., 168

cannibalism, 45
causes, 10n7, 16; first, 41, 74; generative, 27, 45, 161; physical, 41, 68n4
Carrese, Paul, 11n24, 153n3, 182
Ceaser, James, 11n24, 71n47, 129n15,
153n5, 154n10, 155n29
centralization, 95-96, 98n9, 104-5,
108, 123, 166, 173-75, 182, 194
Charlevoix, Pierre, 44-46
checks and balances, 85
Cherokees, 70n26
Chesterton, G. K., 154n14
China, 94
Christianity: in America, 149; as aristocratic, 75; and equality, 21; and li-

French, the, 1, 41, 105, 115-18, 125,
   162
French Revolution, 1, 141-46, 155n32
Frohnen, Bruce, 11n24, 71n37, 190n43

Galston, William, 181
general will, 60, 93
Germanic tribes, 45
Gilson, Etienne, 187
Glendon, Mary Ann, 128n4, 129n16,
   177, 182, 186, 196n2
Gobineau, Arthur de, 188n3
God: and democracy, 135; as Creator,
   75, 97n6, 138, 143-44; idea of, 131;
   as omnipotent, 83; relation to human
   beings, 142, 147; rights of, 148; His
   will, 25, 28, 139
Goldstein, Doris, 37n34
The Grapes of Wrath, 167
Great Depression, 173
greatness, human, 8; and equality, 186;
   and happiness, 22-23; in the individual, 11n27, 62, 121, 123; and legiti-
   macy, 24, 97n2; and liberty, 82; in a
   people, 62, 121, 123; and truth, 87
Greenawalt, Kent, 189n30
Griffiths, Paul, 196n1
Guizot, François, 98n9

Habib, Khalil, 68n5
Hamilton, Alexander, 25
happiness, as goal, 7-8, 48; and education, 179; and greatness, 22-23, 47-
   49; and natural right, 46
Hegel, Wilhelm, 69n10
Heidegger, Martin, 184
hierarchy, 28
Hobbes, Thomas, 3, 48
Holmes, Oliver, Jr., 182
honor, 144-45
humanity, common, 45, 61; fate of, 2;
   and sublime, 48
human nature, its baser side, 23; and
   denaturing of man, 60; and disinter-
   restedness, 119; divided character, 8,
   20, 131; and justice, 7, 42, 172; and
   moral order, 31, 131, 133, 139, 142-
   48, 166; its need for fulfillment, 47,
   102, 137; and pride, 45; and social

state, 74; and soul, 75; and truth, 7;
   its weakness, 51
Hurons, 44-45

ideas: abstract, 16, 39; general, 115,
   123, 131; of moral order, 32, 57;
   "mother idea," 16, 74, 161; and sentiments, 33, 98n26, 114
Incarnation, 146
Indians, American, 41-46, 51-52
individualism, 6-7; American victory
   over, 91, 114; as antithesis of virtue,
   35, 53, 165; consequences of, 92-96,
   113, 132; contemporary, 166, 173-
   79, 181; as error, 101-02, 115, 183,
   195; good individualism, 8, 86, 112,
   165; Tocqueville's opposition to, 48
industrialization, 96, 167
industriousness, 43
inequality: natural, 63, 75-82, 92; as
   social state, 113
Inquisition, Spanish, 87, 140
interests. *See* self-interest
Iraq, 2
Iroquois, 44-45
Islam, 147, 164

Jackson, Andrew, 89, 110, 124, 130n27
Jaffa, Harry, 98n11, 129n9, 181, 185-
   86, 190n44
Jardin, 10n23, 37n34
Jefferson, Thomas, 4, 22, 36n18,
   36n21, 77, 185-86
Jesus Christ, 141
Jouvenel, Bertrand de, 128n5
judges, 125-27, 130n29, 170-72
judicial review, 5, 171, 173
jury, 126-27, 149
justice: definition of, 65; difficulty of,
   7; equal, 167; as fairness, 10n19, 24;
   and greatness, 97n2; and humanity,
   61, 172; and politics, 114, 121; universal, 27, 66-67, 82, 145

Kant, Immanuel, 154n7, 182, 196n3
Kessler, Sanford, 11n26, 37n34,
   156n42, 157n49
Keyes, Mary, 187
Kojève, Alexandre, 69n10
Koran, 147

Index 209

mores, 6, 41; and beliefs, 34, 58; and
laws, 26, 105; and national character,
41; and nature, 42; primacy of, 44;
and self-restraint, 26; and virtue, 8;
and women, 151
Morton, Nathaniel, 57, 156n44
Muller, James, 10n23, 11n24
Mussolini, Benito, 17

Napoleon Bonaparte, 1, 141
national character, American, 164; and
honor, 145; and mores, 41, 53; and
nature, 42; and political society, 52-
53; and prejudice, 51; and social
state, 74-76, 114
Native Americans. See Indians, American
nature: its distortion, 43; as basis of
morality, 33, 44, 102; and history,
69n10; and mores, 41-42; and the
supernatural, 140, 143
New Deal, 168, 174
New England, 54-60, 66-67, 75-78, 88
Nietzsche, Friedrich, 164
Nozick, Robert, 10n18

Obama, Barack, 128n8
order of things, 8, 20, 48, 52, 118-20,
131, 136-39, 177
Orwell, George, 194
Orwin, Clifford, 179

Palmer, Michael, 11n24
Pangle, Thomas, 11n24, 72n49, 184-
85, 196n2
pantheism, 75, 144, 150, 154n13
participation, political, 108, 114,
128n4, 147, 182
parties, political, 109, 111
Pascal, Blaise, 3; influence on Tocqueville, 10n24, 35n4, 154n17
patrie, 109-10, 120-21, 132, 142
patriotism, 110, 120, 131
perfectibility, 144
personhood, 195
philosophy: and American philosophic
method, 92; and art of writing, 16;
and Christianity, 140, 186-87; and
political authority, 64-65, 84-85; and
order of things, 136; and politics,

147; and relativism, 179; and sublime, 102, 137-38; Tocqueville's
view of, 140; as way of life, 48, 92
Pierson, George, 10n23
Plato, 3; on art of writing, 16; on democracy, 71n45; on education, 51;
influence on law, 182; and noble lie,
70n28; on regime, 84-85; on philosophy, 154n20; on soul, 69n15; on
truth, 35n4; on virtue, 65
Plutarch, 3, 36n4
Poletown, 174
political science, 26; Aristotle's, 159;
Hobbes's, 48; and human nature, 42;
and justice, 65-66; Montesquieu's,
159; Tocqueville's distinctive, 7, 28-
29, 31, 41, 46, 127, 133, 160, 187,
191; Tocqueville's new, 2, 8, 26, 59,
86, 103, 111, 122
political society, 44; and absolute good,
48; and pride, 50, 52
political thought, American, 6; classical, 7, 11n24, 15, 36n14, 46, 49, 62,
71n48, 98n8, 146-147, 152, 183-85;
modern, 46, 48, 59, 65, 128n5, 131,
136, 183-85
popular will, 17
post-modernism, 154n20
poverty, 21, 24, 32, 43
pride, 45, 50-53, 69n14, 93, 108, 119,
131, 194
primogeniture, 19
problems, of human destiny, 39, 132,
138-40, 185, 187
progressivism, 189n41
Protestantism, 142-43, 151, 156n44
Providence, divine, and democracy, 25-
26, 161-62; and feudalism, 28; and
Puritans, 57; and science, 41
public opinion, 54, 93
public-spiritedness, 120-21, 165, 177,
181
Puritans, 10n20; as American founders,
30, 40; their mores, 54-61, 67, 75-77,
107; Tocqueville's use of, 70n28
Putnam, Robert, 180-81

racism, 163
Rawls, John, 10n19, 24, 70n29, 193

About the Author

L. Joseph Hebert, Jr. is associate professor and chair of the Department of Political Science and Leadership Studies at St. Ambrose University in Davenport, IA, where he also directs the pre-law program and teaches courses in political thought, U.S. Government, and American law. He received his B.A. in philosophy from the University of Maine and his M.A. and Ph.D. in political science from the University of Toronto. His article "Individualism and Intellectual Liberty in Tocqueville and Descartes," was recently published in *The Journal of Politics*, and his essay "Tocqueville, Cicero, and the Limits of the Polis," is forthcoming as a chapter in *The Citizen of the World: A Critique of Past and Present Political Thought in the Age of Globalization*, edited by Khalil Habib of Salve Regina University and Lee Trapanier of Saginaw Valley State University. Dr. Hebert is currently co-editing a volume of essays on Tocqueville's theory of democratic statesmanship with Brian Danoff of Miami University, to which he will contribute a Tocquevillian analysis of the Second Vatican Council's response to the conditions of modern democracy.

Breinigsville, PA USA
31 October 2010
248299BV00003B/2/P